LIKE IT IS

LIKE IT IS

HOWARD COSELL

A PLAYBOY PRESS BOOK

I would like to acknowledge the assistance of
Peter Cohane, without whose efforts, patience
and help this book could not possibly have been
written.

Published simultaneously in the United States and Canada by Playboy Press, Chicago,
Illinois. Printed in the United States of America. Library of Congress Catalog Card
Number: 74-82482. ISBN 87223-414-2. First edition.

PLAYBOY and Rabbit Head design are trademarks of Playboy, 919 North Michigan
Avenue, Chicago, Illinois 60611 (U.S.A.), Reg. U.S. Pat. Off., marca registrada,
marque déposée.

For my mother, Nellie Rosenthal Cohen, and my late father, Isadore Martin Cohen, whose sacrifices made possible the fullness of my life.

" 'What is truth?' said jesting Pilate, and would not stay for an answer."

Sir Francis Bacon

"Much have I travel'd in the realms of gold,
And many goodly states and kingdoms seen . . ."

John Keats
ON FIRST LOOKING INTO CHAPMAN'S HOMER

Table of Contents

Preface

A man must work at some profession, and the degree of dedication with which he approaches his work is a matter for himself and his conscience. My career in sports broadcasting has crossed two decades, and to survive in so volatile an industry demands a total self-immersion. One cannot hope to stay aware of the countless events, the ever-growing and changing rosters, the exacting and often complex rules which govern the events (not to mention that each name and number has a distinct personality, a unique history worth knowing about), without it becoming his life. And so it has been.

To my delight, the large number of letters I have received since *Cosell* was published have, in the main, been laudatory, and many expressed the desire for a sequel. But most importantly as it relates to this new undertaking, many of those who wrote asked intelligent and incisive questions which merit answering. To those whose letters I was not able to answer personally, I hope that you will accept this book as my reply, with my sincere thanks.

To get the pulse of what is happening in our country, you go to the people. In recent years I have been privileged to speak before dozens of student bodies, civic and social organizations and even committees of the Congress of the United States. Many of their questions are incorporated within this book as well.

The beat goes on. Things change. The people involved and the circumstances that lend impetus to these changes are what make great stories. The past year has been full of them: O. J. Simpson, "Dandy" Don's departure for NBC, Csonka, Kiick, Warfield and the World Football League, Riggs-King and all the rest. In the pages that follow, I tell them the way I saw them.

There is much that is wrong about the sporting profession, about the men who run it, about the men and women who work at it, and about the people who report it in the newspapers and over the airwaves. This should surprise no one if you consider that sport is merely real life in microcosm and, of course, there is much that is wrong about life in our contemporary society.

In every critical piece that I have ever done, I have had two underlying motives: the pursuit of truth, and the correction of wrongdoing. That is what "telling it like it is" really means. That is also what editorial opinion is supposed to accomplish in all journalistic media. To what extent this is done is also matter for this book.

People, opinions, personal philosophies and persuasions. These are the things with which this book deals. It speaks of people whom I love and respect, it answers questions which I found stimulating and topical and it gets to the nuts and bolts of situations which I abhor.

But most importantly, it tells it like I think it is!

LIKE IT IS

PART I

THE BEAT GOES ON

CHAPTER 1

SO LONG, "DANDY"

"Well, we've got to become enemies again."

Your chartered plane flies low over the crest of yet another rolling hilltop and eases into its final approach to the Penn Ridge Air Strip. You are about to land on the outskirts of Elephant, Pennsylvania, population 17. It sits in the heart of Pennsylvania Dutch country in Bucks County amid scores of immaculately manicured farms. The scenery is lush and natural, with stands of virgin timber rising emphatically on the periphery of bounteous fields as though these farms had been scooped out of the wilderness by a great hand, leaving the forests undisturbed. There is a majesty to the place, an innate sense of comfort and serenity of which city dwellers only dream.

It is three-and-a-half miles from the airfield to your destination. En route there are more farms. And in the middle of town, comprising its very center, is the Elephant Hotel, an antiquated structure with an aura of the colonial past. Beyond, there is an entrance drive from which the house is not visible, but which has a sign posted, "Beware of Trained Dog."

At the apex of the 22-acre property stands a charming Pennsylvania Dutch farmhouse, a neatly assembled archetype of ancient stones and hewn beams over a century old. You have arrived at the home of the first family of Elephant, Mr. and Mrs. "Dandy" Don Meredith.

To all appearances, the presence of Don Meredith in a place like Elephant is incongruous. The western attire seems in open contrast to the overalls and black-brimmed hats of the Pennsylvania Dutch farmers. The Texas accent and idiom must be tantamount to a foreign language to these folk. The frivolous, jesting demeanor with which he has become nationally identifiable, and which has cast him as a public figure, appears conspicuously misplaced when compared with the quiet, private and simple character of the region.

I had come to Elephant to do an interview with "Dandy" for my Sunday *Magazine* show. Events of the previous months had led him to sign on with NBC and leave ABC and the *Monday Night Football* package. Rumors were running rampant as to why, and I knew that the only way to meet them was head-on.

When you want to get inside a man's head, especially this man's, you talk with him in the environment in which he feels most relaxed. You meet with him away from the artificiality of the stadiums and studios at his selected retreat. For Muhammad Ali, it is at his training camp at Deer Lake, Pennsylvania, and for "Dandy" Don, it is in Elephant.

To be sure, it is a long way from his hometown, Mount Vernon, Texas, in more than just mileage. There is, as Don says, "a sense of history" permeating Elephant that he finds spiritually replenishing, and an essential privacy in its smallness that he craves. Even Mount Vernon, with its booming populace of 2001 has gotten too crowded for "The Danderoo."

Susie Meredith is a Baltimore girl, and as one she has known and loved this country her entire life. She and Don have recently taken custody of his son by a previous marriage, seven-year-old Michael, and along with the two dogs, about which you were cautioned to "Beware" as you entered the property, you have the Merediths of Elephant.

Susie greeted my wife Emmy and me as we stepped from the car. Nestled in her arms was a tiny, white, puff-ball of fur called Dink. She is of the Chinese breed Shih Tsu, and I call her "The Dinker." Bounding happily around the group was the second Meredith canine, a playful and vigorous Irish

Setter which Don has named, quite logically, "Amigo." Somehow, it fits. These are the animals of which visitors must beware? The Meredith humor would have it no other way.

Emmy and Susie went into the house to visit while "Dandy" and I engaged in the badinage which has become our trademark. The view from the front of the house is one of unobstructed natural life, with a single exception. Far off on a distant hill you can see a dwelling. Don explained that this was the off-season home of baseball great Dick Allen and his wife. He described how he and Susie had stopped by to visit on several occasions only to find that Dick had closeted himself away upstairs. "He's a strange one," Don observed.

The cameras started to roll as we strolled away from the house, down a gradual slope toward a placid pond. Our conversation continued in a light and general vein until we had settled ourselves on the bank of the pond, with Amigo romping happily along its shore. Basking there in the warmth of the oncoming spring's strengthening rays of sunshine, my mind wandered back over the myriad events that had led us to this, "Dandy" Don's exit interview.

Meredith's departure from ABC and *Monday Night Football* may have surprised the sporting public, but it came as no great shock to me. The fourth year of the Monday night package, 1973, had been a difficult one for him emotionally. To understand why, you have to understand Don Meredith. And that is not as simple as it might seem.

He's a complex man, beset by a whole series of swirling currents that seethe within him. On the surface, he is an angular, handsome, fun-loving cowboy with a gift for the quick quip or pun, garnished with Texanese. There is a tendency, therefore, to view him much too simplistically—as if his mind worked in as seemingly artless and meandering a way as a William Blake poem.

Through the years, Meredith has come to learn that some people regard him in exactly this context, and he has developed a deep inner resentment of such an image. In his mind, he sees himself as a thinker and, believe it or not, even a philosopher. In a strange way, and he would never admit this, he views himself as a current-day Will Rogers. He loves country music and attributes a depth of insight to the lyrics of many of the songs that, for me, doesn't necessarily attach to them at all. He can utter a line like "Livin' ain't that easy," and sit back with the satisfied smile of one who has just probed the very heart of Plato or Aristotle.

To prove himself to himself—and he has an inordinate need for such self-regard—he is always questing in different areas of the arts and culture. On one occasion, just prior to the start of the 1973 season, he announced quite proudly to me that he had taken up painting with oils. "You can't imagine the sense of release it gives me," he said. "All that Pennsylvania Dutch beauty around me, I just have to translate it in my own way."

One year, and two years earlier, he was engrossed in the writing of a novel which has yet to eventuate. By the middle of last season, he was exploring with a renewed interest the great classical works of poetry.

The one constant thing about "Dandy" Don as a person is his inconstancy.

His whole life bespeaks the fact. He left the Dallas Cowboys when he still could have played, and played very well. His personal life has been a series of traumas, including two unfortunate marriages. Now, finally, he seems to have found the right girl.

And now, he wants to become an actor.

None of this alters the fact that he is a warm, decent, generous and funny man; a delight to be with, and a man whose charm is totally disarming. What it does indicate is that Meredith requires change at continuing intervals in his life, that he is less than purposeful. This is one reason why he left *Monday Night Football.*

There is another reason, I believe, of which we are both aware, though we have never discussed it openly. "Dandy" Don became a household name in his first year of *Monday Night Football.* He was a whole new thing in the presentation of a sport which had always been celebrated in a holy fashion on the other networks. The American people loved him instantly—his homespun speech, his irreverence and, of course, his humor. At the end of that first campaign he was awarded what to many is television's most coveted prize, the Emmy. It all came so easily to him. And, underlying all of this, the successful emergence of "Dandy" Don, the man "wearing the white hat," embellished by my presence, the "bad guy" in the "black hat."

Under the circumstances, it was only natural that he expected to become a superstar. It didn't turn out that way.

During the next three years, in the whirling complex of public reaction, augmented by the restricted structure of a television format, "Dandy" remained a definitive and tremendously popular personality. But the guy in the "black hat" became one of the most recognized personalities in show business.

In a phrase, Don had become second banana, and while he never evidenced any displeasure towards me by word or deed, he would not have been human had he not nurtured at least some resentment. At different times during the past three years, Roone Arledge, president of ABC Sports, and Chet Forte, director of *Monday Night Football,* have told me privately that this was the case. And once, only once, at a luncheon in Los Angeles on the last day of this past season, did Don ever intimate his feelings publicly. He told the crowd, "Being second banana hasn't been all that bad."

When I did my farewell interview with Don Meredith that day in Elephant, Pennsylvania, he told the truth. In explaining our relationship from his point of view, he said, "The biggest thing we have is respect, man, respect for one another, and what more can you say than that? I think you often say too much and take too long to say it, and I don't always agree with you, but I've learned that you've got a lot to say and I admire that. I particularly admire that you take stands at a time when we've got so many wishy-washy, middle-of-the road people in this country. And you work hard, man, much too hard. You ought to knock it off a little."

That's another thing about Meredith. He won't butter you up.

Now put it all together. A man whose very nature makes it mandatory that he seek change; a man who is a thinker, even if he talks better than he thinks; a man catapulted overnight into national prominence; a man relegated to second banana and inwardly resentful of the fact; a man who doesn't want to be known as "Dandy" Don anymore; a man who who feels that he has far outgrown that image and who has much more to give of himself in public performance. There you've got a man ready to leave the national institution of which he was such a vital part—*Monday Night Football.*

I am told that Don Meredith's new contract with NBC provides that he is never to be called "Dandy" Don over the air again.

Don really suffered last season. He was out of things, didn't really want to be a part of the scene. After our first two games (terrible games: Green Bay 23–Jets 7; Dallas 40–New Orleans 3), Don Ohlmeyer, our producer, held a production meeting in Detroit. His objective was to seek to restore to the package the spark that had existed in prior years. At that meeting Meredith said, "Let's face it fellas, I shouldn't even be here, I shouldn't have started this season. I'm all talked out. I've got nothing more to say about football, the games aren't that interesting."

Privately, I understood exactly how he felt. At given times I have felt the same way. There is a sameness, a redundancy that amounts to a stereotype in professional football. Both Don and I have always shared the philosophy that, "There is more to life than that down there."

But Meredith is a born performer, and was an integral part of something that has become special in America on Monday nights, and so, quickly, Frank Gifford and Ohlmeyer and Forte and I tried to turn him around. For the balance of the season Don performed in fits and starts and had his ups and downs. On one occasion he called Richard Nixon "Tricky Dicky," and the company had him apologize on the air the following Monday night. Some nights he would take exception to almost everything I would say, merely for the sake of taking exception. Part of this was due to his personal discontent, but an equal part was because he was trying to get that old feeling back into the show. Some people at ABC had told him that the way to accomplish this was to continually argue with me.

In Denver, for instance, Don, Susie, Emmy and I were together at the hotel before going out to the stadium. As Don arose to go upstairs to dress for the game he said, "Well, we've got to become enemies again."

Midway in the season, Arledge and I began to feel a very real concern about Don's plans for the future as they related to the Monday night package. We talked at length about a possible successor if one became necessary. As a result of that conversation, I called Joe Willie Namath and asked him to meet Roone and me at my apartment. Namath agreet to come. Arledge made no offer or representation, but we asked Joe about his thinking for the day when he would finally leave football. Namath said that he might very well be interested in a career in broadcasting—one that would not be limited to sports, I might add—but that for the immediate future his life was still in football as a player

In the last half of the season, "Dandy" somehow put it all together again. Maybe it was because the games improved. Maybe it was the magnificent way we were treated in Denver, or the excitement of the city of Buffalo over their improved young team and O. J. Simpson; maybe it was the wonderful contest between Atlanta and Minnesota, or the thrilling finish to the Pittsburgh-Miami game. Whatever it was, I personally felt that Meredith was as good during that stretch as he had ever been. We all looked forward to our fifth year together, or at least I thought we did.

I began to feel uncomfortable again in late December when "Dandy" asked me for my input on a Los Angeles lawyer named Ed Hookstratten. He said that he was considering putting him on retainer. I told Don that Hookstratten was a very good lawyer, extremely well connected with NBC. I told him that it therefore depended upon what he wanted. Don had done an episode in the NBC series, *Police Story,* which had been well received, and this proved to be the surge chamber for Don's newly developed dream of becoming an actor. I said that I was certain that Hookstratten could get him a deal with NBC that would give him an opportunity in areas other than sports. This was becoming increasingly important to Don.

Meredith felt rejected by ABC in one sense. After his first spectacular year on *Monday Night Football,* he was deeply disappointed that ABC made no attempt to use him in prime-time entertainment. I was completely sympathetic to him in this regard, because I felt similarly rejected. Indeed, Don had had an idea for a series in which he would play the hero, a white-suited and invincible cowboy who, on a weekly basis, was called upon to save me, "the hanging judge," paunchy of body but acute of tongue, dressed from stovepipe hat to polished shoes in black. The whole concept would, of course, parallel our roles on *Monday Night Football,* but the project never got off the ground. The point of all this is that while I have had some luck with ABC in the entertainment field, Don has had none.

I knew Hookstratten very well. He is a shrewd, enterprising operator who became Carroll Rosenbloom's lawyer when Carroll acquired ownership of the Los Angeles Rams. He was also the attorney for Dick Martin and Dan Rowan of *Laugh-In* fame and for Dean Martin and Dean's producer, Greg Garrison, as well. Since I appeared often on those shows, I would see "Hooks" frequently and at one point even considered retaining him myself. NBC had expressed interest in me as the host of a weekly, prime-time variety show. I felt certain that "Hooks," who was very close to Herb Schlosser, president of NBC television, could work out a terrific deal for me. Ultimately, I rejected the idea because of loyalty to ABC which has been very good to me over the years and, quite frankly, because of promises made to me in the entertainment field by ABC.

But as I said, I knew "Hooks" and I knew that Don had to be thinking about moving to NBC. I related my talk with Meredith to Roone Arledge, but Roone expressed no alarm, feeling that he was already on top of the situation. At our final game in Los Angeles he had talked with Meredith about the following year, and Don had emphatically stated that he wanted to be on the team again in 1974. As events developed, Roone had two more meetings with Don in January, one at the time of the Bing Crosby Golf Tournament and the other on the eve of the Super Bowl in Houston. At that time, Don was appearing in a second episode of *Police Story.* On both occasions, according to Roone, Meredith committed himself to *Monday Night Football.*

On the Wednesday after the Super Bowl game, Don met me in Honolulu where we were making a joint appearance at a sponsor's sales meeting. He gave no indication that he would leave the Monday night package.

On February 16, he met me in Dallas, Texas. We were to cover an Evel Knievel motorcycle leap for ABC's *Wide World of Sports*. It was here that I learned that he had, in fact, retained Hookstratten. In our conversation that day, Don asked me who Hookstratten should contact at ABC with regard to opportunities in entertainment. I suggested Arledge in the first instance, but added that I did not think that Roone would be upset if he went to Elton Rule, president of ABC, Marty Starger, head of entertainment, or anyone else for that matter. Again, Don gave no indication of an intent other than staying with ABC.

Once again I told Roone what had transpired and once again he went to work. In the unraveling of the events that followed, it became clear that "Hooks" was negotiating with NBC on Meredith's behalf. Due to subsequent talks between Roone and Don, and subsequent actions taken by Roone with ABC's entertainment division, an all purpose deal was worked out for Don that included entertainment as well as *Monday Night Football*. The deal matched NBC's offer in every respect. One might have safely thought that the matter was at last resolved to everyone's liking. But the final blow was yet to be struck.

During the closing week of February, Emmy and I flew to Miami for the annual NFL meetings. It was there that Carl Lindemann, head of NBC Sports, told me point-blank that he thought that his company had Meredith under wraps. By this time, I was sick of the whole affair and didn't give a damn. But I told Arledge about it when I got back to New York. He again spoke to Meredith and received Don's assurance.

Several days later, it was a Friday, I got a call from Lindemann at about 4:30 P.M. He was buoyant as he asked me questions about Meredith. I told him that I had no interest in the matter, hung up, and went up and told Arledge that I was convinced that Don was going to NBC. Roone replied that he had spoken to Don the previous evening, that ABC was in the act of preparing a contract with Don and that Don was jubilant

over the way things were working out. Nonetheless, Roone
called in his aide who was preparing the contract and told him
to call Hookstratten immediately. When the assistant, Irwin
Wiener, reported back, he said that Hookstratten had been
evasive. Arledge ordered him to go to the coast at once to meet
with "Hooks." He then placed a call to Meredith and suddenly
Don was evasive also. Roone advised him that he was flying to
the coast that evening for further discussion. It was a wasted
trip. When Arledge got there, Meredith admitted that he had
already signed with NBC.

The entire charade was an exercise in the chicanery of the
broadcast jungle. "Hooks" was determined all along that Don
go with NBC. NBC was determined to get Don, first because
they believed that he could become effective in dramatic roles
and, more importantly, because they wanted to strike a blow at
the show that dominates Monday nights in prime time. Arledge, determined to protect the show that is the phenomenon of television and the only prime-time production of its ilk
to be among the top-20 rated shows for 1973, went to what he
called "absurd extremes" in order to keep Meredith. Ridiculous money offers are not uncommon in television if competing networks want the commodity. ABC, for example, pays
more for NCAA football than it is worth, but the NCAA has a
hammer over our heads. They can go to NBC or CBS and get
the money they want if we don't pay the piper. Thus, the
Meredith situation; a man with virtually no acting experience
was getting big money offers to become an actor when, in
truth, the aim of the bidding network was to hurt a successful
prime-time show and the purpose of the defending network
was to keep that show intact.

How it will all turn out remains to be seen. In my opinion,
Monday Night Football, now a social institution, will continue to
prosper. Indeed, it may well be that in view of Don's many
distresses during the course of the last year, the time was right
for the change. I remember the furor that followed the replacement of Keith Jackson with Frank Gifford, and yet in the
season that ensued, our ratings continued to rise. I think that
the same thing could happen again. At the present time, if
there is a real threat to *Monday Night Football,* it would lie more
in the departure of great NFL stars, like Csonka, Warfield and

Kiick, to the World Football League, and less in the departure of Jackson, Meredith, Cosell, Gifford or any other single performer on the show. This is because the package is now established as a viewing habit, where originally it needed "personality" announcers to attract viewers. Not that I won't miss "Dandy"; not that the show won't either. We had a chemistry on the air—and it worked. We had the mutuality of respect of which Don spoke that day in Elephant. We had great times together, and I'm sure we will again. And he gave our show a flavor that was unique, which is another reason Arledge tried so hard to keep him. But in our new structure we will concoct a new flavor and, at this stage, I think a better one.

While I didn't like the way Don left, I think he did the right thing for himself. Emotionally, he had to go. As he said in that last interview at Elephant, "My instincts, Howard, tell me it's time to move on. There's a lot going on out there and I want a part of it." Moving on. That's the story of Don Meredith's life.

I hope that things go well for him in the acting field. I think that with tight direction Don can make it. He has the flair. He doesn't really want to be in sports, and he told Roone and me that after his first year at NBC he intends to get out of sports altogether. Yet, NBC is already billboarding him as a sports-caster.

Sometimes you can think you are moving on when you're really moving out. And while there is a lot going on out there, as Don says, there comes a time when you have to decide what it is you want, and settle for it. You can't be a fugitive from life forever, always running away.

Sometimes, too, you can have an image that has made you nationally famous and never escape it. After all, Jim Nabors is still Gomer Pyle. I suspect that Meredith may always be just what he wants most not to be, "Dandy" Don. This is why I closed my farewell interview with him with the lyrics of Bob Dylan's, *Forever Yours:*

> May your hands be always busy
> May your feet be always swift
> May you lay a strong foundation
> When the winds of changes shift.

So long, "Dandy."

CHAPTER 2

SAY HELLO TO "THE HAMMER"

"We got 'The Hammer!' We got 'The Hammer.' "

The moment it became official that "Dandy" Don had left us, the search for his successor began. Roone Arledge had one basic criterion in mind. The person had to be a definable personality, just as Meredith was. But not like Meredith. Don was unique, and a lower-case cowboy type would only emphasize "Dandy's" departure. Certainly, an ordinary jock, an ex-player dedicated to the sanctity and intricacies of the game, would not do. What Roone wanted was someone possessing an admixture of humor, irreverence, candor and football credibility—or as close to having these four qualities as possible.

Arledge's quest lasted four months, and I was engaged in it with him. The first person we agreed upon, and this took place immediately following Don's departure, was Joe Willie Namath. Namath seemed ideal for these reasons: He is the biggest name in professional football, despite the injuries that have felled him during the past four years. It is Namath who they want for the television commercials. It is Namath who they want for the situation comedies and variety shows on television. It is Namath who is advertised for his obvious sex appeal, and women do constitute a large part of our audience. There could be no question of "Broadway Joe's" football credibility. When physically right, he had no peer in his ability to read and pick apart defenses. He had had lots of television experience, including his own syndicated show for a couple of years, so performing was not new to him. He was a personal friend of mine, and had done many shows with me, beginning with the very first time he had ever appeared on television in New York. We used to analyze the Super Bowl games together in a show that was, for a time, an annual fixture. Arledge and I had approached Joe in mid-season the previous year, when it had appeared that "Dandy" had run his race with us. Anyone who has ever socialized with Namath knows he has a good sense of humor. He is a breeze, fun-loving man who is naturally glib, quick at repartee and unafraid to speak out. On all counts, then, Namath seemed to be our best bet.

Because of this, Arledge's negotiations with Walsh and Joe never bore any semblance of reality.

Joe's confusion about his future was compounded by other elements. He is studying acting and wants to be a motion picture and television star when his playing career inevitably terminates. He understood that the American Broadcasting Company could, and would, be helpful in that regard. We would use him in the entertainment area; help him, train him, and he would have the opportunity to grow as a performer. All the while, he would be exposed, for three hours weekly, in prime time on one of the top-rated shows on television, *Monday Night Football*. During the four months that passed before we settled upon the new member of our broadcasting team, Roone met many times with Jimmy Walsh. He brought Jimmy up to our executive offices, introduced him to our top brass: Elton Rule, Wally Schwartz and Marty Starger, all of whom assured him of the company's interest in Namath's long-term future.

The whole thing was ethereal. Joe Namath is a football player. At least for now.

At the very end, before we settled upon our new choice, Arledge had talks with Walsh relative to Joe's playing and doing *Monday Night Football* at the same time. Roone had discussed with Pete Rozelle, the commissioner, the question of whether Rozelle would allow an active player to double as an announcer. According to Roone, Pete interposed no specific objection, implying that such a decision lay primarily with the ownership of the player's team. The Jets' owners objected. They would not let Namath do both. Walsh became furious, insisted that Joe could do both and asked Arledge to go ahead—in effect, to tell the Jets' owners to go to hell. Arledge didn't do it, wouldn't do it, and he was right.

I, myself, was dead set against the idea of using an active player in the booth. There were two reasons. First, I felt such a man could not possibly be objective. He would be handcuffed by loyalties to the players on the field. He would still be one of them in fact as well as in spirit. Second, if our man in the booth had had a bad game on the previous Sunday, or on several Sundays, the sports media people would be entirely justified in saying or writing that our announcer was performing poorly as a player because his concentration was divided. How could Namath, or any other active player, possibly do two demanding jobs at peak efficiency? It simply couldn't be done.

More than that, if we signed Namath, the publicity value would be enormous. The competitive networks would squirm.

For a variety of reasons we never did sign Joe Willie, although we went through nearly four months of talks. I really believe that Joe had an inner urge to do it. I also think that his attorney and close friend, Jimmy Walsh, wanted him to be with us. But their thinking was confused by a number of factors. In Joe Namath's mind, he is still first, and foremost, a football player. Regardless of all that has been said and written about his life-style, about the booze and the broads, the unwavering love of Joe's life has been football. And always, he has had the conviction that he is the best quarterback alive. Whether he is or not, and this is highly questionable because of his beleagured body, the fact remains that Namath believes this.

Namath is a kid where football is concerned. Watching him at Tuscaloosa in the off-season a couple of years ago as he tested his arm, throwing to a group of pick-up kids on the Alabama campus, I could sense his elation at the mere act of throwing a football. He would get it away, with that extraordinarily quick release of his, and then smile slowly—the smile broadening into a delighted grin—as unerringly the ball would rocket squarely into the hands of his receiver. Then he would rub his right arm with loving, tender care.

It will be a very hard thing for Joe Namath to give up football. He has a fixation about it. He wants to win another Super Bowl game. He wants to prove that despite all the injuries that have reduced his effectiveness, he can still be the greatest quarterback in the game. And he wants to use 1974 to find out if it is an impossible dream. Jimmy Walsh, who worships him, feels the same way.

While four months were passing, Roone was not sitting still. He and I were talking constantly about a successor, and we were both being besieged with applications. Strangely, during those months, while we held to a high opinion of Namath's desirability, his potential value to the package declined in both our minds. We began to fear that, following the initial publicity wave that Joe would cause, he might turn into just another jock in the booth, over absorbed with the technicalities of the contest. Employing Joe might be bad for both of us. And, always, we were puzzled by Joe's determination to play another season. It made no practical sense. He is a physically damaged man. His once enormous capacities are now limited. Even worse, he is surrounded by a terrible football team, which cannot possibly give him the protection that his 1968 team did. I am afraid that in the 1974 season Joe will get racked up again, this time forever as a football player. And the opportunity he might have had will have been lost.

The other man I wanted was Burt Reynolds. One of the hottest items on television and in the movies, Burt, it seemed to me, had everything. He had been a good football player at Florida State and had been drafted by the Baltimore Colts, but elected to become an actor instead. Burt has never lost his love for football and, using all of Arledge's criteria, I thought he would be perfect. Roone asked me to call him. The conversation was brief. Burt told me he would love to do it, but that he was tied exclusively to NBC.

Among those calling us were Willie Davis, the former Green Bay great and Sam Huff, the Giants hero. They had no chance. John Brodie, who signed with NBC, was never a candidate, but like Davis and Huff, he, too, would have had no chance. The Bears recommended one of their old stars, Bill George. They were well motivated, but like most owners, they know nothing about the broadcast business and, more specifically, the business of mass communication.

Bart Starr came in to see me. On any list of the world's greatest gentlemen, put him at the top. Bart really wanted the job. He explained to me what he thought he could bring to the package in terms of football analysis. I told him I would talk to Arledge, but that, in honesty, I did not think that Roone would hire him, and I explained the type of performer Roone was seeking. Bart was not considered.

Merlin Olson, the all-pro defensive lineman of the Rams, also came in to see me. He is an old friend for whom I have tremendous respect. A brilliant, articulate and serious man, he was considering retiring from football and he wanted to know what the opportunities might be in sports broadcasting. I asked him if he was talking about *Monday Night Football.* He said no. I told him I was glad about that, because I honestly didn't think he was the man we wanted. Then I called Carl Lindemann of NBC Sports and set up an appointment for Merlin. Carl was very impressed with Olson, and I am sure that when Merlin does retire he will go to work for NBC. But such is the nature of competition between the networks, that even though I sent Merlin to Carl, Lindemann later called me suspiciously and said, "I'm very taken with Olson, but are you guys using me as a beard? Isn't he really the man you want for Monday nights?" I was flabbergasted. Then I laughed and assured Carl that my intentions were strictly honorable.

We called Jimmy Brown in California. To our amazement, because Jim is doing so well in movies, he expressed a mild interest and agreed to meet with us when we came out to the Coast. Roone and I did go to the Coast for ABC's affiliate station meetings, but we never did get together with Brown—which was wrong. We missed connections because our time was taken up with company business at the meetings. Also, we decided that Jim, even if he were interested, was just too serious for the job. Brown is a somber man.

I suggested Dick Butkus. He *is* a definable personality. His body is the image of professional football, symbolizing as it

does the violence and the warfare of the sport. I called Dick
and he came to see us in New York. Poor Dick. As fierce and
unrelenting as he always was on the football field, he is that
lovable a guy in person. He limped into the ABC building.
The football wars have crippled him and he is involved now in
a lawsuit against the Chicago Bears that occupies his mind
every waking moment. We met in Arledge's office for about
an hour and most of the talk was about that. When he left,
Roone and I agreed that visually, Butkus, with his battle-
scarred appearance and his gargantuan body, would bring a
special flavor to the show, but that it would stop there. Verbally, we agreed, he was not ready for prime-time television.

At one point, I had a talk with Bill Cosby and recommended
that Roone see him. That recommendation was buttressed by
another from Chet Forte. Chet had been impressed by Bill at a
celebrity tennis tournament in Monaco. In my own talk with
Cosby, Bill had indicated that he would like to do *Monday
Night Football*. My admiration for Bill Cosby, as a man and as a
performer, is such that I believe he can do anything. Arledge
did not agree. He argued that Cosby would lack football
credibility. "He would have to be funny every Monday night
for three hours," Roone said, "and that's too much to ask of
any man. He would hurt himself and the package too."

While all of these negotiations were transpiring, three other
names were paramount: Paul Hornung, Alex Karras and
O. J. Simpson.

Off camera and microphone, Paul Hornung has always
been a definable personality. "The Golden Boy," as he was
called, has been one of the delightful people of sports. Light-
hearted and carefree, he waltzes his way through life. He has
had his ups and downs, as pro football's most valuable player,
and as a man who lost a year of his football life because of
betting on games in the National Football League while he was
a player. I have known him since 1956, and I believe we have
been friends ever since. Paul and I have gone out together,
played gin rummy together, talked football together and
done shows together. The thrills he gave me as a player, and
the way we both felt about Vince Lombardi will be a bond
between us always.

When he retired from football, he tried his hand at broadcasting. It was not his bag. He was self-conscious; he would clam up, he could not be himself. Paul Hornung, all charm, became Paul Hornung, all stumbles. But Paul is a worker, and he worked at improving himself. I think he has come along very well as a performer. He is one of the radio voices of the Minnesota Vikings, and he has his own syndicated television show—I did one with him—which appears to be successful. Paul felt he was ready for *Monday Night Football* and he wanted the job.

Arledge authorized me to talk to Hornung about it. No representations and no commitments were to be made, and none were. I emphasized to Paul that what we wanted was a man who knew football, but a man who could bring much more than that knowledge to the telecasts. Paul understood. "I can't be 'Dandy,' " he told me, "nor would I try to be. I can only be Paul Hornung, but I promise you, if I get the job, I won't be an Xs and Os guy. You needle me, and I'll tell you I took enough of that stuff from Lombardi."

We weighed Paul very seriously. I would have been delighted to have had him aboard. But after viewing a recent television show that he did in his series, it was decided, unanimously, that Paul simply could not give us the dimension and flavor that we felt had been characteristic of the show. So Paul lost out.

Alex Karras was another matter. For most of the four months until the new man was named, I thought Alex would get the job. His career had gone up, not down, after he left football. He is a funny man, a character, the kind of guy you know is there. He has become an experienced performer, working the television talk and variety shows, and he has done movies. He also did Canadian football. While the reports on his work in Canada were bad, we felt that he didn't have much to work with up there, and that he didn't have the leadership necessary in the broadcast booth to bring out his best assets. We also liked the idea that he had been an all-pro lineman for years. He had some of the visual qualities of Butkus, and we felt that his massive body would evoke the very image of the sport. And no one could question Alex's credibility. Not number 71, a perennial star who had been an All American at the University of Iowa.

More than that, I like Alex Karras. When he was at Iowa in the 1950s, I did his first network interview with him. We became friends. I did a bit part in his David Wolper movie, *The Five Hundred Pound Jerk,* and I did a pilot for him for a television series at my home in Pound Ridge. He appeared on a television "roast" of me. I felt that Alex and I would have a fine chemistry working together; different from my relationship with "Dandy," but just as effective. Arledge agreed and he was on the verge of closing out the issue several times by hiring Alex.

Once, in a conversation with Pete Rozelle, Roone told Pete that he was inclining towards Karras. Karras and Pete have never been known to be fond of one another. When Karras was suspended from football along with Hornung—and, for the same reason—Karras really kicked up a storm. He called Pete a lot of names, and he did it publicly. Rozelle, in his talk with Arledge, told Roone, "You've got the right to hire him, but you'll have trouble with the owners." That fired Roone up and when he told me about it, it fired me up. There was that old question again of owners trying to control announcers. Sure enough, at least a dozen owners spoke to me against Karras, and probably even more spoke to Arledge. They were incensed at Alex because he had allegedly knocked the NFL in his Canadian telecasts. Some of those who spoke to me had never wanted *me* on the air in the first place. Once *Monday Night Football* had become a ratings success, they changed their tune. We're the ones, at ABC, who have to get $100,000 a minute to make back what we pay to the National Football League—not the owners. We're the ones who have to get the ratings to command that kind of money—not the owners. Their idea of show business is to put on a parade of their former players—regardless of their communicative ability —and have them utter silly repetitive nonsenses about the technicalities of football. The owners may mean well, but they just don't understand.

Alex Karras did not get the job, but it wasn't because of the owners. In the final analysis, it was because Roone found a man who he considered better qualified on all counts. Also, Roone had been deeply troubled, as I had been, by the fact that Karras had once associated himself with a weekly football betting sheet and had written a column on how to bet *Monday Night Football*.

O. J. Simspon came into the picture under unexpected circumstances. "The Juice" is in his prime; the greatest, most exciting player in the game. He is young, strong and under a long-term contract to the Buffalo Bills. But when Csonka, Kiick and Warfield jumped to the World Football League, and O. J. found out how much money Csonka was getting, he got a little fidgety.

Simpson is an honorable man, and he is not greedy. He is also human. He gained almost twice as many yards as Csonka did last season. When he signed his contract with the Bills for a span of years, at a salary that suddenly seemed puny next to what Csonka was getting from the new league, he did it because he wanted to prove himself to America as a professional, which he had not yet done. He also has a genuine affection for Ralph Wilson, the owner of the Buffalo Bills, and his current coach, Lou Saban, is his kind of coach. Lou lets him run with the football. Simpson also has intelligence. He knows that at any time, in any game, a knee can go. It happened to Gale Sayers. It has happened to many others.

Thus O. J. decided to attempt to renegotiate his contract with Buffalo. Ralph Wilson is a fine man, and he has a warm affective for O. J. He is also a businessman, and he knows that a contract is a contract. He was hardly disposed to be malleable. Accordingly, he kept putting O. J. off. Simpson grew restive. He began to talk to me about *Monday Night Football*. One of O. J.'s hopes for the future, when he is done playing football, is to become part of the *Monday Night* broadcast team. "I'm prepared to take the consequences and quit," Simpson told me, "if Ralph doesn't agree to give me more money." "That's your business," I replied, "as long as you're willing to take the consequences. But don't use *Monday Night Football* as a bargaining ploy. That would be up to Arledge, not me."

I told Roone of my conversation with "The Juice," and Arledge had subsequent talks with him, apparently in the same vein. Privately, Roone and I agreed that if O. J. ever did quit football, he would be fine as the third man in the booth.

He is already part of the ABC Sports staff—we have been training him—and he is a natural. But we didn't want him to leave the game just yet. Not when he is at his peak, and when bright years loom before him, years which include a movie career. The more attention he continues to get as a player, the more *that* public notice will serve to further his future career in many other areas.

On Thursday, June 27, 1974, Simpson called Roone Arledge from California. In a controlled, measured voice, O. J. advised Roone that his mind was made up. He was going to quit football. As Arledge related the conversation to me, he said, "There was no emotion in his voice, no sign of being upset. He had been thinking it through and he said his mind was made up. Then he asked me if he could get the *Monday Night Football* job."

"What did you tell him?" I asked.

"I told him he always has a home here, and if that is his final decision, he has the job. But I also told him I wanted him to think it over for a couple of more days, because I didn't think he should quit football now."

Two days later, O. J. called. He had met with Ralph Wilson. All differences had been resolved.

On Wednesday, June 26, the day before Simpson called Roone, I was in Roone's office. We were again discussing the candidates for the job. Casually, Roone asked, "What do you think of Fred Williamson?"

I laughed. " 'The Hammer,' you mean?"

"Yes."

"I think he's terrific. I thought about him a couple of months ago but discarded the idea as fast as it came to me. The guy is red hot in movies. I don't think he'd be interested."

"Jimmy Brown was," Roone reminded me. "How much do you know about Williamson?"

"Well, I know all about his football career, and especially the first Super Bowl game. But more than that, we've done shows together. I did the *Merv Griffin Show* with him, and I did my own radio talk show, *Speaking of Everything,* with him when he was in town making the movie, *Crazy Joe.*"

"Well, what do you think?"

"I already told you, I think the guy's great. He's an excellent speaker, an educated man. He's brash, cocky, maybe even arrogant, but some of that is an act. He's a handsome devil, loving his movie success, living it up and he's got the football credibility you want."

"Do you have the tape of your radio show with him?"

"I'm sure we have it in the files."

"Get it. Let's listen to it."

We listened to it, together with Roone's assistant, Dick Ebersol, later that afternoon. It was all in the tape: the articulation, the intelligence, the laughter, the brashness, the success, the remembrances of football, the days on the *Julia* show with Diahann Carroll, the months as an architect in Montreal. Listening to it, I was impressed all over again with Fred Williamson. So was Arledge.

Roone ordered Ebersol to get a print of Fred's new movie, *Three the Hard Way,* with Jim Brown and Jim Kelly, so that we could screen it the next night.

By the time we sat down, on the following evening, to view the film, O. J. Simpson had made his portentous call and we could have been undertaking a hollow exercise. But we did it anyway. The picture was preposterously bad, but Fred Williamson was good. Roone decided that we had to track him down to discover whether he had any interest in doing *Monday Night Football.* Ebersol was assigned the task of finding him.

Dick searched him out in Santa Fe, New Mexico, where he was completing a movie. Williamson was interested. But things would have to move quickly because he had a motion-picture commitment in Europe coming up, and if he were to do *Monday Night Football,* he would have to get out of that commitment. Tuesday would be the deadline.

On Saturday, O. J. was out of the picture—the *Monday Night* picture, that is. On Monday, I was homesick, when I got a call from Roone and Dick advising me that Williamson was flying in on Tuesday. Would I be well enough to come in so that we could all have dinner with Frank Gifford and form a judgment? Yes.

We met for dinner at 7:45 P.M. the next night. But before that I spent an hour with "The Hammer" in his room at the

Warwick Hotel, across the street from ABC's offices. I found him the same challenging man I remembered, full of swagger, and I liked it. He said things like: "Man, that *Monday Night Football,* that's the whole bag. I wouldn't even consider Sunday afternoon."

"You won't be the star with me there."

"I'll be the sex symbol. They won't know Gifford is there."

His eyes flash when he talks, and the grin is always there. He doesn't mean a lot of what he says, and you can tell when he's serious. The smile vanishes and the eyes become thoughtful. I talked football with him and it was clear he had stayed on top of the game.

What I liked about him most of all was the fact that he's a worker. We discussed his days on the *Julia* show, just as we had done on my radio talk show. The man has no patience with people who don't work, who don't seek to meet professional standards. This, as he saw it, was the problem with the people in the cast of *Julia.*

I asked Fred if he knew Frank Gifford, and I was astonished to learn that he had played against him in 1960. Williamson, of course, was a defensive back, 6-foot, 3-inches tall, 210 pounds, marvelously proportioned and reasonably quick. "It was in 1960 when I was a rookie with the Pittsburgh Steelers," he related. "In the final minute of our game against the Giants we were ahead and they threw a long desperation pass to Gifford in the end zone. Dickie Moegle and I had him double covered. Moegle slipped and fell. I was in front of Gifford waiting to catch the ball which was just hanging up there. Gifford kneed me in the leg from behind, and I tumbled down. He caught the pass, the official never called it, and our coach, Buddy Parker, went wild." He laughed. "I never thought much of Moegle."

With that, we picked up Dick Ebersol, and went to meet Frank and Roone for dinner. Frank arrived first and quickly confirmed the story of the Steelers' game. "Buddy Parker has never talked to me since," Frank smiled. When Roone arrived, we all sat down to eat and Fred proceeded to recount the famed Super Bowl I story. "When I joined the Chiefs," he said, "they probably had the best personnel in football, but they were a quiet bunch. Hank Stram got me aside and told me he wanted me to be the holler guy, the team leader. I told him sure, that's what I was. Then, when we were getting ready to play against Green Bay in the Super Bowl, the guys all acted like we were going against a bunch of green monsters. I kept talking about what I was going to do against the Packers. Stram told me to quiet down. This isn't the time to talk, Stram would tell me. Why not, I would ask? Those little green monsters aren't gonna run off and hide, they're gonna show up, and so are we. The writers kept telling me what Fuzzy Thurston and the others were going to do to me, and I just kept laughing and talking. I thought I was getting to the Green Bay guys. At their practices, Willie Wood was wearing a sweatshirt with a hammer on it, and he'd keep yelling, 'We'll get "The Hammer." ' Well, they got me and I was carried off the field. I wasn't gonna get up. But when I got to the sidelines I stood up and looked across the field. There was old number 24, Willie Wood, jumping up and down and shouting, 'We got "The Hammer," we got "The Hammer." ' It was some day, I'll tell you. The funny thing was I never wanted to go to Kansas City. It was the one place I didn't want to go. When I was with Oakland, I told Al Davis, if you ever trade me don't trade me to Kansas City. Davis told me he never would, and then he traded me to Kansas City. What's a guy gonna do in Kansas City?"

We finished dinner and went up to Arledge's apartment. I could see that Arledge was really impressed with Fred and Gifford whispered to me that he thought Williamson was terrific. Roone and I teamed up against Fred and Frank in two games of pool, 25 balls per game. They creamed us. I lost $25 each game to Williamson and blamed Arledge. He blamed me. Williamson, by the way, plays pool like he's acting a movie role. He doesn't even bend over when he shoots. He stands straight up like a black Gaylord Ravenal and just moves the cue in a swift, easy, precise manner, and the damn ball doesn't go into the pocket, it bisects it.

Abruptly, after the two defeats, Roone put away his cue, told Frank and me to play a game head to head and left the room to talk with Fred. I devoured Gifford, 25–8, and as the game ended Roone came in with Williamson and said, "It's done, meet the new member of *Monday Night Football*."

We went into the living room, called the *Monday Night* producer, Don Ohlmeyer, who was in town doing some film editing, and told him to come right over. He was there within five minutes.

We toasted "The Hammer."

There are two similarities between Fred Williamson and the Texan who came before him. Both played professional football; Fred Williamson is a successful actor and the Texan may become one.

All else will be different. *Monday Night Football* will have a new look.

Say hello to "The Hammer."

CHAPTER 3

THE CARACAS CAPER

"I've got a feeling we're never going to get out of this place."

As far as I am concerned, it shall be known forevermore as "The Caracas Caper." I refer to the George Foreman-Ken Norton heavyweight championship fight held in Caracas, Venezuela, on March 26, 1974.

Perhaps the best way to begin in this case is with the ending, because the ending characterized, in its own zany way, the whole comic episode that constituted "the fight" and its surrounding circumstances.

It was the morning after Foreman had reduced Norton to boxing rubble. Emmy and I left the Caracas Hilton at 7:30 along with Terry Jastrow, my producer, and Dorrance Smith, my production assistant. Like everyone else, we wanted to get out of Caracas as quickly as possible, and we were booked on the 9:30 A.M. Viasa flight to New York. While we were driving to the airport I felt an overwhelming sense of relief. Three days in Caracas were over, and suddenly I thought of Woody Allen's classic one-liner in his movie, *Sleeper*. Somebody asked him what it felt like to have been away for 200 years, and he said, "like spending a weekend in Beverly Hills." The three days in Caracas were like being away for 200 years. The way it turned out for George Foreman, the time he spent there seemed like a millenium.

But all that would be behind us now. We bounced into the airport and up to the ticket counter with a whole new verve. Civilization was only four hours away—or so we thought. After getting our tickets validated and our passports checked, we went through customs and were ushered into the VIP room. Joe Louis was there, along with his wife Martha. So were four other Americans, identified with the La Costa Country Club in California. Three of them were booked on a 10:00 A.M. flight to Miami, the other was on our flight to New York. The first thing that happened was that a passenger service agent advised us that our flight was delayed for an hour and a half. We went straight out to the Pan Am counter to check for other flights. No luck. Pan Am had a 4:30 flight that afternoon which was fully booked. Back we went to the Viasa VIP room, there to learn that the passenger service agent was mistaken. It was the 10:00 A.M. flight to Miami that was delayed. "Great," I thought, "Let the others suffer. Just get me out of here."

At 9:20 a Viasa stewardess led us into a minibus and off we drove to the plane. Joe Louis was muttering, "It looks good to me." I knew what he meant. Even a Boeing 707 can look good at a time like that. The plane seemed packed except for four empty seats in first class. Most of the coach space was taken by people from the Carter Underwear Company of Indiana. They had been having their annual sales convention at the Caracas Hilton, and their advertising slogan was "Be smarter, Use Carter." I was to think of that, and a lot of other things, in less than an hour.

9:30 came and went, and we did not take off. Those four seats were still empty. Now it was 9:45 and we were getting restless. 9:55. Finally, the expected passengers arrived. Muhammad Ali and his manager, Herbert Muhammad, Herbert's daughter and a friend, and two of the Ali retinue. Ali, as buoyant and self-absorbed as ever, boarded the plane with a positive gaiety, laughed down the malevolent glares of the rest of us and deposited himself in the row behind me. But now there was a new problem. The flight had been oversold in the first-class section. Ali's group numbered six and there were only four vacant seats. This produced, first, consternation, then panic among the Viasa representatives. Finally, as the minutes ticked away, they decided to approach two of the first-class passengers who had already been seated. Very politely, they tried to induce them to go back to the coach section. The two would not budge. They were a very attractive pair, and I learned later that she was a German woman who had married a wealthy Canadian oil man. Tragically, her husband had died one month ago to that very day in a plane crash. Her companion was a business colleague of her late husband, and her two children were on the plane with her. The Viasa people had obviously tried the wrong pew.

More indecision. It was now 10:20. I turned to Emmy and said, "I've got a feeling we're never going to get out of this place." But Herbert Muhammad came to the rescue. There were still two seats somewhere back in the coach section, and so he had two of the Ali entourage go back there. The Viasa people smiled relievedly, bowed and exited from the plane. The door closed, and we settled back for takeoff . . . . At long last!

The plane taxied to the runway, the engines roared and down the runway we went. We reached the midpoint of the runway and suddenly there was an absolute hush in the plane. WE WERE NOT TAKING OFF! Desperately, the pilot tried to brake the plane. I squeezed Emmy's hand, and she mine. The thoughts that flashed through my mind, in just a few seconds, were ones I'll never forget. Peter and Jill know that Robert Schulman is our lawyer. He'll take care of everything for them. But Hilary is alone in California. Will she hold up? Friends like Carroll Rosenbloom, Don Klosterman, Jim Mahoney—they'll be there to help. My mother will be all right, too. She'll be taken care of financially, and my brother Hilton will be there. But little Justin and Jared . . . Our dream is to see them grow up. Why, oh why, was this happening? And why did Emmy have to be with me? She's so strong, so balanced, if only she were safe at home. She could handle everything, anything. And then, eerily, in a crazy flash I thought, "I won't even get the headlines. Ali and Joe Louis will."

We could feel the plane slowing, but we all knew that the Caribbean was just feet away. I found out later that Joe Louis can't swim. The plane stopped about 20 feet short of the sea-wall. Emmy's hand, encased within mine, was limp. So was mine. We made a turn and started taxiing back to where we had boarded. Not a word, not a single word of explanation from the pilot. But at least we had averted catastrophe, and suddenly the cabin started to hum with conversation, the most notable comment coming from Muhammad Ali. "Howard," he said, "I saved you again. Allah and me. If I wasn't on this plane you'd be in the ocean."

This from Muhammad Ali, who is terrified of flying. He will drive a thousand miles from Chicago to New York rather than take a plane. "You're right, Muhammad," I smiled weakly.

As the plane pulled up to the landing position, we finally heard an announcement: "There will be a fifteen-minute delay to repair a minor instrument."

Immediately after the announcement was made, one of the passengers, a Britisher named John Marshall, jumped to his feet and said, "I'm getting off. I've got to get another plane. I don't care when. I've had enough of Viasa." John Marshall is a producer-manager who, until recently, handled the British actor, Richard Harris. He is currently producing a motion picture on the life of Muhammad Ali; the screenplay is to be written by Budd Schulberg. He is a most engaging chap, looks a little like George Segal and his speech is punctuated by a colorful, clipped, vastly expressive style that smacks of everything one always attaches to the British culture. You close your eyes, listen to him talk and you think you're getting a lesson from Professor Higgins.

At any rate, Marshall was outraged, and even as he was talking, the passenger representatives were boarding the plane and asking us all to disembark. That really did John in. He turned angrily to me, shouting, "What do these stupid blokes think that they're doing. Good Lord, first we must wait fifteen minutes to have a minor instrument fixed. Now we are being asked to leave the plane. Did you see that ground crew before we boarded? Their eyes lighted up when they learned the damned thing could fly. They couldn't fix anything. I am going to insist on my baggage. Will you and your wife join me, old chap? I have absolutely no desire for a watery grave!"

My mood, at the moment, was one of total agreement. But the problem of securing our luggage seemed insurmountable. In any event, Emmy and I joined all the others in leaving the plane. A heavy Venezuelan lady was waiting at the entrance to an auxiliary terminal building about 30 feet from the plane, and she shepherded all the passengers through a seemingly endless corridor into a vast waiting area. Except for John Marshall, what we all wanted to know was what was wrong with the plane and how long were we going to be detained. No answers were forthcoming. The Venezuelan lady vanished, but two Viasa male passenger-service agents did appear.

Marshall went right at them, demanding that they remove his luggage. "There must be another plane," he shouted, "and you chaps have got to get me on it! I've got an afternoon meeting with my attorneys in New York City. It's critical!" The agents nodded in sympathy and assured John that nothing could be done.

Nor could the agents tell us how long we would be delayed. One of them did say that a valve in one engine of the plane had burned, whatever that meant—and it didn't sound good —and all we could do was settle down and wait. There was a bar in the waiting area which was opened for the passengers, and some 200 descended upon it en masse. We decided to forego that scene. Let the Carter Underwear people have first crack.

Everyone of us was disgruntled and nervous over the whole situation: the narrow escape, the absence of any real information, the sense of entrapment in the waiting room and the fear of getting on the plane again even if we were told that it had been fixed. But there was absolutely nothing we could do. There were telephone coin boxes, just two of them, on a wall, and I asked Terry Jastrow to call New York to explain our delay. It developed that one couldn't call long distance on these phones. In fact, we were advised that no long-distance calls could be made from anywhere in the premises. Another comforting thought. And then, as John Marshall and I surrounded the Viasa agents, we were told with finality that we would simply have to wait, that nothing could be done, that we had passed through customs and were technically no longer in

Venezuela. During all this time, Muhammad Ali was signing autographs; Herbert Muhammad was saying, "It's Allah's will"; Joe and Martha Louis wanted soft drinks but couldn't get near the bar. The crowd there was ten deep.

Another 45 minutes had elapsed. Suddenly, a couple of young Viasa stewardesses appeared and ushered a group of us into a small VIP lounge just outside the waiting room: Joe and Martha Louis, Muhammad Ali and Herbert Muhammad, Emmy and I, Terry Jastrow and Dorrance Smith, John Marshall, and the lady whose husband had died in a crash so recently, and her companion. The girls brought us Cokes and sandwiches, and then clustered around Ali. He was not averse. Arms around them, he said, "See, Howard, I'm world famous and pretty. Once you leave America, nobody knows you." No argument.

The food and drink was only a temporary palliative. We were told we had to wait another hour; that the plane was being fixed. The hour developed into an hour and a half. John Marshall suffered through several more tempestuous outbursts and then, suddenly, a Viasa man approached us with a polished, winning smile, and advised us that we could now board. His very manner bespoke pride of Venezuelan efficiency. The only trouble was, as we started back down that tunnellike corridor, none of us felt safe in getting on the plane. This was when I could have used Carter underwear.

The plane took off. It rose peacefully and uneventfully, and we soared over the Caribbean. Another in my long history of flight adventures.

The trip home was not uneventful. Nothing ever is with Muhammad Ali. He had the window seat in the last row of the first-class section. Herbert Muhammad had the aisle seat next to him. The two were engrossed in conversation, obviously about financial matters. I was sitting on the aisle across from them in the row ahead. Herbert had one of those new instant calculators which he was explaining to Muhammad. It seemed to be a clear-cut case of the blind leading the blind. Herbert would talk, Ali would listen and nod. At one point, Herbert called over to me, "Howard, do you put any of your money into gold?" "All of it," I answered airily. "The price of raw gold keeps going up. As a matter of fact, I'm taking a look at silver, too. Lamar Hunt is buying up silver all over the place." Whereupon Herbert looked at Ali triumphantly and said, "What did I tell you? You've got to buy gold."

A few minutes later Ali got up to stretch his legs, walked by me and said, "I've got to buy me some gold." Then he proceeded up the cabin in the splendid manner of a senior partner of Lehman Brothers.

I moved into the now-vacant seat next to Herbert. "Explain the calculator to me, Herbert," I asked. Herbert is a short, pudgy-faced man, with an expression that is very close to jolly. He is extremely mild in demeanor, almost benign. But don't ever cross him. The Muslim training is lodged deep within that smallish body, and I have seen that round, almost merry face harden into a ball of hatred. At this particular moment, though, Herbert was at his very best, perfectly willing to grant me the magnificence of his intellectual largesse.

"Well, as you can see, it's got everything. You can figure out sine, cosine, tangent, co-tangent, even logarithms." I was astonished at the easy, fluid way he threw out terms that hearkened back to plane geometry, trigonometry and intermediate algebra. I wondered when in the world the inner councils of the Grand Prophet demanded a quick figuring of the opposite over the hypotenuse, or the opposite over the adjacent. "When do you need to work with right triangles, Herbie?"

"Not often," he assured me, "it's just good to have it all there."

"Well, what were you showing Muhammad?"

"Oh, that was just subtraction and division. Look. We begin with five million for the Foreman fight. . . . " And then, quickly, Herbert started punching out numbers and subtracting from the $5 million starting figure. He deducted training expenses, his own share as manager, federal taxes, state taxes (estimates, of course), and came to a net figure for Ali of $1.5 million.

"Some of that has to go into gold," he told me.

"Obviously," I agreed. Knowing the ways of Ali with money, I thought to myself that he could, successfully, spend the whole net within a year. Once, in a matter of days, he had run up a bill of more than $100,000 at a Las Vegas Hotel for himself and his ubiquitous followers. Still, it was nice to know that Ali's last fight would give him a chance at the financial security that still eludes him. I went back to join Emmy. "Herbie has become an economist, investment counselor and a mathematician," I confided.

Ali returned from the coach section. He was, as always, restless.

"Those folks back there are crowded, they're uncomfortable. We've got to go back and entertain them. You call me nigger and boy, and we'll do our act."

What I wanted to do was go to sleep, but instead I trailed him into the coach section and we went through a routine reserved for off-camera situations. "Look here, nigger," I would begin. "Did you say Trigger?" he would answer. "Now listen boy," I would say. "You mean Roy?" he would query. And the passengers loved it. I guess after the day they had been undergoing, anything that passed for levity was welcome.

I never did get any sleep on that flight. One way or another Ali was determined to keep us all aware of his presence. He has an energy level higher than that of any person I have every known. He is inexhaustible.

When the pilot finally announced that we were beginning our descent into the New York area, Ali strode quickly forward and went into the cockpit area. This I had never seen before, and I figured they'd throw him out. But they didn't. He stayed in there.

Joe Louis is an observant man with a much underrated sense of humor. He turned to Emmy and me and asked, "Didn't a plane once hit the Empire State Building?"

"Yes," Emmy answered.

"Didn't something else once happen over New York?"

"Yes," Emmy again replied. "Two planes once crashed head on over Brooklyn. Why?"

"Because with Muhammad in the cockpit, something like that's sure to happen to us."

Just as Joe said that, Ali emerged. His terror of flying had reappeared. "I ain't ever gonna do that again," he muttered. "You see too much."

Suddenly he turned to Louis. "Joe, did you ever chop wood when you were in training?"

"Yes, all the time at Pompton Lakes (Louis's old training site)."

"Why'd you do it?" Ali pursued.

"Because they told me to," Joe answered reasonably.

"I think I'll chop wood in Africa before the Foreman fight," Ali said.

"Better chop a lot of it," said Joe.

The plane landed at 5:45 P.M. at Kennedy. "The Caracas Caper" was over.

It had begun in a different way.

Emmy and I were really excited about going to Caracas. We had never been there before, and based upon all we had heard and read, we expected to find it one of the great cities of the world. Emmy had read all the travel brochures and, indeed, all the promotional material read like one long, slick, Doyle, Dane Bernbach ad. You know the kind I mean: clever, suggestive copy, and not too much of it; the brilliant juxtaposition of the words against graphics. The kind of stuff that they've done with the island of Jamaica. The way they made a VW seem like the biggest car in the world despite its small size. That's why we were sold on Caracas.

We took an early morning Pan Am flight on Sunday, March 24. It was a clear, beautiful day and four hours and 20 minutes later, we began our final descent into Caracas. The scene lived up to the promotional material. Majestic mountains lined the shoreline, and then there was the Caribbean itself, splashing up on sandy beaches bleached white by the tropical sun. Visions of Hawaii danced through my mind, especially with a heavy mist settling in on the mountain tops. It almost looked like a whole series of Diamond Heads. The airport itself is at the very tip of the shore, jutting out into the sea.

Terry Jastrow had arrived the previous day, and had arranged to have a driver at the airport for Emmy and me. After clearing customs and picking up our baggage, we set out on the 50-minute drive on the relatively new highway which wends its way through the mountainside in an ever-climbing pattern toward Caracas. Caracas, the capital city of Venezuela, sits at an altitude of 3000 feet above sea level, cradled among mountains which soar ever upward.

As we made the drive, there were few homes to be seen, and those that we did see were, in the main, tiny huts of tin and discarded boards like those you see in and around Mexico City. Finally, as we entered the city of Caracas, any visions of Hawaii were banished forever from my mind. There, surrounding the city, were the tiered shanty dwellings which served as homes for the multitudes. The squalor was foremost; then the sight of lines of wash drying in the torrid sun. This was Mexico City all over again, poverty everywhere, circa 1968.

We drew up to the Caracas Hilton which is set in the heart of Caracas, surrounded by tall office buildings and high-rise apartment dwellings. I don't know if you have ever seen the Kahala Hilton on the island of Oahu. But it is one of the world's most beautiful hotels, in a paradise-like setting. I suppose we had expected that the Caracas Hilton would be something like that. Instead, I felt as if we were in the old Hotel Astor on Times Square.

We stayed at the Caracas Hilton because this was the headquarters for the Foreman-Norton fight. After check-in, we went straight to the pool which was one flight above the lobby. It felt like being in a public bath. Turn one way and you were confronted with the office buildings, turn another and you'd see wash hanging from a thousand lines. In all of the promotional brochures that I had read about the Caracas Hilton, I had never seen a mention of any of this. We got settled in pool chairs and lay back to get some sun. Suddenly, the wind whipped up, black clouds rushed in and we had a downpour. I was to learn that this happens almost every afternoon in Caracas.

I had viewed Caracas as a much-needed vacation. I didn't have much interest in the fight because I was convinced that Foreman would knock out Norton within three rounds and had made a prediction to that effect on the air before I left the States. But now, disenchanted with my early experience with Caracas, I elected to join the fight mob in the lobby.

The fight crowd, at any important heavweight event, never changes. There are always past managers, trainers, ex-fighters, the camp hangers-on, the publicity people and, of course, the writers. And you know you are always going to see some of them either in the lobby or at the bar of the hotel where the fight is headquartered. At Muhammad Ali fights, there is usually a step up in class. Some of the more sophisticated and famous writers will be in attendance, like Norman Mailer and Budd Schulberg. But in this case, they were conspicuous by their absence.

The one landmark figure through my nearly 20 years of covering boxing is Harold Conrad and, sure enough, he was the first person I met in the lobby. Harold can be classified professionally as either a publicity man or a press agent. In either case he is extremely effective. He knows everybody there is to know on the fight scene. He knows how to handle the press and keep them happy. He has personal quality, because he is himself a competent writer, has been a columnist in his time, has written screenplays and is at conversational ease on any level of company.

Conrad's personal appearance is astonishing when contrasted with his age. Now well into his 60s, he remains trim, almost sleek, walks tall at about 6 feet 1 inch, and looks to be in his late 40s. His dress is impeccable, his manner urbane, his tongue witty, his moustache carefully styled. He reminds me, in a way, of the old Edwin Arlington Robinson poem, *Richard Cory* which began, "Whenever Richard Cory went downtown, we people on the pavement looked at him . . . He was a gentleman from sole to crown, clean favored and imperially slim. . . ." That's Harold Conrad, definitely out of place in the boxing business, but cursed forevermore as a part of it. I am sure, however, that he will not come to Richard Cory's end. For Richard Cory went home one night and "put a bullet through his head."

In any event, I asked Harold to fill me in on what was happening. He told me that, for the first time within memory, he was having nothing to do with the promotion of a heavyweight championship fight. But he said, "There is a storm brewing over the referee."

It developed that Foreman's manager, Dick Saddler, had brought his own man to Venezuela to referee the fight, a fellow from Washington State named Jimmy Rondeau. The Venezuelans had another idea. They wanted a Venezuelan to referee the fight. The Norton people had still another notion. The whispers went that they wanted a German who lives in Puerto Rico to be the referee. This chap was a friend of Bill Daley, who also lives in Puerto Rico. Daley is an old-time fight manager whose reputation has been subject to question from time to time (that's a careful understatement), and, reputedly, he had a behind-the-scenes ownership interest in Norton. So everyone wanted a piece of the act, and what else was new? This kind of nonsense (strategic and often undercover attempts at maneuver) is deeply rooted in boxing history. There has never been very much about the business that is savory. And I have never seen a championship bout fail to take place because of a squabble over the referee.

I was more interested in the story that had broken just before my arrival in Caracas, a story concerning the Ali-Foreman fight in Zaire, Africa, on or about September 30, with each fighter getting a guarantee of five million dollars. Conrad assured me that the story was true, which disconcerted me even more than the Caracas Hilton. "How the hell do you get to Zaire? Where do you stay? How do you get out? What shots do you need—cholera, and what else? And who needs the whole damned thing?" This is what I was thinking as Harold talked, and in the back of my mind I could hear my boss, Roone Arledge, telling me in his persuasive, guileless way, "You've got to go, Howard. You were there in the beginning with Ali, you've got to be there at the end." "I'll be there," I muttered, to myself.

"Maybe Norton will win," said Conrad.

"Fat chance." I went to the bar.

Things were not all bad at Caracas Hilton. They make a good vodka martini, straight up with a lemon twist. And they have good peanuts. I munched a few of them and idled through my drink. A Boston attorney named John Cronin,

whom I had known for years, came up to me and invited
Emmy and me to a dinner party he was giving at the hotel.
Cronin is another of those who tenants the big fight scene. He
is a rabid boxing fan, but more than that, a most successful
attorney who has had professional ties with boxing people for
many years. I thanked him, told him we might drop by, had
another martini and went up to join Emmy. Caracas was
looking better.

We went to the party that evening and had a delightful time.
The food and wine were excellent. So was the water. Unlike
Mexico City, there is no water problem in Caracas. And the
occasion was enlivened by the arrival of Angelo Dundee and
Dr. Ferdie Pacheco. Angie has been Ali's teacher and trainer
throughout the "Great One's" entire career. He has also
managed a whole host of fighters, some of them champions.
Pacheco, a close friend of Dundee's, is Ali's doctor. The two of
them must be regarded as notable figures in the backstage of
boxing.

Dundee is one of the shrewdest men in boxing. What sets
him apart from the average manager or trainer is his personality and his personal class. By this, I do not mean that Angie is
either an educated or a cultured man. He is not. He is a bright
little fellow with a sparkle about him that glows in his eyes. He
knows fighters, boxing styles and clever matchmaking (the
right kind of opponent for his particular fighter) about as well
as anybody in the business. He has an uncommon fidelity to
his fighters, and an ability to get the most out of them. He did a
superb job, for instance, with the heavyweight Jimmy Ellis,
and actually guided Jimmy to a bogus World Boxing Association heavyweight title during the years of Ali's enforced idle-
ness. Ellis, in my opinion, never really believed in himself, but
Angie, taking one fight at a time, would give Jimmy the tactics
to win. A prime example was the Quarry fight in 1968 when
Ellis confounded Jerry by the simple tactic of mixing it up,
and then suddenly backing off.

Dundee is not a whiner or a complainer. He has never been
paid the money he has deserved by Ali and the Muslims, but
he has never let this disappointment affect his devotion to
Muhammad. He is what he is—a boxing man. As such, he is
human. He will work hard to build up a fight. He will color his

appraisal of a situation to enlarge the appeal of the contest. Before Ali fought Henry Cooper, for instance, Dundee was a model of open worry. He studiously proclaimed Cooper the greatest left hooker in boxing. Cooper, of course, was the greatest bleeder in boxing and became, for a time, an object of British medical interest because of his extraordinary capacity to endure terrifying losses of blood.

Angie is also a past master at selling himself on his own fighters. This can be good or bad, depending on the circumstances: good, if the opponent is as bad as Angie inwardly thinks he is, or bad, if Angie is overrating his own man and underrating the other. All in all, though, if I had a son who turned to boxing—perish the thought—I would want Angie to manage him. And Angie has a great sense of humor.

I suppose that, in the long run, happiness for Angie is the Fifth Street Gym at Miami Beach, a fleabag upstairs joint where his fighters train. This is where he develops his young fighters, and when he discovers a good one, he hoards him like gold.

Pacheco is, without question, one of the most interesting men I have ever met in sports. A balding man, with a ready, open smile, he is warm, entertaining, informative and even intellectual. He is a man of many parts. Professionally, he runs a medical clinic in the Miami ghetto. He does truly noble work there, but his interests extend to many other things. Boxing is just one of them. Ferdie is a good writer, and has had a couple of books published. He composes poetry. He has a fine ear for dialogue and is an engaging storyteller. He has a positive passion for acquiring antique cars, and once drove Emmy and me to the Miami airport in an antiquated limousine which he proudly described as "the personal transport of Al Capone." He also draws and paints. His conversational range can lead anywhere, from politics and government to law to the stage and screen. When he goes into a city that is new to him, there's a good chance you'll find him at the museum. Together, Angie and Ferdie are a unique part of the special color that marks boxing as a sport. It was nice to have them in Caracas.

Not that their arrival had been any more inspiring than ours. When they got to the front desk of the hotel to register, they were told, politely but firmly, that they had no reservations. This can be a shock when you have your confirmation in writing. Pacheco whipped his out of his pocket and snapped, "Here's my reservation, confirmed."

The clerk smiled pleasantly and said, "Sorry, we're out of rooms."

Somebody in the lobby got the word to Ferdie and Angie. "For an extra 50 they'll find rooms."

Pacheco swallowed his indignation, pulled 50 dollars out of his wallet and said, "Maybe this will help."

It did. A lot of extra 50s passed across that front desk on Sunday, March 24, and Monday, March 25.

They didn't try that act on Muhammad Ali, though, when he arrived the next night.

Monday, March 25, was my birthday. But it was also Dick Saddler day. So was Tuesday. In fact, as I had learned, every day in Venezuela had been Dick Saddler day from the moment of his arrival in that country. It changed the day after the fight, when it was learned that George Foreman would not be allowed to escape the country until he coughed up some $270,000 in "taxes." Poor George, whose young life has been plagued by a series of mishaps, both financial and marital, was in his own terms, "gangstered." He was, in effect, incarcerated in Caracas through the following Monday.

But make no mistake about it, Dick Saddler was the king of the fight. The importance he assumed in Caracas had been a long time in coming. Saddler is an old-time boxing man, both as a trainer and a manager. He knows every sweaty, smelly gym in the country, every tank town, every crooked promoter. And he can smell out a hustle the way hunting dogs can pursue a scent. His life has been dotted with struggle, with failure and with disappointment. Once he managed the late Sonny Liston and he has no hesitancy in telling you how Sonny never paid him what he owed him. Join the list. Still, he owed something to Sonny, because it was through Sonny that Dick latched on to Foreman. Foreman had been, as a veritable child, a sparring partner for Liston, and George admired Sonny's fighting abilities tremendously. To this day, Foreman regards himself as a boxing disciple of Liston's. And that's how Saddler discovered George.

Many people were surprised when Foreman hired Saddler as his manager after the Mexico City Olympics of 1968. I, myself, was surprised. I had thought that Foreman's Olympic boxing coach, "Pappy" Gault would inherit George. But once again, in the subterranean shenanigans of boxing, the obvious did not prevail. Dick Saddler got the fighter.

And Dick Saddler knew what to do with him; how to train him, how to develop him. Dick made all the right fights in all the right towns. This bum here, that bum there. Foreman's knockout record grew and grew, but his reputation did not, because of the caliber—or absence thereof—of the opponents Saddler carefully chose for him. But Dick knew what he had. A fighter with pulverizing power, whose fists seemed not to be fists at all, but a pair of clubs. And he watched Foreman's self-esteem grow and grow. He also knew that if ever there was a fighter tailor-made for George Foreman, it would have to be Joe Frazier, the then heavy-weight champion of the world. Just as there are horses for courses, so are there fighters for fighters. And Joe Frazier, with his wading-in style, was bound to be a human punching bag for Foreman. Nobody believed this when Dick Saddler told them, but they found out on January 22, 1973, on the island of Jamaica.

The wonder of it was that Foreman ever got the fight with Frazier. But this was where Saddler hit it lucky. The late Yancey Durham, Frazier's manager, never wanted Joe to fight Foreman. Yancey knew it was too great a risk when a return bout with Ali was in the offing and for much more money. And Ali's style was much more suited to Joe's than to Foreman's. But such was Frazier's personal distaste for Ali that he insisted on the Foreman fight. It cost Joe his title and millions of dollars, and it gave Saddler a lifetime dream, possession of the heavyweight champion of the world.

The only trouble with all this was that Saddler, in some ways, was unequipped to handle the fighter. It is one thing to select opponents and to prepare a fighter for a match. It is quite another to cope with the complex business and economic circumstances that surround so valuable a property as the heavyweight champion in this day and age. Saddler could not deal effectively with such matters as ancillary rights—closed-circuit and home television—for the simple reason that he had no background in such affairs. And so, Foreman became involved in some unfortunate deals that were costly to him. Foreman himself was not without blame. He allowed personal friends to bleed him. One of them, for instance, apparently took $100,000, personally, out of a seedy promotion in Tokyo when Foreman disposed of somebody named Joe "King" Roman in the first round. Saddler suffered and almost lost the fighter. Foreman said he would be his own manager, and that Saddler would be the trainer.

In Caracas, however, Saddler was in his element, especially with so simple an issue as who would be the referee. Norton seemed a respectable opponent, based upon his two fights with Ali, and Saddler wanted to take no chances. He wanted his own man, Jimmy Rondeau.

So Saddler played it tough. This is where he can be deceptive. On the surface, Saddler seems an easy-going man with a lazy tongue. And one gets the feeling that he's an old-time song-and-dance man. Indeed, he plays a good piano—the left hand isn't bad—and there's nothing he enjoys more than sitting down and banging out an old tune with a Teddy Wilson rhythm. Nothing, that is, except showing his muscle in a boxing situation that allows for it.

All day Monday, Saddler showed his muscle. The weigh-in was uneventful, though both men were a little heavier than I had expected. The only matter of note was the continuous meetings Saddler was having with the Venezuelan boxing authorities, the World Boxing Association and the World Boxing Council. Then there were Saddler's laconic asides to the press. The open hints that the fight might not take place. The referrals to the contract for the match itself, and the insistence that the terms of the contract were being violated. "I'm not going to let my title rest in the hands of a Venezuelan referee," Saddler told me. The Venezuelans kept insisting, as a matter of national pride, on a countryman being the referee. The WBA and the WBC people kept wringing their hands, though neither group really matters. Both are merely initial organizations, usually disregarded, and without any real jurisdiction or authority, especially in the United States. How-

ever, Bill Brennan, a very decent fellow, and the past president of the WBA, would report to me periodically, "We're
going to work this thing out. The fight will go on." On that
Monday I never doubted it, though some of the scribes were
now beginning to take Saddler seriously.

By seven o'clock that evening, I was bored with the whole
mess, and Emmy and I went out to dinner with Dundee,
Pacheco and Terry Jastrow. I was, in fact, hopeful that the
fight would be called off, so eager was I to get back home.
Besides, I felt the cancellation of the fight would make a better
story than would the fight itself.

Tuesday, the day of the fight. The possibility of cancellation
suddenly assumed credibility. At the Caracas Hilton we got a
report that George Foreman had half limped and been half
carried into a taxi and taken to a local hospital. The report said
that Foreman had injured his right knee on a stairwell that
morning at a police station where he had gone to visit with
some youngsters. Saddler, at the same time, was quoted as
saying outside the taxicab, "This doesn't mean the fight is off!"
Well, what the hell did it mean? A tactic in the fight over the
referee? Was the knee really hurt? A report of the latest
happening went out over the wire services. I started getting
calls from ABC affiliates promptly. Was the fight off? I
doubted it. Could I give an eyewitness report on Foreman
going to the hospital? No, he left from the Avila Hotel. I was at
the Caracas Hilton. Could Foreman beat Norton with a game
leg? How the hell did I know?

The next thing we heard was that Foreman was back at the
hotel with his doctor and his friend Leroy Jackson told those
members of the press who were there that there would be a
statement at 2 P.M. Dick Saddler, in the meantime, was
holding court in a meeting at El Poliedro, the handsome new
arena where the fight was to be held. He was still hassling over
the selection of a referee. Virtually every writer in Caracas
headed for the Avila. I went over with Ferdie Pacheco and
Jerry Izenberg of *The Newark Star Ledger* and Jack Murphy of
The San Diego Union. We waited in the lobby as 2 o'clock
came and went. At one point, I got Foreman's room number
and went up with a couple of others to see if I could visit with

him. Leroy Jackson came to the door and said that George was resting. He could see no one. "Will there be a fight?" I asked. "There'll be a statement soon," he said. We went back downstairs to mill around in the packed lobby. There may have been a record number of disgusted, disgruntled people there.

Finally, Bill Caplan, Foreman's publicity man, led everyone into a large meeting room to start a press conference. He really had nothing to say other than that Saddler was in meetings which he, Caplan, had just left, over the selection of a referee. But what about Foreman's knee? Well, that was up to George's doctor. At about this time, Terry Jastrow ran in to tell me that Saddler had just arrived at the hotel. Some of us got to him as he went into the elevator to go up and visit Foreman, and suddenly somebody said, "The fight is on." So momentous was the announcement that I felt we had unraveled Watergate.

In a matter of moments, Saddler came back downstairs and joined the press conference. He spoke for 22 minutes, in a wandering exposition that was a repeat of what he had been saying for days: How he had signed a contract in good faith, a contract agreed to and recognized by all the appropriate authorities; how the contract was not being abided by; how he would not let a foreign referee strip him of his title. (Always, according to Dick, it is "his title.") None of the questions on everyone's mind were being answered: Would there be a fight? Would there be an American referee? What about George's knee? Saddler hedged on the first two questions and said that only Foreman's doctor could tell us about George's knee. The doctor was at the press conference and, in what I considered a shamefully unprofessional display, said he could give us no information on the knee at that time. He would examine George later. In all my years of covering boxing, this was as bad a scene as I had ever witnessed. To add comedy to the occasion, Chris Dundee, Angie's brother, was there. Chris is a Miami Beach matchmaker, and he had a couple of closed-circuit locations for the fight. With his mind focused squarely on his ticket sales in Miami Beach, Chris loudly counseled the room that Saddler was a promotional genius, that we should lay off him, that the fight would go on. Chris has never won any awards for subtlety. Privately, he was muttering, "What the hell is the guy up to?"

The "press conference" broke up in an atmosphere of chaos. I went back to the Caracas Hilton and left Ferdie Pacheco in the act of trying to convince Foreman's people that he should be allowed to examine Foreman's knee. Maybe he would be able to help.

At 7:30 P.M., Emmy, Angie Dundee, Ferdie, Terry Jastrow and I left the hotel for the arena. Surely, the fight would take place. We got into our seats at ringside and Bill Brennan of the WBA came over to talk to me. The referee had been decided on an hour earlier. The referee's name? Jimmy Rondeau. Hail to Dick Saddler, king of the referees! But the fight would be judged by three Venezuelan judges. So, national honor would be maintained. And boxing had another idiotic, inglorious chapter to add to its crummy history.

But what about Foreman's knee? We would have to wait. He wouldn't be coming into the ring for a couple of hours. Sitting through preliminaries is usually an exercise in boredom. But I must say that in the final prelim before the main event, they had a pretty good fight going. It was interrupted, however, by the arrival of Muhammad Ali. The crowd, such as it was—the arena was only half-filled—went wild. Ali was up to the occasion. He has done his instant replay a thousand times. In this instance, his foil was the Argentine relic, Oscar Bonavena, who Ali had disposed of three years earlier. Now we had to endure the whole act again. Ali threatening Bonavena. Bonavena being held back. Ali being held back. And no longer was anyone watching the two kids in the ring.

Mercifully, the preliminary ended. Kenny Norton entered the arena and moved on up into the ring. One of his owners, Aaron Rivkind, spoke to me briefly. "Kenny will beat him," he said. "I've never seen him so confident, so ready." I never did get to ask Rivkind why he had accepted Jimmy Rondeau as the referee. Nor did I ever get to find out from Rondeau why he had accepted the assignment. That very morning, in the hotel lobby, Rondeau introduced himself to me, and confided that he no longer wanted the job. "In this mess, I'm better off without it." But there he was in ring center.

It seemed an eternity before Foreman appeared, and when he did, there was no trace of a limp. He went through his act, which has now become familiar. The baleful stare at the opponent. A throwback to Liston.

The fight got under way. Norton, supposedly confident and ready, fought like a drugged man. Foreman seemed mildly sluggish, but stalked Norton steadily and completely dominated the round. It ended in the second round. Thank God. It was no contest. What had all the furor been about? Jimmy Rondeau? He did a lousy job, I thought, as the referee. He seemed incapable of determining when a knockdown was a knockdown. On two occasions I thought he looked to Norton's corner for instructions, and he was supposed to be Saddler's man. Why not? Everything else was screwy in this damned thing.

I got the real lowdown from Foreman in my interview with him in the ring after the fight ended. Prayer that afternoon had healed his knee, he told me. "Just prayer?" I asked. "Just prayer," he said.

Then I spoke with Muhammad Ali who confirmed that his fight with Foreman would indeed be held in Zaire, Africa. There would be a confrontation in the Congo. "And you can't come over there agitatin', Howard. The Lumumba boys is over there, and you'll get cooked."

I left when Dick Saddler said, "I have created me a monster."

During the ride back to the hotel, Angie Dundee kept saying, "I liked what I saw. Foreman is made to order for Ali." That sounded familiar. The last time Angie had said anything like that to me was before the first Ali-Norton fight. "A perfect setup," he had said. "No way Ali can lose." That was when Ali got his message from Allah, a broken jaw.

Terry Jastrow just kept shaking his head. He was new to boxing and he couldn't fathom Angie. He knew what Angie had said on the air after the first round, "This is not the same George Foreman who fought Joe Frazier. Norton can get lucky and win this fight." Less than two minutes later Norton was gone. "Terry will learn," I thought.

As we approached the Caracas Hilton, some of the colorful phrases that have characterized past heavyweight championship fights kept running through my mind: "The Rape of Shelby" (Dempsey vs. Gibbons); "The Long Count" (Dempsey vs. Tunney); "The Invisible Punch" (Ali vs. Liston at Lewiston, Maine); "The Hernia Fight" (the Ali-Liston fight that was cancelled in Boston when Ali underwent surgery for a hernia).

What did we have now? "The Battle of Wounded Knee," Pacheco suggested.

"Hell, no," I answered. Now we could see the Caracas Hilton. "We've got to call it 'The Caracas Caper'."

CHAPTER 4

KING VS. RIGGS: MALE CHAUVINISM NEVER DIES

"I'll never understand why Riggs went into the tank . . ."

It is right to begin, I think, by placing Billie Jean King in perspective. There are some things she is not. She is not Betty Friedan. She is not Gloria Steinem. Those two ladies were staunch leaders in the combat zone for women's rights long before Billie Jean beat Bobby Riggs in a tennis match, and the war they have waged on behalf of women has never been limited by the chalk-line boundaries of a tennis court.

They are the ones who have endured the years of work, the years of trying to educate people—not just men, but, almost tragically, women themselves—the years of recruitment, the years of grappling with ignorance and the years of suffering ridicule because of that ignorance. They are the ones who have been totally committed to the fight for equality for women: equality of opportunity, equality of pay, equality under the law. They are the ones who have sought the right to control their own bodies, to change ancient abortion laws, to eradicate the archaic sexual attitudes toward women. They, and some others, have been the intellectual and motivational core of the continuing growth of the women's rights movement in this country.

Billie Jean King has come to the wars lately, but on a vastly different battleground. Her forum was the sports arena. With a record tennis crowd of more than 32,000 people in the Houston Astrodome, and a viewership of some 40 million television watchers at home, she scored, tellingly, for the women's movement. Her achievement: raising the consciousness of women about themselves, and uplifting them by puncturing the long-adhered-to chauvinist theory that any male could defeat any female in athletic competition regardless of age differentials. There was nothing intellectual in the accomplishment, unless one would call all of the psychological maneuvering prior to the match against Riggs an exercise of a superior mentality. But, of course, it was hardly that. It was Billie Jean King doing her thing with a racquet and a ball.

I can tell you some of the things Billie Jean is. She is a lot better looking than she photographs. In fact, she's a damned attractive woman even if her thighs are a little too thick. "I've always had that problem. Nothing I can do about that," she says airily. She is pert, she is spunky and she has sparkle. In any crowd you'll know that Billie Jean King is there. Her eyes flash, her teeth are beautiful, her smile makes you warm to her. But she is tough. She never forgets anyone who she feels has wronged her. She carries a grudge like a time bomb waiting to detonate. On the tennis court there is a fierceness about her. Her concentration is absolute. Her disgust with her own errors is palpable, and her intensity toward her opponent is unrelenting. She is like a shark, eager to devour the prey. She radiates good health, although before the Riggs match she had been ill and some questioned her physical capacities going into the contest. She loves tennis the way Ellington loved the piano. She never tires of talking about the game, of playing the game. And she glories in the perfectly executed placement or the volley the opponent can't return. "You have no idea what a beautiful thing it is," she will tell you. "It's as fulfilling as a great work of art."

Her life has changed in a score of ways since she beat Bobby Riggs. Always concerned about women in sports, always determined to make women's tennis important to many millions of Americans, she has grown a very great deal since the Riggs match. She understands that her victory has become a symbol to countless women, that it has given them a new and perhaps inspiring feeling that women are, as a sex, different yet equal. As a result of this, she feels a sense of responsibility to all women that transcends the obligation she still entertains toward women in sports.

But her new responsibilities have produced new problems and new dangers for her as a person. So many activities are absorbing her time and attention that she is on the way to becoming a human computer.

She is a pioneer in World Team Tennis, the playing coach of the Philadelphia Freedoms. She is putting out a new magazine for women in sports. She still travels the women's pro-tennis tour. And there are dozens of other commitments, speechmaking being just one of them. She is becoming personally inaccessible. One must go through a Maginot Line of secretaries, public-relations people and tournament directors to try to get to her. The odds are that you never will. Billie Jean King faces the peril of becoming a permanent symbol for American womanhood and an IBM-type conglomerate at the same time. This would be a crime because she's got too much bounce, too much verve and too much pure spirit and personality ever to let that happen.

She didn't plan it this way.

Billie Jean King never thought about playing Bobby Riggs, and never would have played him if Bobby had not crushed and humiliated Margaret Court, the great champion from Australia. Once that happened, Bobby became the hottest sports promotional item in the country, and women tennis players became butts of his and most of American males' wit. Billie Jean seethed. She knew she had to turn it around. She knew she had to play Bobby Riggs. She also knew that she could beat him and, in the process, expose him.

So she agreed to the match.

For Bobby Riggs at age 55, it was a dream come true. A lifelong hustler, a born charlatan, a once superb tennis player, a man gifted, despite his advancing years, with a repertoire of shots that were at once devastatingly effective and humiliatingly amusing, a player with uncanny court strategy and, in the fullest sense, a male chauvinist, Bobby understood the sensational show-business value of a tennis battle of the sexes.

He knew the worth of Billie Jean King as an adversary in terms of the box office. Margaret Court was colorless, dull, and the name meant nothing in the United States. But even for that match, Riggs was able to attract a great deal of national attention. With the colorful Billie Jean King against him, the whole country would respond to the match. And Bobby would promote the hell out of it. In the long run, he was sure he would make it into a million-dollar hustle.

He was not alone in this belief. A very smart Hollywood agent-manager, Jerry Perenchio, who had had prior television experience with supersports events, agreed with him. Jerry, working in tandem with Jack Kent Cooke, had bought the theater-television rights to the first Muhammad Ali-Joe Frazier fight. It was Perenchio who had seen merit in the Riggs-Court match and who put it together. He represented Riggs. Now he viewed the King-Riggs match not as a theater-television attraction, but as a prime-time television entertainment special. He knew what he had going for him in Bobby Riggs, and while he didn't know Billie Jean King that well, he had a clear picture of the overtones that would make the match a mass communication attraction of tremendous impact. So it was Jerry who promoted the King-Riggs match. It would be man against woman in an age of women's lib, and a 55-year-old tennis relic would touch base with people all over America, hissing through his teeth as he spoke, belittling Billie Jean King and serving as the authoritarian voice of male chauvinism.

In his negotiations for the sale of the package, Perenchio dealt primarily with two networks, CBS and ABC. CBS seemed to have a leg up because they had carried the Riggs-Court match and, indeed, there apparently would have been legal ramifications had Jerry tried to sell the package elsewhere. But he liked the idea of doing business with ABC for two reasons: First, ABC is number one in sports, and ABC had proven it could make sports prime-time entertainment in the case of *Monday Night Football*. Second, and there is much irony here, he wanted me to host the show.

I say there is irony here because, when Jerry had the Ali-

Frazier Super Fight One package, I was his fall guy. He made public statements to the effect that he would not hire me to do the fight. He made his client, Burt Lancaster, one of the announcers for the fight and, in the days before the match, Lancaster issued statements to the press about how he would do the broadcast. "Not like Howard Cosell," he said. Some time after the fight had taken place, Perenchio openly stated that he had been in error and that I should have done the telecast. Now, he wanted me for the *Battle of the Sexes.*

ABC Sports got the package. The match was set for September 20, 1973, in the Houston Astrodome.

Instantly the publicity wheels were set in motion. ABC Sports set up a closed-circuit telecast of a press conference for ABC's affiliate stations. The telec st was for the dual purpose of announcing to the press, and to our stations, that ABC would be carrying the match in prime time.

The telecast originated from Studio One on West 66th Street in New York City. Studio One is our largest facility and the place was jammed with members of the press. Bobby Riggs and Jerry Perenchio were present, along with Roone Arledge. I conducted the proceedings. Billie Jean King participated by way of a split-screen appearance from Denver, Colorado, where she was playing in a tournament.

The thing began routinely. Arledge made the announcement that ABC Sports had acquired the rights to televise the match. Perenchio expressed his pleasure at that fact, and then we got to the two contestants. Riggs went through his whole act, talking about how everybody was out to get him, making the point that the match was on a best of five sets basis, and that this would favor Billie Jean because she was so much younger than he. "They're out to get me," Bobby said, never meaning a word of it. In fact, the moment he finished talking about everything that had been stacked against him, and while the cameras were elsewhere, he leaned over and whispered to me. "You don't really think she has a chance, do you?"

Billie Jean just listened to Bobby rant on and on as she sat and watched on the split screen. When I asked her what she thought of Riggs's statements, she said, "I think he's crazy. He's an old man."

We got to the question of what Billie Jean would wear at the match. She had not yet thought about it. "What do you think Bobby should wear?" I asked. She chuckled, and then she said, "I don't think I should say it on television."

"Go ahead," I urged her, "this is only going out on closed circuit."

With a broad grin she responded, "I don't care if he only wears his jock strap." That crack broke up the joint.

During the question-and-answer period given over to the press, Nora Efron, a bright and talented writer, asked Roone Arledge if he were going to have a woman commentator on the telecast. Arledge didn't commit himself, but admitted he was thinking about it. Billie Jean made it clear that she wanted a woman commentator on the show, and I made it clear that nobody had authority to name the announcers but ABC Sports, that the contestants had no right of approval over the selection of announcers. This whole issue remained very important right up to the moment of the match.

The press conference got tremendous coverage in the newspapers and the promotion for the match was under way.

In the days that followed, Bobby Riggs seemed to be everywhere. One television appearance followed another in city after city throughout the country. He appeared at Ethel Kennedy's charity tournament at Forest Hills. He was on the air with me at half time of a preseason NFL game in Kansas City. He played tennis with Harry Reasoner on *The Reasoner Report.* He gloried in showing all his court tricks, placing chairs all over the court as self-imposed obstacles, racing around them to get at his opponent's shots and delighting all who watched with his shot-making antics. Bobby can do tricks with a tennis ball. The "English" he can get on the ball is unbelievable. He is a master of the chop, the drop shot; the spin he gets on a ball is utterly frustrating, and he executes placements as though the chalk lines were designed for his personal convenience. Everyone who watched him play and listened to him talk was convinced that Riggs would do to Bille Jean what he had done to Margaret Court. Or so it seemed.

And how Bobby loved it—all the attention, all the noise, and all of it on behalf of Bobby Riggs, the sure perpetrator of a million-dollar hustle. Privately, Bobby would think of all the years past. How he had won at Wimbledon, and what had he gotten out of it, really? How he was gradually forgotten. How all of his hustles, in tennis, golf (he *is* a good golfer) and even in pool, had been executed in anonymity. Bobby loves public notice almost as much as he loves money. Almost. But now he had the impossible dream. He had both. And it would be only the beginning. Billie Jean King would be a stepping stone. Chris Evert would be next.

When I was with Bobby during those days, I found myself laughing with him, listening to him and subconsciously nodding my head in agreement with him. "How can Billie Jean possibly beat him?" I thought. I watched him toy with Alan King and Bill Cosby at Forest Hills, captivate the crowd at the Ethel Kennedy tournament, make the ball dance in strange and mystifying ways, and I found myself falling prey to the growing legend. Against a woman, any woman, Bobby was invincible.

My thinking was also influenced by some of the male tennis players. Gene Scott, an attorney now, but previously a fine player on the amateur circuit, had written a new book on tennis. I did a radio show with him about the book, and we got into the King-Riggs thing. Gene explained to me, patiently and almost patronizingly, how Billie Jean did not have a chance. He told me of the 21-point match he had played against her at an earlier date. It had taken place on Long Island, and he had spotted her ten points and service. He won, 21–17. "My God," I reacted, "this is a guy who knows." And then he carefully detailed exactly how Riggs would play the match, how he would bewilder Billie Jean with his incredible variety of shots.

Billy Talbert was another, and there is nobody in tennis I respect more than Talbert. "It's a matter of styles," he told me. "The only woman who would have a chance to beat him is Chris Evert." I thought of Chris, staying at the baseline, expressionlessly returning ball after ball, seemingly tireless, and I decided Talbert might be right. Chris could wear Riggs down, but Billie Jean's all-court movement would enable Riggs to destroy her with his clever court tactics.

Jack Kramer did not mince words. The match would be a

joke. Bobby would toy with Billie Jean the way he had with Margaret Court.

So it went during the long buildup for the match. And everywhere that Bobby went, the press was sure to go. In Los Angeles, for instance, Pete Axthelm of *Newsweek* and Nora Efron, for *New York Magazine,* were with Riggs, doing features on him. This was in August. Pete was both amused and fascinated by Riggs, and he was astonished at the apparently inexhaustible energy of the little man. Bobby would take all his pills every day (vitamin pills, salt pills, pills and more pills), and if you were with him long enough, you began to get the feeling that, damn it, there's something to it, the guy doesn't act like he's 55, and maybe you should start taking the pills too.

Nora Efron wanted Billie Jean to win. She wanted her to win so much she even bet on her. But Nora, while doing her story on Bobby, confessed to me at the Beverly Hills Hotel, "I'll probably lose my bet."

The thing that amazed me about Bobby during those weeks of buildup for the match was the way people bought his act. Everywhere he went he said the same thing, over and over. "I'll cut her up. They're sticking it to the old man, making me play five sets. Women should be in the kitchen. . . ." On and on he droned; for me, he had become a frightful bore.

But I had to admit one thing. If I wanted to hire a salesman, I'd hire Bobby Riggs. If I wanted to buy a self-generating publicity machine, I'd buy Bobby Riggs.

I sure wouldn't hire Billie Jean King. After that opening closed-circuit telecast, she didn't do one damned thing to help the promotion on or off the court. On the court, she began to have unexpected troubles, physical difficulties. Playing in the U.S. Open at Forest Hills, she had to walk off the court and default to Julie Heldman. Apparently prostrate with heat exhaustion, Billie Jean was taking a longer rest during the match than Julie thought she was entitled to. Billie Jean told her, "If you want it that badly, it's yours," and she left.

Then, at Hilton Head Island in South Carolina, she got sick again. She lost a match to Chris Evert that she had all but won and was obviously struggling in a physical sense. Her husband, Larry, issued a statement about her health. Billie Jean was to undergo tests, the statement said, and it confused everyone because it seemed to imply and deny illness at the same time.

With the Riggs match only a couple of weeks off, I began to wonder if it would be postponed or called off altogether. But then came assurances that Billie Jean was fine and so that issue faded into the background.

At Houston, in the days just preceding the match, the striking contrast between Billie Jean and Bobby came into vivid focus. They would practice only a short distance from the Astrodome in a "bubble," part of the whole complex that had been the accomplished dream of the late Roy Hofheinz. Spectators and, of course, the press were on hand to watch the practices. The moment Billie Jean was finished, she would shower, change and flee the scene. Answers to questions from the press were perfunctory; so brief as to be almost meaningless. But Riggs was always available to make up for Billie Jean's shortcomings. He was appearing everywhere, partying everywhere and such was his apparent confidence that one had to figure he knew what he was doing.

I knew at least one thing that Billie Jean King was doing. She was worrying about Jack Kramer, maybe even more than she was thinking about Bobby Riggs. Earlier on, I mentioned that Billie Jean is a great one for bearing a grudge. Jack Kramer is the prize example. The reason she was concerned about Kramer was that he had been hired by Roone Arledge to be part of the telecast. So had Billie Jean's close friend and fellow professional, Rosemary Casals. Rosemary was just fine, Billie Jean thought, but she didn't want Kramer anywhere in the vicinity. She had a long-standing feud with Jack that stemmed partly from his opposition to World Team Tennis, which Billie Jean fervently supports, and also from an incident at a tournament in California some years past when Jack allegedly disparaged her and Rosemary. To Billie Jean King, Jack Kramer is the original male chauvinist.

The way Arledge had structured the telecast, I was to be the host of the show, Kramer would be the male "expert," Rosemary the female "expert" and Frank Gifford would do celebrity interviews on the sidelines. Personally, I didn't like the whole set-up. I felt that there were too many people on the show, that the whole approach to the show should be one of humor. I thought the so-called experts would only get in the way of a smooth, evenly paced telecast. On a personal level, Jack Kramer has been a friend of mine for 20 years. I hardly knew Rosemary Casals, having met her only briefly on several occasions. I *did* know that she had very strong feelings against Riggs and the manner in which he'd been publicly parading his male chauvinism. But that's the way Arledge wanted it, and that's the way it was.

It was not the way Billie Jean wanted it. She wanted Jack Kramer off the program, and she let her feelings be known. Some of the newspaper writers dropped little items to the effect that Billie Jean objected to Jack Kramer's participation in the telecast, and hinted that he would be taken off the show.

Arledge and I were deeply upset by this because, while it didn't matter one bit whether Kramer was on the show or not, there was a major underlying principle involved. In the history of the sports broadcast business, networks have habitually given to commissioners, owners, promoters, sponsors, whomever, right of approval over the announcers to be selected to do a telecast. Arledge has led the way in breaking this unwholesome practice. In the multimillion deal that he made with the NFL for *Monday Night Football,* he absolutely refused to give NFL Commissioner Pete Rozelle a veto voice over announcers. Recently, when Arledge acquired the television rights to the Kentucky Derby, he again refused to allow Churchill Downs a veto voice over announcers—a right that the track had always possessed heretofore. Thus the thought of allowing a competitor in a tennis match a right of veto over an announcer was intolerable. And so the matter of Jack Kramer mushroomed, climaxing the night before the match.

Arledge and I were staying at the Warwick Hotel, and as I look back upon it now, it seems to me that we were in endless meetings on the subject. Phone calls went back and forth between Roone and Jerry Perenchio. Jerry wanted Kramer dropped from the telecast and the matter put to an end.

"Nobody gives a damn whether Kramer's on the show or not," he argued. "We've got the biggest event of the year. Why screw it up?"

Meanwhile, Billie Jean King steadfastly maintained that she could not perform at her best if Kramer did the show. Her mental distress would be such, she said, that her concentration would be divided.

Arledge refused to waver. "I think we should drop the telecast," he told me. "It's a damned irony that this comes up over Jack Kramer, who isn't even an ABC performer, who we've just hired for one show. But that doesn't matter. The principle does. We've got to back him up."

Then Arledge went to a meeting at the Astroworld Hotel with Perenchio and Billie Jean and her husband, Larry. Arledge demanded to know if Billie Jean adhered to her position that she could not perform at her best in the match if Kramer were part of the show. She said yes. Roone then asked if she or Larry would make that statement on the air as part of the show. Again, they said yes. Arledge said that under those circumstances Kramer might voluntarily withdraw from the show, but that he would not ask him to. When he got back to the Warwick Hotel, Arledge and I called Jack Kramer. We told Jack exactly what had happened, and what Billie Jean King's position was. Roone then told him that we would back him to the hilt and cancel the telecast if Jack wanted us to. Jack said, "Hell, no. I really appreciate ABC's position on this, but I want to see Bobby beat the hell out of her. I'll withdraw from the telecast."

Arledge reemphasized that ABC would stand by Jack, and Jack, in turn, said that he wouldn't be responsible for the cancellation of the telecast or for giving Billie Jean any excuses for losing. Roone then told him that Larry King was going to videotape a statement to be played at the top of the show in which he would explain why Billie Jean objected to Kramer's presence and how it would diminish the quality of her play. Arledge asked Jack if he wanted to go to our Los Angeles station and videotape his own statement of withdrawal. Jack said yes.

The whole thing had become a behind-the-scenes *cause*

célèbre—absurd in the light of what happened when the match was played.

With that matter resolved, we had to get a replacement for Kramer. I recommended Gene Scott because he had actually played and beaten Billie Jean King; because he had called tennis matches for WNET-TV in New York; because he was gaining public attention with his excellent new book on tennis. Scott was contacted, and arrived in Houston only hours before our production meeting the morning of the match.

Chuck Howard was the producer of the show. Chet Forte was the director. We met at the Hyatt House and everybody was there except Rosemary Casals. Forte was in a disgruntled mood. "We don't have the camera positions they promised us," he complained. "It'll hurt the whole damn telecast." Since there was nothing we could do about it at the moment, that matter was tabled. In the long run there was nothing that we could do about it anyway and, as a consequence, the pictures weren't as good as they should have been. When Rosemary finally arrived, she met everybody, but Scott and me, for the first time.

Chuck outlined the format of the show to everyone, and he stressed to Rosie that if she had strong feelings about women's lib, she should not hesitate to express them. As it turned out, Rosie hardly needed that urging.

The meeting broke up, and I went over to the Astrodome that afternoon to look at the videotaped statements of Larry King and Jack Kramer and to watch Bobby Riggs practice. The place was already flooded with celebrities. Andy Williams was there, George Foreman and Jim Brown were there, as were, literally, dozens of others. As I watched Riggs practice, he suddenly looked old—very old. I thought back to the way Muhammad Ali had partied the night before his first fight against Kenny Norton and how, on the day of the bout, there was no fight in him. I wondered about Riggs in the same vein.

That was some night in the Houston Astrodome! Tuxedoes were our ordered dress for the event. When I arrived with Emmy, Frank Gifford was already there. After I got Emmy seated, Giff took me back under the stands to a place adjacent to the Houston Astros' clubhouse where there was a table stocked with sandwiches and soft drinks. Giff and I each had a sandwich and a Coke, and I went into the Houston clubhouse where the attendant told me that we had just missed Leo Durocher. Leo was in his waning days as manager of the Astros. Then I went back out onto the playing field and looked around. It was a rich, plush crowd that was arriving. How different, I ruminated, from the day the Astrodome had opened. I was there on that day for an exhibition baseball game between the Yankees and the Astros. I was covering the opening for *Wide World of Sports*. The crowd was shirt-sleeved then, and beer was the popular refreshment. I remembered getting Roger Maris and Rusty Staub to hit fungos in an attempt to reach the roof of the Astrodome. They failed miserably.

Tonight was a "happening" of another sort. The drink of the evening was champagne. At least it was for those seated in the $100 chairs along the sidelines of the court. Formally dressed waiters came walking past with trays of filled champagne glasses, "beaded bubbles winking at the brim," and the patrons in the expensive chairs reached for them happily. Many thought, in view of the price of the tickets, that they were a Jerry Perenchio treat. But no, the cost was a dollar per glass.

A wooden platform had been constructed for the announcers and those of the television crew who would be working directly with us. We were situated at about where second base would normally be. We faced the court diagonally behind one corner of the playing surface and our vision was poor, almost as poor as most of the $100 seats. Even worse, as it turned out, the acoustics were terrible, and we couldn't hear the official on the public-address system. Worse yet, we couldn't see for ourselves whether a ball was in or out.

But, of course, none of this mattered to the crowd in the Astrodome, and it didn't really matter that much to us either. We were all caught up in the extraordinary, almost bizarre setting. The uniqueness of the scene: The Astrodome is a place for baseball and football, even for basketball. But tennis, who'd ever have dreamed of it? And the crowd, peopled with an array of celebrities that would have challenged one of those old-time Hollywood premiers. Flashbulbs popping everywhere. Lots of expensive and garish jewelry adorning the women. Those Texas oil millionaires do, in fact, exist!

Gene Scott tried to measure the size of the crowd. He and Rosie Casals never thought when they became tennis players that they would ever see one like it at a tennis match. It made Wimbledon, the diamond of the tennis world, seem puny. More than 32,000 were present, the largest crowd ever to see a tennis match. The ultimate word for the occasion would be "gala." It had the atmosphere of an international ball.

To add to the festive air, the way the contestants came on to the playing surface was a combination of P.T. Barnum and Flo Ziegfeld. Billie Jean was carried out by four men whose bodies resembled those of professional football players. She was wearing a white tennis dress dotted with blue sequins. Bobby Riggs came out in what appeared to be a chariot drawn by a group of young girls, each of whom was wearing a yellow T-shirt with the words "Sugar Daddy" inscribed on it. Bobby, himself, was wearing a yellow jacket with the same words. Right up to the end, Bobby was a promoter and a hustler. "Sugar Daddy" is a huge candy lollipop that he was advertising. And then Billie Jean presented a small, live pig to Bobby. She had topped him at the very beginning. The symbolic meaning of the pig was unmistakable.

By this time I was on the air. The show had opened, the entrances had been described. Then I led into the Jack Kramer matter and we played Larry King's statement followed by Jack's. After that I introduced Gene Scott, who picked Riggs to win easily. And then I brought on Rosemary Casals who picked Billie Jean to win in three straight sets.

I had planned on treating the match with a light touch. All the weeks of buildup, of promotion, of emphasis upon the battle between the sexes seemed to be part of a hoax—another Bobby Riggs hustle. But suddenly, as Billy Jean and Bobby started to warm up, the circus atmosphere evaporated. There was an abrupt development of tension throughout the arena. The crowd was intensely serious about this match. It was more to them, much more, than tennis. It was a woman against a man; an event to be equated with one of the principal contemporary forces in American society: the quest for equal rights for women. All of the Bobby Riggs's put-downs of the female sex had taken hold. The thing was for real. The air was so heavy with anticipation that one would have thought a heavyweight championship fight was about to begin.

There could be no joking about this match now. Not yet, anyway. Not unless developments warranted it. Not unless Bobby's boasts came true, and he could play the role of comedian in victory.

Billy Jean served first. In a cautious initial game she held service. So did Bobby. Ali and Frazier were feeling each other out. The first to break through was Bobby. Billie Jean seemed tense and a little uncertain. Bobby looked taller, somehow, after the breakthrough. But there was no clowning yet, and there would be no clowning at all this night.

Billie Jean became aggressive and broke through Bobby's service. The women spectators erupted with a delighted roar. Billie Jean held her own service and did it confidently, assuredly, easily. She was moving all over the court now, and was not afraid to follow her service to the net. The diversification of her game was becoming evident and the crowd could sense it.

So could Rosie Casals. As Billie Jean assumed control of the first set by breaking through again, and as the crowd burst forth with vocal elation at the miracle that was happening, Rosie began to snipe back at Bobby for all of the barbs that he had manufactured against the fair sex in all the weeks before the match. Billie Jean won the first set 6–4.

Gene Scott felt sheepish. His theories were being disproved. Rosie, a little firebrand who had been waiting a long time for this, was ebullient. As Billie Jean breezed through the second set, 6–3, Rosie would not let up. She laughed at, and even mocked, Riggs's futility, and derided him as an old man. She reminded the viewers of some of Riggs's remarks during the long campaign before the match. She was winning the battle, but losing the war. She was accomplishing exactly the opposite of her intentions. She was creating sympathy for Bobby Riggs among 40 million viewers. Several times I sought to get her to cut back with remarks like, "Don't you think you're being a little harsh on Bobby?" "Don't you think you're overdoing it a little?" "Why don't you let him get off the floor just once?" "You won't let the poor fellow up, will you?"

But Rosie was not to be deterred. It's possible that she was enjoying the victory even more than Billie Jean. When, in the third set, Bobby was an obviously beaten player—looking like the 55-year-old man that he was, sitting on a sideline chair while a doctor worked over a cramp in his leg—Rosie's merriment reached its apex, and based upon the phone calls and wires ABC received, it was at that point that the resentment of the viewers toward Rosemary achieved its climax.

As Billie Jean ran out the match 6–4, 6–3, 6–3, I recollected that these were the exact scores predicted by Rosemary Casals.

I have not had the opportunity to speak with Rosie since that night, though I suspect that the subsequent furor about her performance on the air both hurt and puzzled her. Billie Jean later told me that Rosie said she had only done what the producer had told her to, in other words, don't be afraid to speak out as a women's libber. If that is the case, then there had to be a misapprehension, at least in terms of degree of speaking out, of what Chuck Howard had told her in the production meeting. Whatever the circumstances, I felt sorry for Rosie and didn't blame her. She is not a professional announcer, trained to be objective and sensitive to audience reaction. And the ones who are to blame for her performance are the ones who hired her.

There is also this to say about Rosie. She overstated, and yet the things she said were the things that most women were thinking during all the months that Bobby was practicing his act against them. Her mistiming and her incessant carping were what undid her, because there was a lot of truth in the things she said.

Rosemary Casals may have created sympathy for Bobby Riggs during the telecast that night, but certainly she had nothing to do with the attitude of the crowd in the Astrodome. That, too, underwent a subtle, curious change as Billie Jean mercilessly took Riggs apart in the third set. While he sat there on the sidelines, during changes of court, having his cramped leg worked on and swallowing still more pills, he suddenly seemed a pathetic figure, laid bare for all to see him as he really was—a weary, beaten, 55-year-old man who was no match for a great 30-year-old woman tennis champion. There could be no more bravado, no more barbs. The "quips and cranks and wreathed smiles," as John Milton once wrote, would have to give way now to the proper acceptance of defeat. In other words, he would have to eat his words as gracefully as possible.

I felt sorry for him, and I could sense that the spectators did too. When he would win a point in that final set, they would applaud him as they had not done earlier in the match. And, somehow, they understood the truth about Bobby Riggs —that underneath all that layer of talk, all that boastfulness, he wasn't a bad guy. He was an actor who hadn't meant many of the things he said, but who loved being on stage and who loved a hustle even more. Now his act was over. He could never be on center stage again. For six months of his life, at an age when it didn't seem possible, from the time of the Margaret Court match up until this night, the night of the great debacle, he had what he never had when he had been a Wimbledon champion. He had the whole country in his hands. But the death of his million-dollar hustle was all that remained. That, and a broken dream.

Bobby took the defeat well. I have seen him reasonably often since the match, usually in Las Vegas where he is the resident tennis pro at the Tropicana Hotel on the Strip. He laughs, he kids around, he is always in his tennis shorts, but he is, in a way, a sad figure. His legs seem spavined, like an old race horse ready to be put to stud. And his eyes seem somehow lonely. In fact, this is what he seems to be most of all, lonely, even though his girl, Sandra Giles, is there with him. He appears deserted, even when there are people around him. He still gets occasional television commercials in which he says, "Remember me, I'm Bobby Riggs, the guy who lost to Billie Jean King. . . ."

He is back where he began, working the quiet, unpublicized hustle; working it wherever he can, at the Tropicana, the Riviera, Caesar's Palace, all along the Strip. You pick the game. Tennis. Golf maybe. Or maybe even pool. Bobby can do it all. But never again before 32,000-plus people and 40 million more at home. "Life is but an empty dream."

Billie Jean King's life will never be the same again. It couldn't be. She had two immediate feelings as the match ended—elation and, above all, release. She showed both in the embrace she gave her husband, Larry, immediately after the match had ended. Gone was all of the tension leading up to and surrounding the contest. And gone was the artificial game of psychology, of off-court tactics she had played in the weeks preceding it. She had not lent herself to the publicity campaign, she had not been available for appearances, she had seemed almost uncooperative for one reason: She would not let Bobby Riggs psych her out. Nothing would impair her concentration. Billie Jean King lives on concentration, on the fulfillment of purpose.

But now, at last, there would be surcease, relief from the unremitting pressures of a unique situation in sports history—indeed, in the social history of this country. And she was ready for it. There would be no rematch or anything of the sort. She would never play against a man again. She would go back to work on the things that mattered to her: World Team Tennis, her new magazine, *Woman Sports,* the pro-tennis tour. She had made her point, and she had never claimed that a woman could beat a man of comparable age in any sport that required physical strength. There was nothing left to prove.

But Billie Jean had become a superstar overnight, and that was why her life could never be the same again. She had become a very special superstar, a symbol for American women. Life would have to be more than tennis, which was all she ever wanted it to be. She would have new obligations and new responsibilities.

Except for the fact that she has so many things going for her, and despite the fortress of people she has working for her, which makes it so hard to get to her personally, Billie Jean, on the surface, does not seem to have changed since she beat Bobby Riggs. She still has that natural, winning air. There is no pretense about her. She remains a girl for blue jeans, and hates to dress up. I was with her in Orlando,

Florida, when she was a co-speaker before the managing editors of the nation's newspapers, and that's the way she arrived, in sweater and jeans. But her words command an audience now, and that never happened before. She knows it. She knows that people don't listen to her merely as Billie Jean King the tennis player. They listen to her as Billie Jean King, the woman who upheld women.

This has Billie Jean thinking. I caught up with her in Akron, Ohio in March 1974. It was just another stop in her pro tour. She was staying at one of those uninviting, Main Street-type Holiday Inns, just across the street from Akron University where the tournament was being played. We walked for more than an hour and covered a wide range of subjects.

One was politics. "Yes," she said, "I've been thinking about it. Larry says I'm a natural for it."

"What would you run for?" I asked. "The Congress? The Senate?"

She threw her head back, laughed, and said, "You know me. Probably for president." And then she added, "We'll have a woman president, you'll see."

That's when I asked her about the changes in her life, and she said that tennis continues to be the dominant force in her existence. But so many people demand so much of her now, and she is involved in so many projects, that she has felt compelled to build an iron curtain of people around herself. "If I didn't love tennis so much, why would I be here in Akron?" she asked. "Why would I be staying at the Holiday Inn, and then traveling on to the next stop? It's tennis, and tennis is beautiful."

There have been many gossip stories about her marriage to Larry King. She talks about it forthrightly. "We love one another. We talk on the phone together every day, but it is very hard for us to be together. He is busy on the coast with the new magazine, and he runs everything for me in a business sense. That is why I once said we might be better off if we just lived together, instead of being married."

What about children? "I've thought about it. But the way things are now, with so much to do, I don't know." She laughed again. "But I'm 30 now, and if I'm ever going to do anything about it, I'd better get the show on the road."

Where do you go next? "New York, believe it or not. I have
to get fitted for an evening dress for a magazine cover. I can't
stand the thought of it. You know how I hate to dress up. And
then we have a tournament in New York. That's one I've got
to win."

As she walked off toward the Akron gymnasium in a sweater and tennis dress, carrying her racquets, she looked like any
other girl on her way to a set of tennis. But within 20 yards, she
was besieged by women and men who wanted to know about
the match against Bobby Riggs. "That's the way to go, Billie
Jean," one woman said. "Show those men up."

Billie Jean grinned. "We've done it already."

Some men will never admit it. At the Alan King Tennis
Classic in Las Vegas in May 1974, Ted Schroeder, the old
champion of the late 1940s, was talking with me.

"I'll never understand why Riggs went into the tank in that
match against Billie Jean," he said. "Bobby must have had
some bet on the line. I happen to know that he took 32 salt pills
in his dressing room before the match. Do you know what that
does to the body? Still, I have to wonder why he did it?"

"To lose a million dollars and become a nobody," I
answered.

Male chauvinism will never die. But Billie Jean King dealt it
a helluva blow.

CHAPTER 5

THE CASE OF THE JUMPING DOLPHINS—AND THE CASE OF JUMPING JOE

"In an hour or two we will all be members of the Toronto Northmen."

Sunday morning, March 31, 1974, was a perfect time to bury one's self in *The New York Times.* This is exactly what I did. The weather outside was typical of late March in the big city. It was cloudy, damp and penetrating. Occasionally, the splatter of rain on our apartment terrace would interrupt my absorption with the crossword puzzle, and a look out the windows would confirm the prediction of showers throughout the day.

The Times Sunday crossword puzzle is always a challenge, but it's a comfortable one. I usually sit in the den, curled up in a large wing chair, and forget about the outside world. This happens only after I have carefully poured over the "Week in Review," the "Book Review," the "Arts and Leisure" and the "Sports" sections. Once you've done that, you're entitled to put the world to rest. My only problem on that Sunday morning was the upper right-hand corner of the puzzle, and my frustration was growing. I even began to wonder if I should cheat, if I should sneak to the bookshelves and, without Emmy hearing me, quickly scan *Webster's Unabridged Dictionary* for synonyms that would give me the key to the undone remainder of the puzzle.

I have done this in the past, and then trumpeted triumphantly to my wife that I had once again prevailed. Sometimes
she has caught me during my surreptitious invasions of
Webster. So now she is suspicious of every victory I claim. But I
wasn't going to do it that day. I was just too content being back
from Caracas, and our day was carefully planned so that even
the rain couldn't bother us. Between 10:30 and 11:00 we were
going to go over to the ABC Television Studios where I was to
record a telephone conversation with George Foreman, still
being held tax hostage in Caracas. The phone call was to be a
last minute update on our *Wide World of Sports* show that
afternoon, when the Foreman-Norton fight would be shown
on home television for the first time. After playing the fight
telecast, which I had covered the previous Tuesday night in
Venezuela, we would discuss George's problems and then let
the viewers hear our telephone talk of that morning.

The rest of the day would be perfect. Emmy and I were to
meet Roone Arledge for brunch at the Plaza, one of New
York's more civilized and pleasurable haunts, and after that,
the three of us were to go to Madison Square Garden to watch
Billie Jean King play in the finals of a women's professional
tennis tournament.

Except for the phone call to Foreman, none of it worked
out.

At 10:35 A.M. as we were getting ready to leave the apartment, the phone rang. It was long distance calling from Toronto, Canada. The operator could not pronounce the name
of the caller. In the background, I could hear him trying to
clarify the name for her. It wasn't necessary. I could tell it was
Larry Csonka. "Put him on," I said.

"Zonk" got right to the point. "Howard, I'm at the Sutton
Place Hotel with Jim and Paul [Kiick and Warfield] and Ed
Keating, our manager. In an hour or two we will all be mem-
bers of the Toronto Northmen of the World Football League.
I wanted you to have the story."

While I had known of Larry's publicly expressed willingness to listen to the blandishments of the new league, I
couldn't believe my ears. I had thought that Larry had been
talking about jumping to the World Football League only as a
bargaining lever against his boss, Joe Robbie, the principal

owner of the Miami Dolphins. And I had never entertained the notion that three of the leading stars in pro football would leave the world champions at one and the same time. But there it was, and the story was certain to be one of the major disclosures of the sports year.

I asked Larry what room they were in and jotted down the number. I then asked him to stay right there until I could call him back within the hour, explaining that I would try to find a way to put Jim, Paul and him on television live that very afternoon on my weekly *Sports Magazine* show. "Zonk" agreed to stay put, and said he would advise the telephone operator to put through a call from me. He told me that they were not otherwise accepting calls.

Now the languid pace of a leisurely Sunday morning was transformed into the quick, bustling, almost frenetic energy that goes into the pursuit of a breaking story. I don't care how long one has been in the business, or how many stories you've been out on or what your past successes have been. The excitement, the inner pulsation of knowing that you can bring to the American viewing public information that no one else has yet been able to gather and transmit, is a supreme accomplishment to one whose life's work is that of a reporter. The thrill of such an achievement never dies. It is always there, to be savored over again in the years to come and to hone the reporter's energies for the next big scoop.

Emmy and I were at the studio in eight minutes.

In the control room were Dennis Lewin, producer of *Wide World of Sports*, Terry Jastrow, producer of my *Magazine* show, several production assistants and Bill Caplan, George Foreman's publicity man who had left Caracas the previous day. I burst into the room and told Caplan the phone call to Foreman would have to wait. I told Terry Jastrow that we would have to table our *Magazine* show which had already been taped for play that day at 4:15 P.M. And I told Dennis Lewin, who literally goes crazy every weekend cutting *Wide World* to time—frequently when the show is already on the air—that I would get to the Foreman phone call as soon as possible. Then I explained the situation. The reaction of everybody was the same as mine had been: Disbelief. But these young men are the greatest assets ABC Sports has, and they are quick to respond efficiently and cooly to the demands that are placed upon them. I told Terry to make immediate arrangements for a charter flight from Toronto to New York for about 1 o'clock in the afternoon. Also, he had to make instant arrangements for a studio and for our *Magazine* show set to be struck. If the three Dolphins left by 1 o'clock, they would land at La Guardia airport at two. We would have a limousine pick them up and have them at the studio by 2:30 or 2:45. Then we would have a choice of either taping the show, or going live. So Terry had to order a limousine, too.

Then I told one of the production assistants to call Roone Arledge and explain the flow of circumstances to him. "Tell him Emmy and I will meet him at the Plaza in forty-five minutes."

Then I called Csonka in Toronto and spoke with him and Ed Keating. They were of the opinion that the contracts would be prepared and signed by 12:30 so that all parties would be able to fly by charter to New York at 1:00 P.M. New York time. Paul Warfield, however, had a problem. He had to make an appearance in Cleveland that night. I assured Larry and Ed that the charter would wait until after the show was done and would then take Paul on to Cleveland. I further told them that Terry Jastrow would call them with instructions to the hangar where the plane would be waiting for them at the Toronto airport. I filled Terry in on my conversation while he was in the midst of a telephone call to a charter airline that we regularly use.

During all of this, Bill Caplan, Foreman's man, stood by patiently and understandingly. George Foreman, locked in the Avila Hotel in Caracas, could not possibly have been so patient or understanding. As a virtual captive in a foreign country, he was himself a continuing national story.

Caplan accompanied me into an announcer's booth adjacent to the control room and placed the call to Foreman. I got on the phone with George and did the interview, but the sound quality was substandard. So we did it again, and this time it was fine. George couldn't have been more cooperative despite his obvious resentment and chagrin over the way the Venezuelan authorities were treating him.

Dennis Lewin was now set with his *Wide World of Sports* show for that afternoon. Terry Jastrow informed me that studio facilities had already been arranged, and that the chartered plane was in the works. Emmy and I left for the Plaza, and on the way, we were still figuring that if things worked out as planned we would still get to see Billie Jean King.

Arledge never did get to the Plaza. He called me there and said he would meet me at the studio. He wanted to be there personally to insure that everything would go all right. Emmy and I made brunch a quick affair, and we were back at the studio shortly after 12:00 noon. Roone hadn't even gotten there, but Terry had disconcerting news. Ed Keating had called and things were progressing much more slowly than planned. He wanted to talk to me immediately. I called Ed and he explained the problem, which was ridiculous, but fact nonetheless. They were working out the final details of the contract with John Bassett, one of the owners of the Toronto franchise, but it was Sunday and there were no stenographers available. They would have to handwrite the agreement, and there would be no way to make the plane at 1:00 P.M. New York time. Toronto, by the way, was on standard time, one hour behind New York. Obviously, then, we were (to put it mildly) in deep logistical trouble. Keating had another dilemma, one which I readily understood. The Canadian press wanted the story and Bassett wanted them to have it lest he alienate the Canadian newspapers. At the same time, Keating, mindful of the American press, was concerned about protecting his clients from the wrath of sportswriters over the delivery of an exclusive story to the competitive medium, television.

"I understand all of this, Ed," I said. "To protect the guys once the contracts are signed, why don't you let the press have the story? That should be about 2:30 P.M. New York time, or maybe a little later. What I want is to have the three players on my *Magazine* show at 4:15 P.M. New York time. John Bassett owns our affiliate TV station in Toronto. If you can get the fellows there by 3:45 P.M. New York time, I will try to get facilities for a split-screen interview."

"I absolutely guarantee that," Keating answered.

"I'll call you back," I told him, and hung up.

Terry Jastrow was equal to the occasion. The charter was canceled, the limousine was canceled. Terry put Pat Shearer, our sports operations man, to work immediately on arranging the split-screen interview. Within 45 minutes, Shearer had coordinated the facilities problem with our Toronto affiliate, and we were all set. I called Keating and so advised him. "Don't worry about a thing," he said cheerily. "We'll be there."

At 3:30 P.M. New York time, I was seated in our studio, and Toronto technicians were seated in a Toronto studio. The split screen was set and ready to go. We checked pictures. We checked sound. 3:45 came and went, but Csonka, Warfield and Kiick had not arrived at the Toronto studio. 3:50 and still no sign of them. It may have been damp and cold outside, but inside that studio we were sweating. 3:55. 4 o'clock. 4:05, and at last, there they were. There would be no time to videotape now. We would have to go live. The three players were seated, and again we checked sound. We had about three minutes for some preliminary talk, but that was in the nature of just kidding around. And then we hit the air.

For the first time, the public saw and heard the three men tell what they had done, why they had done it, how they thought their Dolphin teammates would feel about it, what their attitudes would be in the remaining year they must spend with the Dolphins, the general range of what they would be paid by their new owner, whether they had given the Miami owner an adequate chance to meet their demands and whether they thought they had defied ethical and moral principles in doing what they had done.

I concentrated on Csonka during the interview, although I had known all three for a number of years and was aware of the fact that each was an expressive man. Warfield has been doing broadcast work for a number of years, and seeks a future in the field. Kiick is a carefree rebel with a definable personality and has a way of putting words together. But Csonka is, in my opinion, one of the most articulate athletes I have ever known, and one of the most forthright. I felt that by focusing on him, after establishing all three with an individual question or two, I could bring clarity and continuity to the story. Larry did not let himself or the others down.

And so the show was done and ABC Sports had another broadcast exclusive, thanks to Larry Csonka.

But there was one thing more to be done. The *Magazine* show went off the air and *Wide World of Sports* came on. Roone Arledge told Dennis Lewin and Terry Jastrow that he wanted about three minutes of the interview excerpted and replayed on *Wide World of Sports*. Terry shot over to the videotape editing room and went to work. Lewin immediately started to figure out what to cut out of *Wide World of Sports* so that the excerpted interview could be slotted in. Donna DeVerona, our hostess for the shows that day, would lead into it. With the precision of a Swiss watch, it all pieced together.

By the time we finished, Billie Jean King had won her match and had left the Garden. It was not the day we planned, but both Arledge and I felt it was one of our most satisfying days in television. We thanked those young people for their superb efforts, and then we went over to Roone's apartment for dinner. He loves to cook, and he is so good at it that there have been times in my life when I have thought that he would make a better chef than he does a sports-broadcast executive.

What really pleased us most was that we had demonstrated how television can be immediate and flexible. We had tabled a show that was already prepared for broadcast. We had survived a series of hectic exigencies and had gone "live" with a breaking news story. This, we felt, is what television is, or should be, all about.

But upon reflection, the core fact remains that we got the story because, and only because, Larry Csonka called me at 10:35 that Sunday morning. And that call, why and how it came about, provides a significant insight into the making of a scoop.

To be effective, a reporter, any reporter, must have connections in the field in which he works, because these connections can do one of two things: (1) They can contact you with a breaking news story, as in the Csonka case. (2) They can keep you steadily informed from the inside on a continuing story, as "Deep Throat" did with Carl Bernstein and Bob Woodward in the indefatigable chase by those two men for the truth about Watergate. There is nothing new in the need for sources. Political reporters and sports reporters have always recognized this. So one job of a reporter as he covers his beat is to develop contacts, gain their confidence and their respect, and draw upon those contacts at the appropriate time. In doing this, the reporter faces a basic problem within himself. He must resist the tendency to forfeit his reportorial integrity when he faces the problem of making disclosures or writing unpleasant truths about those contacts who, in the past, have helped him. Each reporter must make this decision when the question arises, in his own way, according to the dictates of his own conscience. Again, the contacts are necessary not only for real reportorial results, but all too often for mere survival in the competitive world of reporting.

In this, "The Case of the Jumping Dolphins," Csonka, with the consent of Warfield and Kiick, did not call me by accident. In the first place, the three young men had their own motivation, their own ax to grind. They wanted to explain their action to millions of American people, and they knew that I had the forum to enable them to do exactly that. They also trusted me because of the relationship which I had developed with them over many years.

Warfield, for instance, has had his own television and radio shows. He wants to make broadcasting his future. He has had many talks with me on the subject, and when I did a TV special on the Miami Dolphins, it was Warfield who interviewed me, rather than the other way around. Warfield is not like Csonka and Kiick. He is a quiet man, a private man. Even though he wants to perform on the air, he is not by nature an extroverted man. He carries himself with great personal dignity, and is extremely articulate and thoughtful. Once he confessed to me that his wife was home in Cleveland, not with him in Florida, because neither of them felt at peace in the Southern atmosphere of the peninsula state. Since the owner of the Toronto franchise also owned a television station, it was clear that Paul was getting two things when he jumped to the World Football League—a lot more money and a long-term broadcast opportunity. Also, he couldn't help being enamored of the fact that Toronto is a northern city, a very beautiful one and close to his native Ohio. I wonder how

Paul feels now that the Toronto franchise has moved to Memphis?

Csonka andKiick are very different from Warfield. They are a pair of noisy nonconformists, not necessarily with a cause. The one thing they share with Warfield is football excellence, a willingness to place demands upon their bodies that seem almost masochistic. Csonka's capacity to endure pain is amazing, and he has transmitted at least some of this to Kiick. The two of them love football. "If I didn't," Csonka says," there is no way in the world I'd go through the pain of these feet." Then Larry looks down at his feet. They are something to see. They are gnarled, pigeon-toed and don't really seem strong enough to carry that hulking 6-foot, 4-inch 240-pound frame. When he walks, it is almost like a shuffle, tenderly executed as if each step were an ordeal to be painfully undertaken. On the football field, it somehow vanishes.

Csonka, when you first meet him, overwhelms you with his size. But then you forget about that size as you become enveloped by the warmth, geniality and softness of his personality. There is laughter in this man; he loves a practical joke, relishes defiance of the establishment and particularly likes to torment his coach, Don Shula. He will complain about Shula endlessly, but when it comes to football, his respect for Shula is enormous.

Kiick is a perfect mate for Csonka. He enjoys the same defiance of authority—almost flaunts his beard in Shula's face, fights with Shula over whether the beard is to be trimmed, respects Shula the way Csonka does, but resents Shula because Mercury Morris was moved into the starting lineup ahead of him. Like Csonka, Jim is a practical joker, and the two, together, are past masters at finding ways to embarrass or even frighten Shula. Yet each man has a high degree of intelligence and a great deal of sensitivity. Sensitivity is the common bond among Csonka, Kiick and Warfield.

I spent more time with Csonka during the past year than in all of the prior years of our relationship. I guested with him and Kiick on the *Irv Kupcinet Show* in Chicago as we talked about their book, *Always on the Run*. I did my own radio talk show with Larry about the book. I was with him during much of the week leading up to the 1974 Super Bowl. During the NFL meetings in Miami Beach in February 1974, Larry was with me constantly. Each day he would fly a charter with me from the Opalocka Airport in Miami to Rotunda, Florida, where ABC Sports was taping the finals of *The Superstars.* Larry's teammate, Dick Anderson, was in the finals and Larry wanted to make the scene with him. When you spend this amount of time with a man, you get to know him. Every time we would go to a restaurant, Larry would insist on taking the check. He would sign it, "Don Shula, Coach, Miami Dolphins." A quick grin would always flash across his face as he did it. "The son of a bitch owes me that," he would say. And then Larry's big mustache would quiver, the hairs almost smacking together with relish at the thought of Shula's discomfort when he would get his monthly bills containing items from restaurants he had never patronized. Shula once told me, "That big goof is crazy. He may wind up in jail. If he doesn't, I may put him there. But only when he's done playing."

Csonka loves to hunt in the Everglades. His partner on most such occasions is Manny Fernandez, the extraordinary defensive lineman of the Dolphins. Fernandez is the strongest man on the team. Although he is not as heavy as many other defensive lineman in the NFL, he has developed his upper body strength to astonishing proportions. One day Manny and Larry were in the Everglades when suddenly the two of them heard a rustling noise. "Hold this," Fernandez whispered to "Zonk" as he handed him his gun, and shot off into the thick of the surrounding swamp. Larry stood immobile, clutching two guns, as the minutes passed. He became uneasy, and began to think terrible thoughts of Fernandez dying somewhere out there in that wilderness. And he didn't feel any better about being alone, even though he had two guns.

Suddenly, Fernandez reappeared. Manny had company. He was carrying an alligator and he said, "This is the bastard who took a swipe at us." Csonka was terrified. Like most of us, he doesn't like live alligators. "What are you doing with that son of a bitch?" Larry asked him.

"Hold him for a minute," Fernandez said, "I want to tape

his jaws and bring him back to camp."

"I'm not touching that damn thing," Csonka said. "This isn't a baby alligator we're dealing with."

Fernandez persuaded Csonka to hold the alligator's tail while he encased the jaws in his arms. They carried the alligator that way to the car. Fernandez freed one arm to get heavy masking tape, and actually succeeded in taping the alligator's jaws together. Then they threw the alligator in the back of the car, drove back to the Biscayne College training camp, and secretly, that night, carried the 'gator into the shower used by Don Shula and his chief aide, Bill Arnsparger, now head coach of the Giants. The next morning while the members of the team were dressing, Shula and Arnsparger went into the office they shared. The shower is adjacent to the office. Within seconds the two burst from the office screaming like deranged men. "Get the goddamned alligator out of there!"

When order had finally been restored, the alligator disposed of and the Dolphin players had stopped roaring over the incident, Shula mustered up a semblance of cold dignity, walked into the dressing room and went straight to Csonka and Kiick. "This time you guys have gone too far," Shula began threateningly. Kiick didn't give him a chance.

"Coach, every time something happens around here you blame Larry and me and it's not fair. I don't know one damn thing about that alligator. If you want to know the truth, I hate alligators. They scare the hell out of me."

Csonka was quick to chime in. "That's the truth, Coach. You're always blaming us. Big as I am, you know damned well I don't have the strength to handle an alligator."

Shula looked at the two of them. He didn't want to admit it, but what they said made sense. Only one man on his club had the physical strength to handle an alligator. Shula whirled around. "Fernandez," he shouted, "where the hell are you?"

Larry Csonka told me that story as we were flying from Miami to Rotunda. During that stay in Florida he told me many more. He has an irrepressible sense of humor, and yet he has a very deep sincerity. We talked often during those days together about the World Football League. One night, he and his wife, Pam, were our guests at the Diplomat Hotel for *The Sammy Davis Show.* Included in the party were Don Klosterman, general manager of the Rams, Carl Lindemann, head of NBC Sports, and his wife, Cissy, and Sig Hyman, administrator of the NFL pension fund. We got to talking about the World Football League and Larry told everybody there that he was interested in what they had to offer; that he hadn't heard from the Dolphin's owner, Joe Robbie, since the Super Bowl. The next morning, when Larry and I landed at Rotunda, some members of the press were there, including Will Grimsley of the AP. They asked Larry about the World Football League. Csonka didn't mince words. He told them he was interested, and that he hadn't even heard from Joe Robbie. My own thought, still, was that Larry, deep inside, was using the World Football League as a bargaining lever with Joe Robbie.

That night, back at the Americana Hotel in Miami Beach, I told Don Shula about Csonka's public statements concerning his interest in the World Football League. Don was not disposed to take them seriously. "That big goof," he said. "He just likes to sound off."

It's history now. Csonka did more than sound off, and so did Jim Kiick and Paul Warfield. When those three appeared together live on the ABC-TV network before millions of people they brought the World Football League instant credibility. Since that day, player after player, some of the great players of the NFL, have jumped, and with the new credibility, new investment monies have come into the new league. And why not? They don't make superstars in the world of football any bigger or better than Larry Csonka and Paul Warfield, nor are there many better all-purpose players than Jim Kiick.

Looking back, I am glad I've spent all those hours and days with Larry Csonka. He has become a very good friend, and he is one fine man. I consider this far more important than the story of Sunday, March 31. But the journalistic fact is that ABC Sports got the story, not by accident, but because one of its reporters had developed the trust and friendship of Larry Csonka.

"Why did you call me ignorant?"

The phone call from Larry Csonka was one way to come upon a breaking news story. On January 24, 1974, I found myself suddenly, and unexpectedly, in the middle of another. This one involved Joe Frazier and Muhammad Ali.

On Saturday, January 26, 1974, we were going to show for the first time ever on home television, *Super Fight One,* the first fight between Ali and Frazier. ABC Sports had been looking forward to this for a long time because the fight was a classic; public interest was tremendously high, and the show would undoubtedly get an enormous rating. Remember, *Super Fight One* had been seen only by a relatively small percentage of the national population on closed-circuit television in theaters.

We planned the telecast so that Ali and Frazier would be in the studio with me to comment of the fight round by round as it progressed on the screen for the home viewers. We were to tape the show on Thursday, January 24. Arrangements were made well in advance for Ali and Frazier to be in the studio at 1:00 P.M. that day. Members of the sporting press were to be present in the studio during the taping.

On Wednesday, January 23, a hitch developed. I received a phone call from John Martin of ABC Sports. He informed me that Joe Frazier did not want to appear to do the show, and that Joe's manager, Eddy Futch, did not want him to do it either. Martin told me he had just been advised of the situation by Robert Arum, Ali's lawyer and president of Top Rank, Inc., an organization tied in with the promotion of the impending second fight, and holding theater-television rights to the contest. Martin asked me if I would talk to Frazier in an effort to get him to reconsider and appear on the show.

I immediately called Arum who confirmed what Martin had told me. I asked Arum if there were anything he could do, and he told me that he had tried but failed. "Frazier doesn't want to go on with Ali," Arum said. "He feels that Ali abuses him and, as you know, he despises Muhammad."

Arum spoke the truth, although "despises" may have been a harsh word. Frazier is a completely decent man, and while he has seething resentment toward Ali, it is hard to conceive of a man as kind and as open as Joe nurturing hatred for another human being, and in this case the word "despise" connoted hatred.

The truth was that Joe was no match for Ali verbally, and he knew it. The truth was, also, that Ali had downgraded—if not ridiculed—Joe many times in the past, going back to before the first fight. And the final truth was that after the first fight, Ali, with his native genius for personal public relations, actually sold millions of Americans on the idea that he, Ali, had really won the first fight but that the officials had cheated him out of it. This rankled Frazier above all else, and caused him to smoulder inside at the very thought of Ali. Now, on January 23, 1974, he did not want to undergo the risk of being humiliated on national television by Muhammad.

Knowing that background, I called Frazier at his gym in Philadelphia. He was in the middle of a press conference but subsequently called me back. I spoke to him at length about the show, and told him that I wanted to stick strictly to commentary about the first fight and that I had no intention of letting Ali wander off into a stream of endless diatribes against Joe. I would do all I could to prevent such an eventuality. Frazier said it was up to his manager, Eddy Futch, and he put Futch on the phone. I told Futch exactly what I had told Frazier. Eddy, also a decent man who had managed Norton to a victory over Ali, agreed to allow Joe to do the show.

On Thursday, Ali arrived at the studio with his brother, Rahaman, Dr. Ferdie Pacheco and others. Angie Dundee, Ali's trainer, did not arrive till much later. Frazier arrived with Futch and some others including David Wolfe, an investigative reporter who has been working for a long time on Frazier's life story. A large number of sportswriters were also present, among whom were Dave Anderson, the splendid columnist of *The New York Times*, Rich Talley of *The Chicago Tribune* and Grimsley of the AP.

Dennis Lewin was the producer of the show. He had three chairs placed on stage. I assumed I would be in the middle, but Dennis informed me that he wanted Joe in the middle with Ali to his right for camera purposes. I would be on camera left.

Later, in the light of what occurred during the taping, some writers wrote that I was to blame for what happened because I had not sat in the middle. Obviously, they were totally unfamiliar with the fact that the producer makes such decisions, not the performer.

We got the show under way, and everything was proceeding smoothly. As the early rounds unfolded, I would lead each fighter with questions and they would take over with comments. Joe seemed a little tense and uncomfortable at the very beginning because of his concern about Ali's possible misbehavior. In truth, on a number of occasions, Ali did begin to ramble and each time I would cut him off by insisting that he stick to analysis of the fight itself. I did this five times by actual count. In the meantime Frazier relaxed perceptibly, so much so that by the sixth round Joe interspersed the words, "I didn't think I would enjoy this, but I'm having a good time." He said it with a big grin on his face for all the viewers to see, because his face appeared on the upper right-hand corner of the screen over the action when he made the remark.

A few rounds later the explosion came. Joe, himself, made a remark about Ali having to go to the hospital after the fight. At this point Denny Lewin was using the technique of having a head insert of both fighters in the upper corners of the television screen, so that the viewers could follow the verbal interchange exactly as it took place. Immediately after Frazier made the remark about Ali having to go to the hospital, Muhammad sounded off. "Why'd you say that about the hospital, Joe? Why'd you bring up the hospital? I wasn't gonna talk about the hospital. Everybody knows I went to the hospital for ten minutes. You were in the hospital for three weeks. I wasn't gonna talk about no hospital." And on he went. I was remonstrating with him, trying to get him and Frazier back to the subject of the action in the fight, which was still playing on the screen. But this time there was no stopping him. He said, "You're ignorant, Joe," With that remark, Frazier abruptly jumped to his feet and stood over Ali. The word "ignorant" was the trigger, and there could be no mistake about the fury in Joe Frazier as he loomed over Ali, who was still in his chair. Frazier exploded, "Why did you call me ignorant?" If there's one word in the English language that Joe Frazier will not accept from Muhammad Ali, it is "ignorant." Frazier is a proud man.

At this juncture, Ali's brother moved on stage and approached Frazier. Frazier looked at him and asked, "You want to get in this, too?" It was then that Ali leaped out of his chair and started to wrestle with Frazier. Each still had on his microphone and earpiece. As the two wrestled off the stage and on to the ground the earpieces and microphones were ripped off. Camera bulbs flashed. People rushed in to separate the fighters. And Frazier, in a rage, left the studio followed by Futch.

The whole incident happened so swiftly, so suddenly, that everybody was thunderstruck. I stayed glued to my chair and quietly described the ugliness of the scene. The fighters could have been hurt and I must say I had no desire to get between them and wind up being the recipient of any blows that might be struck. While I am 6-foot-1 and 188 pounds, one of Joe Frazier's arms is as big as my two thighs put together. And one of Muhammad Ali's hands would make three of mine. Also, the two men were itchy and tense with the bout only four days away. They were sharp, ready for battle. If Dennis Lewin made a mistake in judgment by not seating me in the middle, I was, at that moment, grateful for it! As Frazier was leaving the studio, I told him how deeply I regretted the incident and recapped for the viewers the fact that Ali had called Joe "ignorant" and that the use of this word was what had prompted Joe's emotional upset.

Some ten minutes after Frazier left, I resumed the show with Ali and explained to him that I would serve as devil's advocate on Frazier's behalf. Ali continued to allude to the fracas. I would either seek to cut him off or to challenge his statements, and the show was finally concluded.

The story was grist for all of the assembled sportwriters. Some had spoken with Frazier and Futch, and then they all crowded around Ali. It got a tremendous play in the newspapers that night and the next day. The New York State Athletic Commission held a hearing the next day and fined both fighters $5000. The fine was announced by the chairman of the commission, Jim Dooley. And then one of the commissioners, Kenneth Sherwood, who happens to be black and who is the successor on the commission to Jackie Robinson, made a statement in which he, at the very least, implied that I had been the agitator in the incident. He had not been present at the studio during the taping. He had not seen the tape of the show, nor had he even called ABC to request the opportunity to view the tapes. He also said that I had caused enough trouble for Muhammad Ali in the past with my interviews with him.

Suddenly I had become the issue, Robert Arum was outraged. He denounced the fine as he spoke in the hearing room, labeling it a defiance of due process. He then expressed his resentment of Commissioner Sherwood's remarks about me, pointing to the fact that Sherwood hadn't even seen the tape of the show so that he could not have known what happened. Then, Sal Marchiano, a sports reporter for WABC-TV in New York, went after Sherwood with both barrels. He demanded to know how Sherwood could have made the statement about me without seeing the tapes. He demanded to know what Sherwood knew about the relationship between Ali and me, and he pointed out that I had defended Ali against the very action taken by that commission when they stripped Muhammad of his title and his right to fight. All of this happened at noon on Friday, January 25. Sal went on local television that night, and excoriated Sherwood with a biting commentary.

Roone Arledge and I viewed film of everything that had happened in the hearing room at about 3:30 P.M. that Friday afternoon. We were enraged and shocked by the absence of responsibility shown by Sherwood in his capacity as a public servant. We were equally shocked by his ignorance. I kept thinking, "Good Lord, this man sits in the chair held by one of the closest friends of my entire life and one of the greatest men I have ever known, Jackie Robinson. How can this be?"

Arledge went to a phone and called Sherwood. He was out, but he called back later. Roone didn't mince words with him. He told him point-blank that as a public servant he should have called and asked to view the tape before he made any statement. He also advised him that I had been, perhaps alone among all national broadcasters, the one to support Ali in his darkest hours against the action taken by the very commission of which Sherwood was a part. He further told Sherwood that the tape of the show would reveal that I had made every possible effort to control the fighters in their conversation during the course of the taping. Sherwood hedged and said he would view the show at home the next day.

Meanwhile, around the country many people (understandably because of the whole sordid history of boxing, with its false publicity buildups) took the incident with a grain of salt. "Just another stunt to promote the fight," they thought. But the writers who were in that studio wrote the truth and nothing but the truth. They knew that they had witnessed a tense and ugly scene which harkened back to a similar confrontation between Ali and Ernie Terrell.

They wrote it like it was, and several of them later expressed to me their own sense of shock and dismay that some of their colleagues who had not been present in the studio that day, blithely wrote that the whole thing was a publicity plant to stir up more public interest in the fight.

On Sunday, January 27, the weigh-in for the fight was held at Madison Square Garden. The fighters were brought in separately so that there could be no repetition of what had taken place in the studio on the prior Thursday. I was at the Garden that day originating my *Magazine* show with George Foreman as my guest. Subsequently, I originated live at the weigh-in on *Wide World of Sports*. It was at this time that Commissioner Sherwood introduced himself to me, told me that he had viewed the show the previous day on our Saturday *Wide World of Sports* presentation and apologized for the remarks he had made in my direction. I asked him if he wanted to go on *Wide World* with me and make that apology public in the light of the vast publicity that his statements about me had already been given in print. He said he would be glad to do so, but that he would stand by the fines the commission had imposed on the fighters. I told him I had no quarrel with that at all. And so he did make a public apology.

The whole thing added up to another major sports story.

An authentic happening, unplanned, unexpected and unwanted with yours truly somehow in the middle. But I've been there before.

Yes, there are a lot of ways a reporter can get a scoop.

CHAPTER 6

1974: YEAR OF THE SUPERSTAR, THE DAREDEVIL AND THE ODDSMAKER

The people. They are the soul of sport. They are the essence of what you find in sport, of what you get out of life. Each is a distinct personality, a whole complex of emotions, talents and intelligence worth probing and comprehending.

Every year my profession brings me into contact with dozens of these people, and the past year has been no exception.

There are some whom I've come to know more intimately than others, and always there is the intense satisfaction at having had the opportunity.

The following character sketches are good examples. In their own way, they represent a broad spectrum of what sport really is to the American public. They are the Superstar, the Daredevil and the Oddsmaker. They are my friends.

"It is his physical presence," Burton related.
"He is a dominant man."

O. J. Simpson is unquestionably one of the greatest running backs ever to have played football. He is superb. His instincts are uncanny, his intelligence exceptional. His change of speed and change of direction manifest this. Often you will see him behind the line, slowed down to a walk, and then, suddenly, he will be fairly flying through a hole that hadn't seemed to exist. His use of his blockers is a priceless work of art. He knows exactly what Reggie McKenzie, his principal scythe, can do.

He knows Reggie's speed, his strength, the comparable strength of Reggie's opponent on a given day. He knows Reggie's moves, his habits, and he knows how to take advantage of them. In the same way, he knows the qualities of all the other men in his offensive line and utilizes them to the utmost. This is what you call intelligence.

Equally important, O. J. is uniquely attuned to what he, himself, can do. His instincts tell him where the tacklers are, when to make his move, when to switch direction, when to accelerate his enormous speed so that abruptly, instead of being entrapped, there he is, alone, storming downfield with that joyous, unfettered stride of his, all the while laughing that infectious laugh that captivates people. Speed and strength. Those are critical assets that belong to "The Juice," as they call him. He is as strong as he is fast. He can break a tackle almost as effectively as Csonka, but because of his speed and guile, he doesn't have to resort to raw power the way Larry does.

"The Juice" is fearless. He lives with the illusion that he is impervious to injury and, indeed, the injuries have been few. He reminds me of Jimmy Brown in that way, and sometimes he will do the very thing that Jim was famous for. He will get up from under a pile of bodies ever so slowly that you will think to yourself that this time he has had it as he laboriously, painfully pushes his body back to the huddle and then on the very next play he will kill you. Like Jim Brown, he is a master at giving you that leg and then taking it away. But he is faster than Jim ever was.

"The Juice" never stops analyzing. He sat with us in the broadcast booth throughout the Green Bay-Jets game in 1973 and heard us praise the middle linebacker of the Packers, a highly regarded player named Jim Carter. In a long discussion the morning after the game, O. J. carefully explained why Carter, in his opinion, is not an exceptional player. "I can kill him," O. J. said simply and without arrogance. "He plays too far off the ball. Just run sweeps, give me the one key block, and Carter won't see me all night." "The Juice" then proceeded to explain that this is a major, but unnoticed, failing in many NFL linebackers. They play too far

off the ball in their determination to defend against the run
and the pass at the same time.

I have never known a more confident athlete than "The
Juice." There isn't any player he doesn't think he can beat;
there isn't any team he doesn't think his team can beat.
Throughout the 1973 season, O. J. was steadfast in his belief
that Buffalo would make the playoffs. They didn't quite do it,
but the Bills did remarkably well for the young team that they
were. I personally believe they did as well as they did because
Simpson's confidence was contagious. He is the unquestioned
leader of the team, and it is quite possible that the self-
assurance he transmits to the others has been as important to
the success of the club as his own vast running abilities.

"The Juice" is a selfless player, and his teammates love him
dearly for it. Throughout the whole incredible season of
1973, while Simpson was accumulating a record total of 2003
yards gained rushing, all he talked about was his offensive
line. People nobody ever heard of, names like Reggie McKenzie, Dave Foley, Joe DeLamielleure, suddenly became recog-
nizable. Foley was a reject of the Jets. At dinner functions,
O. J. would turn to Weeb Ewbank, the Jets' coach, and kid-
dingly thank him for letting the Bills have Dave. But Reggie
McKenzie, number 67, out of Michigan, is Simpson's pride
and joy. "I take him everywhere, won't let him go to lunch
without me, can't let him out of my sight. He's my man," O. J.
says, and McKenzie beams. When O. J. passed the 2000-yard
mark in his final game of the season at Shea Stadium, all he
still talked about was his offensive line, "the men who made it
possible." And the way they hugged him on the field was
unnecessary evidence that the feeling was mutual. It's what
Lombardi used to call *love*.

"The Juice" is more, far more than just a great runner. He is
an exceptional blocker who will fling his body at the target
with unsparing violence and without thought to potential
damage to himself. It is partly because he does this that his
own forward wall is so dedicated to him. He has never asked
anything of them that he has not asked of himself.

O. J. is a marvelous receiver. His hands are good, he runs
patterns well, his timing is special and, of course, once he

catches the football he is without peer as a breakaway threat.

As a player, there have not been many, if any, better than O. J. Simpson.

The kind of player he is reflects the kind of man "The Juice" is. If there is one adjective to describe his personality, that would be the word "engaging." He kind of sweeps you up. Unconsciously, you think of Sinatra singing the Sammy Cahn lyrics to one of Frank's favorite songs, *The Tender Trap.* You remember how it goes:

> You see a pair of laughing eyes . . .
> And suddenly you realize . . .
> They're part of the tender trap.

That's the way it is with O. J. He does have a pair of laughing eyes, big brown ones. He is almost never without a smile; a wide, warm smile that makes you feel good just to be around him. He is a tender trap. He is a terribly good-looking man, with a large head and a body to match. He stands slightly over 6-feet 2-inches, weighs about 210, walks with a lazy, loping slouch that has become a familiar mark of identification to football fans everywhere. He walks the way he runs —deceptively, easily. Everything about "The Juice" is relaxed. He is enjoying life, he is enjoying being a superstar. And he has never changed. I have known him since he was a junior at the University of Southern California. He refuses to take himself seriously.

Simpson is a kind man, a thoughtful man and a sensitive man who cares about people. He's an ambitious man. The night before the season finale against the Jets in 1973, "The Juice" was at a New York dinner party with my wife and me. We left together and started to walk down Central Park South toward the Essex House where the Bills were staying. Every two steps O. J. would be stopped by fans. He ate it up, signed autographs for them, talked football with them. Nothing synthetic about him. He enjoys it.

Then, as we got to the Essex House, he said, "Will you do me a favor? Reggie McKenzie is up in the room resting. He'd get a great kick out of it if you went up to see him."

So up we went, and quietly, stealthily, Simpson opened the door for me and then ducked. McKenzie was lying in bed with his right elbow encased in a hot towel. Reggie, who is a man of warmth and humor, looked up and casually said, "You looking for the man?" "Hell, no," I replied. "I'm looking for you. The man's nothing without you." McKenzie roared. And then O. J. walked in. "Looking for me?" he asked. "No, I'm visiting the man who makes you tick," I answered. Whereupon Simpson laughed, turned to Reggie and said, "Howard's the only one who knows the truth. I was a bum before you came along." McKenzie would block a pair of charging bulls for O. J.

I'll never forget the time when O. J. went with me to Joe Namath's saloon, Bachelors III. "The Juice" was a college senior at the time, winner of the Heisman Trophy, a star in his own right. Namath arrived after we got there, and I started to tell Joe that Simpson was with me. But O. J. restrained me and softly said, "Howard, don't ever rush the great ones." That incident, I think, says a lot about the man.

O. J. wants to be an actor. He also wants to be a sportscaster, and, as discussed in an earlier chapter, thought about retiring as a player to join Frank Gifford and me on *Monday Night Football.* Roone Arledge made him a part-time member of the ABC sports team a couple of years back, because he recognized that the man has a big personality. In January 1974, O. J. became more than part time. He became the host of our weekend shows and I spent a lot of time in the studio with him. He has a peculiar physical habit on the air. His body sways back and forth, and his wife, Marguerite, and Roone and I would kid him unmercifully about it. "It's a new version of Swing and Sway with Sammy Kaye," I said. O. J., with that rare capacity to laugh at himself, would smile sheepishly and say, "I don't understand why I do it. I don't do it in football. But you've got to admit it's different."

There is in Simpson a competitiveness, a desire to excel that all but consumes him. This even applies to such minor pastimes as gin rummy and pocket billiards. Each weekend, at the ABC Studios, he would play gin rummy with the stagehands between on-the-air stints. Personally, I think O. J. is a lousy gin player. But he plays the game with the airy assurance of one who knows what he is doing. He will sit forever with a six, seven and nine of diamonds, waiting for an eight that will "gin" him. Most of the stagehands were equally bad players, and somehow, O. J. would get the needed eight. Then he would smile at me as triumphantly as if he had just won the Super Bowl. "They can't touch me," he would laugh. And then, in mock Ali fashion, he would add, "I am the greatest." He was, with that bunch, until he got involved with one stagehand who happens to be a hell of a player. He skinned Simpson; he really did. By the end of Simpson's broadcasting chores for the winter, O. J. could only moan the lament of all failing gin players: "He's a lucky stiff. I can't get any cards at all." To this day Simpson is convinced that he can kill the guy.

One night we were playing pool in Roone Arledge's apartment against Roone and Marty Starger, the head of ABC's entertainment division. Simpson was terrible and we all kept needling him. "I'll show you guys," he said. Damned if he didn't run off six balls. I had the uncomfortable feeling that if he spent two weeks at the game he'd be good enough to play Jackie Gleason or Leo Durocher, two of the more classic pool hustlers of our time.

But even O. J. can become careless. At Rotunda, Florida, he was competing in the finals of *The Super Stars,* a hit show that we had recently developed, and he was facing some of the finest athletes in the world. O. J. was absolutely certain he would win the competition. He had it all worked out in his own mind. But he lost the competition in the very first event, when Kyle Rote, Jr. beat him in tennis. Kyle is a remarkable young athlete, but O. J. had him whipped. He was leading young Rote four games to one and became overconfident. He started to wink at me and others during the course of the match, to take shots for granted, to lose concentration, and suddenly, Kyle caught and passed him, and won the match. Since it was only the first round of the tennis competition, Simpson scored no points. Rote went on to win the tennis competition, scoring ten points, and Simpson was dead. O. J. was enraged at himself. He knew exactly what he had done. "As long as I compete, that will never happen to me again," he vowed.

When his playing days are over, it remains to be seen whether O. J. will become a full-time sportscaster or an actor. As a sportscaster he has exactly the right combination of humor, insight, knowledge and irreverence. Most of all, he is outspoken. He would never be afraid to say exactly what's on his mind.

But I think O. J.'s real future is as an actor. I base my judgment on a visit to Oroville, California, where the movie, *The Klansman* was being shot. I went to Oroville—and it's not easy to get there—to do my *Magazine* show with O. J. He plays an avenging black in the movie and was surrounded by heavy company in terms of the rest of the cast: Richard Burton, Lee Marvin, Linda Evans and Lola Falana. The movie was directed by Terence Young, one of the finest directors in the motion-picture industry.

I was simply astonished at Simpson's acting abilities. I watched him do a couple of scenes, one by himself—an action scene—and one which he did with Burton and Lola Falana. The man has a natural presence given to few. He has honest emotions. He is a quick study. He takes direction very well. And, perhaps above all, he is unawed by the presence of established greats around him. Picture, if you will, a man who sprang from the black ghetto into his first major movie role completely confident and secure in exchanging dialogue with one of the greatest Shakespearean actors who has ever lived. Simpson did it.

Terence Young is not a director who will risk a multi-million-dollar movie on an inexperienced performer whom he doesn't believe in. Young believes in Simpson so much that he increased his role as the movie progressed. "I believe that O. J. is destined to become a great actor," Young told me. "The time will come when Simpson will be able to say, 'Sidney Poitier, move over.' "

Lee Marvin, an old personal friend of mine, who never wastes time kidding anybody, including himself, said, "The man's a born actor. I was with Jimmy Brown when he made his first movie, *The Dirty Dozen,* and Jim impressed me, but not like O. J."

Marvin was a great help to Simpson. Not only did the two get along very well, but Lee taught O. J. things. "Don't worry about using the exact words of the script," he told him. "Capture the thought, the mood, the feeling, the emotion, and then do it your way." That's just what O. J. did. Instead of becoming stilted, and placing all of his concentration upon trying to remember words, O. J. became the character he was scripted to be.

It was not an easy movie set for a rookie actor to be around. Burton and his wife, Liz Taylor, had their final breakup there, and there were some ugly scenes. Burton himself, apart from reported romances with a pair of local girls, had been indulging his fondness for vodka. When Liz left, she had everybody's sympathy; Burton, beset by his own problems, was inevitably delaying shooting and causing budget problems. In this atmosphere, according to Lola Falana, it was a delight to have O. J. around. He would kid everybody and leaven the tensions that were enveloping the company.

Except once. He didn't much care for Burton, and one night Burton started to needle Simpson with some talk about "bronze heroes." I must say that if I have ever known a black man without any emotional hang-ups over being black, it is O. J. Simpson. He is not, in any sense, an "Uncle Tom." He is simply not absorbed with, nor does he necessarily agree with, black militancy as a way of life. But don't insult him or his race. He'll go at you. So he gently pushed poor Burton to the floor.

Later, when I interviewed him for the *Magazine* show and asked him about his scuffle with Burton, O. J. just laughed and said, "Oh, Burton's all right. It's just that sometimes he gets diarrhea of the mouth."

In fairness to Burton, he developed a real respect for Simpson's performing abilities. "It is his physical presence," Burton related. "It is almost as if he were on the football field. He is a dominant man."

"What a great way to put it," I thought. O. J. Simpson is a dominant man. Lola Falana also said something that I will always remember. She spoke of O. J.'s energy level. "The man can go forever, work forever. I have never seen anybody with his energy level except for Muhammad Ali. He works here from Monday through Friday, flies all night on Friday to New York to work for ABC and then flies back Sunday night to begin working here Monday morning. And he never even looks tired!"

I couldn't agree with her more. I marvel at the fact that O. J. seems inexhaustible. This is related, unquestionably, to his ambition. I go back to what Terence Young said. If acting is what O. J. Simpson wants, Sidney Poitier, move over!

And I do think acting is what O. J. really wants. He has thought it through very carefully. He could have taken roles during the current black movie rage that would have brought him a lot more in the way of immediate money. You know the kind, the *Shaft* series and others. But O. J. wanted to learn how to act. He wanted to be around the Marvins and the Burtons. Never mind the money. I asked Lee Marvin if O. J. was getting paid what he deserved. Marvin, with that crisp, even bristling delivery of his snapped, "Of course not! With Marvin and Burton around, there's nothing left for anyone else!" Then he flipped his cigarette away, patted O. J. on the shoulder and said, "The chump will make more in future pictures because of what we're doing for him."

O. J. knows. His new picture is called *Towering Inferno*. Some of the people in the cast are Paul Newman, Steve McQueen and Fred Astaire. O. J. is learning, all right.

Maybe the best tribute to O. J. Simpson as a football player is a banner often seen in the great, new Buffalo stadium: "Miami has the oranges, but Buffalo has 'The Juice.' "

Maybe the best way to describe O. J. as a player and as a man is to apply the late Branch Rickey's characterization of Roy Campanella: "He is as fine a man as he is a player; and he's all there is of both."

"*If I miss the jump and hit the canyon wall, it really makes no difference....*"

I first met Evel Knievel in January 1974. I went to Dallas, Texas, to meet up with "Dandy" Don. Our assignment was to cover a motorcycle leap to be attempted by Knievel over a long series of Mack trucks, presumably for a world record.

I did not relish the assignment. I had the feeling that motorcycle leaping was for kooks, and that it was beneath my dignity to report the event. I also had a preconceived image of

Evel that was distasteful. You know what I mean: the black leather jacket, the boots, the gloves, the kind of image conjured up by Marlon Brando in *The Wild One,* or by the marauding motorcycle gang called the "Hell's Angels"; rebels without a cause, a danger to society, violent, a bad influence on young people and all the rest.

When I first met Knievel I was surprised. He was not as I had envisioned: cocky, tough and defiant. On the contrary, I discovered he was a most attractive man with sensitive eyes, very light brown hair, a face and mouth that seemed too soft for the daredevil character he portrays, and he was dressed in white, almost carefully so. His speech is excellent, his grammar good.

He was openly thrilled about appearing on *Wide World of Sports.* He wanted to cooperate with the telecast in every way he could.

He carried with him a diamond studded cane. Expensive canes have become a Knievel trademark. After one of his many injuries, he explained to me, he needed a cane to help him walk and the cane has been a security blanket ever since. He has, literally, dozens of them, all very expensive and very fancy. Some are diamond studded, others gold plated and still others are made of exquisite ebony. Most of the time he wears a handsome, costly, white leather jacket with blue and red trimming with his name written across the heart. He told me that there were only six or seven in the world like it. He had it custom made. He also said that some of his canes had been sent to him as gifts. Some he had purchased. He is always on the lookout for more.

During our first meeting, he wanted to discuss two things. First, there was the question of world records in motorcycle leaping. "Records were hazy things in this business," he said. And there were many claims of records that had no authentication. "Yet this leap tomorrow will be a world record," he insisted, "and I hope you will report it that way." Second, he asked us to consider his relationship to youngsters. Knievel feels strongly about this. Everywhere he goes, he stresses that young people should not seek to do what he does, should not, if they have motorcycles, try "wheelies" or leaps or excessive speeds, or any of the other antics generally identified in the public mind as dangerous and, somehow, gangsterish.

Then we talked about the leap itself: the problem of the takeoff, at what speed to approach the ascending ramp, at what speed to actually make the leap, the attitude on landing, maneuvering on the landing ramp and, of course, braking. We also discussed the possible effect of wind, should there be any.

He knew his business. He detailed every problem, every inch of the way. "When you've had nearly every bone in your body broken and had it happen as many times as I have, you've got to know what you're doing—or else, you're gone." Knievel has had any number of mishaps. It is a miracle that he is alive. He cracked up in a jump in Las Vegas, and it looked for a moment as if he couldn't possibly survive. But he did. As he describes his many injuries, you would think you are looking at a series of X-ray plates.

He is a curious admixture of carefree spirit and nervous tension. His movements are quick and jerky as he talks and his speech is in rhythm with those moves. He likes to say, "My name is Evel Knievel. I'm a professional daredevil." And then he will tell you his philosophy about life and death, and he will do it in a way designed to convince you that he has a contempt of fear; that death is an afterthought, and that he is forever death defying.

I don't think he believes this at all. I think, like all of us—only perhaps more so because of the peril in what he does—he is gripped by fear and anxiety. When we parted after that first meeting, I realized that Evel Knievel was far more than a kook. "He has to be crazy to do what he does," I thought. But oddly, I felt he had a sense of purpose, an intelligence, great personableness, and I liked him. I also respect any man who is willing to put his life on the line. And Evel is first and foremost a showman. He constantly talks of his continuous flirtation with death. The way he does it suggests high drama. Even his white helmet expresses the flamboyance of the man. "Color me lucky," it says.

The day after that first meeting, "Dandy" and Emmy and I drove 20 miles outside of Dallas to a little suburb where the motorcycle raceway was located, the scene of Knievel's leap. It was really incredible: cars lined up as far as the eyes could see. Twenty thousand or more people were jammed into the rickety wooden stands; flags and pennants everywhere; a state fair atmosphere, and everybody waiting for the hero, Evel Knievel. I had thought that all of the spectators would be youngsters. Many of them were, but there were many more adults than I had expected. I turned to Meredith and said, "This is your country 'Dandy.' Is it always like this?" I've never been to one of these things before," he said. "But I know they go mad for him. This is Middle America, man, and they just eat it up."

We went over to Knievel's camper to observe him before his leap. The camper itself is extraordinary. Knievel claims it's the largest in the world, and that it cost him more than $90,000. I believe it. The interior contains several couches, a bar, a large refrigerator; all of these in what constitutes a combined living room, kitchen and dinette. Then there is a reasonably large dressing room in the back that is cut off from the living area by drawn curtains. Just behind the curtains, on either side of the camper, are wardrobe closets containing Knievel's many attires, his canes and the rest of his personal accoutrements. The camper had four state troopers posted around it as security guards, and there were more down the road to ensure that fans would not be able to get too close to the entourage.

Inside, Knievel was behind the drawn curtains getting dressed. In the living area was his wife, Linda, to whom he's been married for 14 years. She is a most attractive woman, and the Knievels have three children. Looking at her, you wouldn't believe it. There were five others in the room; friends of Evel's who like to be present at every leap he undertakes. They laugh with him, tremble with him and share in the excitement and fear for his life.

It is in this camper before the leap that the nerves of Evel Knievel burst out. He put his head through those drawn curtains, spoke sharply to everyone around him, screamed about the wind (and it was windy, with gusts of up to about 40 miles per hour) and started to rant about his way of life. "There's no money in the world worth it," he moaned. "A man can't go on this way, taking his life in his hands." Knievel's own hands, at this point, were shaking unmistakably.

He withdrew behind the curtain and occasionally you could hear him muttering and then he would shout, "Are those guards out there? Are they keeping people away? I've got to be left alone. I've got the worst leap of my life out there today. It's for a world record."

Finally, he came out, resplendent in his all-white garb. "People have no idea what I go through," he barked. "This is no way to live." All his movements now were cryptic and there was no attempt by him to disguise his nerves with a pretended calm. Instead, he took two long shots of Wild Turkey Bourbon, and then grabbed his cane and walked off into the neighboring woods with one of the security guards. This is how he seeks to compose himself before the jump.

Meredith and I walked over to the raceway. We were now caught up in the mystique of the man and the drama of the situation. "Damnedest thing I've ever seen," said "Dandy." "The clubouse was nothing like this, not even before a championship game."

The crowd was festive. They had no idea of what went on in that camper, and they couldn't have cared less if they had known. They recognized "Dandy" and me, gave us loud cheers and chanted, "Where's Evel?" We were transmitting live on *Wide World*, and Evel was timed out to appear for his warm-ups at a precise moment. Out he came and from the roars that greeted him you would have thought that 100,000 people were there. His bike seemed gleaming and ready, precision tuned for the challenge. It has been carefully prepared by Ray Gunn, who, in the beginning of Evel's career, had lent Evel some money and has been with him ever since. Sometimes, too, Evel's machines are maintained by Roger Ryman, an old-time rider who is part of the Knievel entourage.

Knievel took his "show business" warm-ups, crowd-pleasing antics that included "wheelies." Those trucks seemed endless, insurmountable. The winds were constant and disturbingly strong. As Knievel drove up to us after the warm-ups he was edgy. He shouted at the raceway security people, "Get these people away, all of them! A man's about to risk his life."

Then he did a short interview with Don and me and, for a moment, he seemed to relax. He wound up asking me to ride off on the back of his bike. Judiciously, I refused and suggested "Dandy" as a substitute. Don was equal to the occasion. Wearing his now famous cowboy hat, he got on the back of the bike, rode off with Evel and then doffed his hat and waved it to the crowd.

The whole exercise seemed good for Evel. The showmanship in him, the ego, had come to the fore. He was doing his thing live on national television and so, momentarily, the tensions were dissipated.

But not for long. The leap itself was about to take place. He returned "Dandy" to our camera position and off he went for the real warm-up. Two practice runs, then a third and then the leap. After each practice run, he would talk briefly with Ray Gunn. And then, with a startling suddenness, he was on his way and in the air. Only at that last moment did the crowd grow quiet; did their gaiety depart as they were struck by the macabre possibility that Evel could be killed.

Not this time. The bike soared high over that line of Mack trucks but then, because of the strong winds behind him, Knievel's landing attitude and distance were slightly off. The machine landed heavily on the ramp and too far down. Evel's body shot up off the seat, then down, then up again and then down as he struggled for control of the bike. He won. He braked the bike, and rode back to me. We talked, and he told of the problem the wind had created. I didn't realize the agony that he was suffering at the time.

I did later, much later, back at the hotel. Evel couldn't straighten up. "It's my back," he said. "Something happened when I landed. I can't go to the bathroom." He wanted to wait before seeing a doctor, hopeful that the pain would go of its own accord. But even with his ever-present cane, he could hardly walk.

My wife and I had a dinner engagement that night in Dallas, and we got back to the hotel at about 11 o'clock. There was a note in my message box from an old friend, Murphy Martin, the anchor man for WFAA news in Dallas. He had taken Evel to the hospital. Emmy and I waited for them to come back. It was nearly one in the morning when Evel arrived. He was almost bent over in two. The lowest vertebra in his back had been broken. "I've had it before," he told me. "It's no real problem. It'll heal by itself. What's killing me is that I can't go to the bathroom."

Evel is right. It's one hell of a way to make a living.

Because of his pride, because of his braggadocio and because of the romantic notion that he has of himself as the world's incomparable daredevil, Evel has trapped himself. As this is being written, he is scheduled to jump the half-mile-long Snake River Canyon at Twin Falls, Idaho, in September 1974. He is supposed to do it with a jet powered machine, and his safety factor is supposed to be parachute equipment that will enable him to eject himself if the machine does not achieve sufficient arc to make the landing. Don't ask me what happens if he makes the landing, and don't ask me what happens if he has to use the safety factor because the parachute might not have time to open and enable Knievel to glide safely into the canyon. The whole thing seems an exercise in suicide.

But Evel is hoisted on his own petard. Some time ago, as he was building his reputation, he said he wanted to jump the Grand Canyon. The then secretary of the interior, Stewart Udall, prohibited him from doing so. So Knievel leased the property in Twin Falls from which he will essay the leap—if he ever does. I have talked with him about the leap and tried to dissuade him. So far, no luck.

What he says publicly about the leap is this: "If I miss the jump and hit the canyon wall, it really makes no difference, because I'm just gonna get somewhere quicker than where you're going some day. And I'll wait for you. Dying is a part of living, and while I'm alive, I'm gonna live it to the hilt."

But remember, that's what Evel says publicly. That night in Dallas, shot full of pain, Evel began to wail about the fact that he had committed himself to the canyon jump. I sensed then, with positive surety, that he doesn't want to make that leap, that he wants to get out of it, but that he is afraid to face the consequences of not making it. He is distraught with the fear that the image he has built of himself, for himself and for his public, would be destroyed. And yet there is enough of the gambler in him to impel him to attempt the jump. He is the kind of man who can lose himself in the fantasy of joyous thought. One can see him sitting there, dreaming, a slow smile coming across his lips, breaking into a wide grin as he rhapsodizes the scene—the smooth take-off, the unbelievable landing, the deed accomplished for all the country to see on television, the absolute grandeur of the achievement. Then there would be no argument. Evel Knievel would be the greatest daredevil who has ever lived.

That's the dream that may impel Evel to make the leap. But sometimes the dream vanishes in the face of haunting reality.

Knievel has a blustery ego, but he will rise to the occasion and pay homage to another man's accomplishments in the same field. We were in Toronto together to televise a motor cycle leap by a young man called "Super Joe" Einhorn. Einhorn was going to jump over a long series of minitrucks in a very confined physical area in the International Trade and Exposition Building. Einhorn was claiming that the leap would be a world record.

When I got to Toronto, I met Knievel and John Martin, director of program planning for ABC's *Wide World of Sports*. Evel was almost frenzied in his behavior. He paced the room and said he could not go ahead with the telecast. "I've worked a lifetime to build a reputation," he cried. "And I can't go on television and credit another man with a world-record leap when it isn't a world-record jump at all. I've been over to that building, and I've measured that damn jump, and it's thirty feet shorter then the one I made in Dallas. I can't go through with it." Martin and I listened to him patiently. His energy temporarily spent, he sat down and I assured him that all he had to do was follow my lead on the show, and that there would be no statements made that would be false or that would be designed to embarrass him.

We went over to do the show.

I couldn't believe the nature of the leap when I got to the Trade Building. The space was narrow . . . I mean it was *narrow*. And the hall didn't seem long enough for "Super Joe" to brake his machine in time to avoid crashing into the wall. Even Evel admitted to me that it was a devilish challenge, although clearly, it did not seem to be as long, in distance, as Knievel's leap in Dallas.

Evel was still uneasy about doing the show. But once Einhorn began to take his practice runs, Evel became absorbed in the show, performed remarkably well and showed qualities of compassion and generosity toward young Einhorn. "Super Joe" had no sooner started the motor for his first practice run than Knievel said on camera, "Is something wrong with his machine?" Evel is so expert at what he does, so acute in his perceptions, that he knew it even before Einhorn did. Then Einhorn tried another practice run and still the cycle was not performing right.

"He'll have to try another bike," Evel said. "He must have another bike here."

But no, Einhorn tried the same bike for a third time and rode back to us shaking his head. It still wasn't right. Now he would try another bike. Knievel knew the dangers of a new bike. It should be warmed up for a long time, tested and retested. The feeling would be alien. We interviewed Einhorn and "Super Joe" said, "Frankly, Mr. Cosell, I'm scared to death. But I'm going to try it with a different machine."

This was where Knievel jumped in and told Joe that he was a great performer and if he wanted to go ahead with a new machine, he was sure that he would make it. Then Knievel told him that if he decided not to make the jump, he didn't have to apologize to anybody. "You've proved your courage a hundred times, Joe," Evel told him. "This is a very difficult jump, and I know that a new bike can be troublesome. So whichever way you go, everyone will understand." "Super Joe" straightened up, went off to get his new bike, took his practice runs and made the leap successfully. Knievel had made him feel ten-feet tall. Evel embellished it in his congratulations to the young man. "One of the greatest leaps I have ever seen," Evel called it. All of his prior talk in the hotel room was forgotten. The man is, by nature, a gentleman.

With us in Toronto was a close friend of Evel's, a fellow I remember only as Joe. What I remember most is that Joe was a bartender in Butte, Montana, where Knievel grew up and still lives. Once when Evel needed money, Joe lent him $500 That loan has long since been repaid, but Evel feels he can never really repay Joe. Joe has cancer and is given only six months or a year to live. Knievel is taking him everywhere with him during Joe's remaining time. "Color me lucky," Evel says. "I want Joe to have some of it."

Knievel tries to do too much. He is his own business manager, runs his own business affairs but he isn't really qualified to do so. He wants to write a book about himself and he asked me about it. I told him I thought he had an interesting story to tell. He said that publishers had contacted him and asked me whom I would recommend. I put him in touch with a publisher, and the two made a deal that called for the payment of an advance to Evel. Within a matter of 48 hours, Evel was calling the publisher and demanding to know where his check was. The publisher patiently tried to explain to Evel that the business didn't work that way, that contracts had to be drawn and signed and that the matter was in process. Knievel is a wild man in matters like these, and can only hurt himself. He should have proper representation.

He has many avenues of income, not the least of which is the Evel Knievel line of toys, some of which are truly fascinating. He is enormously proud of those toys, pointing out how kids love them and, he argues, they learn about motorcycles in a clean way. They don't think of the bikes the way many of their parents do, as symbols of violence and rebellion. He is probably right about that. My two grandsons, Justin and Jared, play with the things for hours at a time. They love them.

He is a phenomenon in contemporary American society, and he must be recognized as such. There is a whole cult of young people that follow him, believe in him and love him.

The last time I was with him, I said, "Evel, you've got a big responsibility to the youth of this country. You're the one who created your image. Now you've got to live up to it. With your daredevil attitude, your good looks and your whole flair for living, you're a current day Douglas Fairbanks, Sr."

"Never heard of him," Knievel replied. "I'm Evel Knievel, vintage 1974. The kids don't have to worry."

"Mr. Jim Snyder, you know, the man who does all those political polls."

Despite a common misconception, Jimmy "The Greek" is not a bookie. He is an oddsmaker, and more than that, he is a fascinating man.

Years ago, two young men grew up in the town of Steubenville, Ohio. One was named Dino Crosetti. The other was named Demetrios Synodinus. Both dreamed of getting into sports. Dino Crosetti became a singer named Dean Martin, and was never heard of again. Demetrios Synodinus became Jimmy "The Greek" Snyder, and everybody knows who he is.

The first thing that impresses you about Jimmy "The Greek" is that he is a quiet man, soft-spoken and very gentlemanly in his behavior. He dresses mainly in sports clothes, jackets and slacks, and in a way, looks like a gambler. This is all right because he has been, in his lifetime, one of the biggest gamblers in the country.

But not a bookie. He has bet, head to head, against men who make book, but he has never practiced the habit of making book himself.

He always liked to bet head to head. He became interested in sports early. Back in Steubenville he was a natural-born gambler and started to bet. He learned a lot about sports and in the course of study learned a lot about how to evaluate contestants, what the yardsticks should be and how they should be weighed in measuring and assessing the opponents. People began to ask his opinion about contests. When he finally gravitated to Las Vegas, Nevada, it was only logical that he would become *the* oddsmaker in the nation's gambling capital.

I mentioned that Jimmy likes to bet head to head, or, at least used to. He doesn't bet any more. He hasn't bet since 1951, and there's a good reason. In 1950 he lost a $275,000 bet on the Sugar Bowl game. So he went into the oil business in Texas and hit 22-straight dry wells. That's why he went to Las Vegas. But in the old days, he used to bet with H. L. Hunt, the oil multimillionaire of Texas, father of Lamar Hunt, president of the Kansas City Chiefs. H. L. and Jimmy would bet on college football every Saturday. Each had the choice of three games, and each would pick the winners of the three games they selected. The other would have to take the other team in those games. They would bet $50,000 a game.

There was no way Jimmy could lose. H. L. was an S.M.U. alumnus, and every week one of his selections would be the S.M.U. game. Now S.M.U. has had, in its football history, such notables as Doak Walker, Kyle Rote and Don Meredith, but in the years that H. I. was betting on S.M.U. against "The Greek," the Mustangs were not prospering. Neither was H. L. Hunt. I still wonder how much H. L. lost to Jimmy during those days.

But what the hell did H. L. care? When a reporter told him that his son was losing a million dollars a year with the Chiefs, H. L. answered, "At that rate, he'll be broke in 200 years."

If there is one thing Jimmy resents, it is being thought of as a bookmaker. Very carefully, he will tell you that he is an oddsmaker, and he will explain the difference. On the question of whether or not, by setting odds, he is encouraging gambling on sporting events, Jimmy will tell you that the gambling goes on anyway, and that since it does, he wants to service the public by providing the most scientifically derived information possible.

Sometimes Jimmy can be uncanny. When Howard Samuels began his administration of Off Track Betting in New York City, he brought Jimmy "The Greek" into New York and asked for his projections of what OTB would gross the very first year. "The Greek's" estimate proved to be almost exactly on the nose. At the same time, "The Greek" can miss, like anyone else. And he knows how to take it with good grace.

He was the one who made the Baltimore Colts 17-point favorites over the New York Jets in the 1969 Super Bowl. A lot of people took off on Jimmy for that, but all he did was smile and go down to Texas to accept "The Bonehead of the Year Award."

His operation is an interesting thing to see. It is in the Tropicana Hotel, right on the Strip, which he represents in a public-relations sense. In his office is a huge desk, surrounded by plants, set upon a platform a step above the rest of the room. Jimmy will tell you that there is nothing psychological about this, that he has no desire to sit up there in the guise of a king, overseeing his disciples. As a matter of fact, Jimmy is quite the opposite. He is not only the soft-spoken, perfect gentleman, but he is utterly without airs. He likes people, and he wants people to like him. It doesn't matter whether they're important or unimportant. He is a family man. He and his wife, Joan, have three children, and he is terribly proud of them.

You get an insight into Jimmy as an oddsmaker when you view his operation firsthand in his office. In professional football, for instance, you read his sheets on which his rating system is set. He breaks down the different elements, according points to each. First is speed; second, the defensive secondary; third, the front four; fourth, the quarterback; fifth, the running game; sixth, the special teams; seventh, the home team; and eighth, what he calls the intangibles.

Jimmy rarely goes to a regular season NFL game. He does go to preseason games in order to take a close look at the rookies. He knows that every team drafts to repair weaknesses, and he wants to ascertain whether or not the rookies drafted by a team have the ability to do that.

College football presents a bigger problem for "The Greek" because of the abundance of teams and games, but he has more than 30 "stringers" around the country to assist him in assessing the teams in conformity with his rating system. It is on the basis of this system that Jimmy arrives at his odds.

The thing that impresses one most of all in Jimmy's offices is that fact that oddsmaking is only a part of his operation—and not the biggest part. At this stage of his life, it is what he least wants to be known for. Jimmy wants to be known as a diversified businessman, and he is entitled to that dignity. He writes a daily syndicated column. He does a daily national radio show. He is a public-relations advisor to a number of major corporations like Lum's, S.T.P., and two divisions of Nabisco, the candy division and Aurora Toys. He knows a lot about marketing, and within the past year has helped Aurora devise three games bearing his name. He has done commercials on television, and done them very well. But at this point, despite many offers, he is not doing any more. He is determined that his ultimate image be that of the broad-based public-relations and business advisor who is also an expert on sports. He is, in fact, now contemplating moving out of Las Vegas to Florida. He has had it with the faceless town and faceless people, the one-armed bandits, the dealers who never see you but dispense the cards with their slick fingers and stony eyes, the garish hotels with their ornate lavishness and the always available women.

Jimmy is an astute political pollster, and he wants his business to be involved more and more in this. He is beginning to get increased recognition in this area and has been called upon to give expert testimony on poll taking before a committee of the Congress. This is what he truly enjoys. He has a vital interest in politics and discusses it often. One of his public-relations clients is John Y. Brown, the man who made Kentucky Fried Chicken into a national institution and who now runs Lum's. John Y. is politically oriented himself, and he may declare himself a candidate for the 1975 gubernatorial race for the Democratic party line in Kentucky. You can be sure he is consulting "The Greek."

For a man who travels as much as "The Greek" does, he is terrified of flying. Once we flew from Las Vegas to New York together, and we played gin rummy all the way. The flight was a little bumpy, and Jimmy was so frightened that he lost all concentration. In four-and-a-half hours in the air, he didn't win a total of ten hands. I had been afraid to play him for money, and I've regretted it ever since.

Jimmy has a swarthy complexion. His hair is combed back with a middle part; the hands are manicured with the long, slim, tapering fingers of a cardsharp; the smile is rare, the face serious. When first I met him, his six feet carried 238 pounds. Now he is down to 206, and he has spent some time at the Duke University Medical Center seeking to lose still more weight.

People are interested in "The Greek." Even though they have often seen him on shaving-cream commercials, he remains a mysterious figure to them. They think there is something shady, manipulative, behind-the-scenes about him. It's that old matter of image again. I did a *Magazine* show with Jimmy. It got one of the highest ratings of the series.

"The Greek" knows all of this. He wants to be around a long, long time, and he wants that image changed. He thinks about meeting people and being introduced as "Mr. Jim Snyder, you know, the man who does all those political polls. . . ." I hope it happens. I like him very much. I like his brains, his courtesy, his considerateness and his directness.

But I suspect, when all is done, that just as Don Meredith will always be "Dandy" Don, Demetrios Synodinus will always be Jimmy "The Greek," and he won't be less of a man for it.

CHAPTER 7

STAR TRACKS

"Knock it off. You're Howie Cosell, and you

never had it so good."

I think everyone enjoys recognition and approval. I don't think you can be human and not relish the gratification that comes with being recognized everywhere you go; whether it's Des Moines, Iowa, Denver, Colorado, Birmingham, Alabama, or Buffalo, New York. It is nice, too, to be able to get the right tables in restaurants, careful service at airports, extra concern from salespeople, bowls of fruit from hotel managers, and all of the other bonuses that stem from being known. But in the long run, these things are superficial. And as I have grown older, I have had many doubts about the joys of being a celebrity.

One doubt is intellectual. Despite all the vanity I am supposed to have—and I do have my share of it—I have an inner insecurity about my status. I never dreamed that I would achieve the recognition I currently have, and I am not truly comfortable with it. One of the compensations for being well known is the opportunity to meet notable people in all avenues of life, from Frank Sinatra to Supreme Court justices to George C. Scott. These people seem like towering figures to me, and I think back, invariably, to my beginnings in Brooklyn and wonder what I am doing with them. And I wonder what a "celebrity" is, really, and whether a sports commentator should ever be entitled to celebrity status. So many people are so much more important and never become notable in a public sense. Fine teachers, research scientists, skilled surgeons, are some examples. I realize, of course, that in the American scheme, that's the way it is. But I can never be satisfied that that's the way it *should* be.

On a personal level, being a celebrity carries with it an obvious benefit. Your value increases as a performer, and you make a lot of money. When I was a kid growing up on Eastern Parkway, I would look at the better apartment buildings that some of my friends lived in, admire the cars that their parents could afford, the fact that they could go to camp in the summer, belong to Union Temple where they could swim and play basketball, and I dreamed of some day being able to afford all these things for myself and my children. If I can ever make $100 a week, I used to think, I can have it all. Now, I often look back to those days and wonder at my naïveté. I marvel at the absurd amounts of money I command for merely saying a few words. But I know how hard I have worked to get to this point, how I have scraped and struggled, scrambled and survived. Once, my wife and I wanted to go shopping. We checked our assets. Two dollars. That was all we had in the world. So the monetary rewards that spring from national renown are easy to take.

But there are disadvantages, too. Your private life is destroyed, just destroyed. People chew you up. However well intentioned they may be, they absorb you and there is no way out. You can't eat a quiet meal in a restaurant. You can't walk a street or stroll in Central Park unnoticed. When you go to a sports arena you are so mobbed that your physical well-being is jeopardized. Autograph hounds surround you, pour over you; there is no way to escape them. Turn one down, try to get away and you'll be abused by them. Some of them will write to a newspaper or a magazine telling how cruel you are, how their children look up to you and how cold and uncaring you are in return. Some will insult you and if you retort, you are in danger of a lawsuit against you—a lawsuit that becomes a subtle form of blackmail. Because you are a public figure sympathy is with the "little guy." Then, too, you are handicapped in such an instance because you don't want bad publicity.

I receive dozens upon dozens of letters and phone calls every week of my life asking me to make appearances all over the country on behalf of local charitable functions. It is simply expected that I will come. But it is impossible for me to come, in the face of my broadcast commitments. I have made as many appearances as I can, to the point of my health breaking down in December 1973. But turndowns are never understood. And, suddenly, a column will appear somewhere on the theme that you have grown too big, that your ego has carried you away with yourself, that you owe everything you have to "the fans," and that you have no right not to appear at the affair you were asked to come to.

At one press conference in Toronto, Canada, for instance, in November 1973, I faced the typical attitude. I was there to make the principal speech on the eve of Canada's championship professional football game, the Grey Cup. It was 6:30 P.M. on a Saturday night. I had to leave Toronto at 6:30 A.M. the next morning for San Francisco because there was a *Monday Night Football* game there the next night. By itself, this is pretty good evidence of the schedule I keep. Yet a writer at the press conference demanded, literally demanded, to know why I had declined to attend an affair held some weeks earlier in Nova Scotia. "After all," he said, "it was for charity." You try to explain. But what more can you do?

All of this leads to another point. Once you're on top, you're going to get worked over, people are going to try to shoot you down. This is especially true when you are in the performance business. If you're a professional, you try to harden yourself to it, but it is never easy to do this and I shall never personally be successful in doing it. Television is a cruel business. There is no other way to put it. You kill yourself trying to get to the top. The odds are that you'll never get there. But if you do, you have to understand that your tenancy is temporary. You are a transient. You are surrounded by envy and by weakness. Others want your position and, understandably, think they deserve it. Still others resent your success even if they're not in competition with you. And very often they are executives in your own company who can hinder your progress when you're on the way up and who seek to undo you when you finally arrive as a major talent. This is what I mean by weakness: those people who find their own security in undercutting others. The net result is that you feel your skin is being peeled off, layer by layer.

On top of it all, as a celebrity you are constant copy and a constant target for the print medium. Here your family enters into it; your wife and your children, especially your children. Your wife lives with you and she develops a sense of balance about things that are written; a better sense of balance than you will ever have. But it's different with your children. They reach a point where they don't want to look at a newspaper or a magazine for fear they will read something ugly about you.

This has all happened to me, but I do not express it in a whining, complaining sense. Harry Truman put it best: "If you can't stand the heat, get out of the kitchen." I don't intend to leave the kitchen voluntarily. I'll take the heat, and live in the broadcast jungle. While these are the disadvantages of being a celebrity, while there are days when I want to tell everybody, "Leave me alone. Who needs you? I'm sick of all of you," I inevitably return to the basic proposition: "Knock it off. You're Howie Cosell, and you never had it so good." And I can't kid myself, I have an innate need to perform and be recognized.

When David Frye, Rich Little and the rising young Garbiel Kaplan take off on me, I enjoy it immensely. The fact that they do so means that I am a distinct, definable personality, and not a run-of-the-mill talent who nobody can identify or remember. And I also like the fact that kids everywhere try to imitate me. Basically, it means that I'm getting through to them, and it reminds me of Woody Allen's quote: "Howard is every kid's dream of what a sportscaster should be.

But the serious question is, at what point do I become a parody of myself? Going out to Hollywood as often as I do, guesting on as many shows as I do—always playing myself and possessed of a distinctive speech rhythm—I am always in danger of becoming a parody of myself. Especially, since most of the roles I play involve humor.

I do think I have a good sense of humor and a quick wit. I love the challenge of going against Don Rickles or Johnny Carson or anyone else for that matter. I don't think I take myself too seriously. Humor provides surcease from day-in-day-out boredom. But doing all those shows, in effect mimicking myself, gives me pause for thought.

But I am a man who wants to be taken seriously when I am talking about serious things. I don't want my own credibility impaired by audience laughter when I'm talking about issues, and taking a position and explaining why. Yet this can happen to me and has happened to me on occasion, because some people automatically think that I am putting them on. When they think that, I have it coming to me because I am frequently putting people on. And when I do it, I do it with a veneer of the utmost seriousness. And so, there is a fine line, a sensitive balance, between and among self-deprecating humor, put-on and absolute sober expression meant to be taken seriously.

Overall, I hope and believe that I have achieved the right balance among the three, but you never really know. One of the most encouraging things to happen to me in this regard has been the reaction to my statement that I was considering running for the Senate. I have received literally thousands of letters and phone calls, from people not just from New York State but from all over the country, urging me to make the race and offering to come to New York to assist me. Perhaps that's evidence of my credibility with regard to serious matters. And I would like to think that their support stems from the many forthright positions I have taken on the issues in my field.

Because I am an easy figure to caricature, and appear often these days in cartoons, it seems to me that I must be on guard against the self-parody problem. This also relates to the question of over exposure on television. There was a time when I was on so many shows, week in and week out, that I couldn't look at myself. And if that's true for me, it certainly figures to be true of the American public.

Thus, I have cut back on appearances. As to why I made so many in the first place, I would have to admit that that stemmed from an inner insecurity that besets many perform ers. "Get on there and stay on there," you tell yourself. What you really do is destroy yourself through oversaturation. I think I've learned that.

So my motto now is: "Pick and choose, and be on guard."

In sports broadcasting, being in the middle of things can sometimes be frightening. I don't mean that I enter the arena actively fearful, but I do mean that I have had enough experience with aroused crowd behavior to know what can happen.

A good example would be the ring scene after the Foreman-Frazier fight in Kingston, Jamaica, on January 22, 1973. That was a night I'll never forget. I was lucky to get out of that ring alive. The security officers simply could not hold off the crowd that surged into the ring when the fight ended. I had to try to interview both fighters and was literally submerged by the mob. I remember some young islanders actually grabbing me, trying to throw me out of the way as I struggled for balance and tried to keep the telecast going. At the time, I had an instantaneous fear of falling to the floor and being stamped upon; worrying at the same time about Emmy, who was at ringside. Somehow, I extricated myself from the situation, and got the interviews done.

Then, humor interposed itself in a sick form. The ring mélée was such that my director, Chet Forte, didn't have pictures of the fighters and me. He had the audio, of course, but all you could see on-camera were milling, flailing bodies and George Foreman being carried by jubilant fans out of the ring and up the aisle toward his dressing room. It was a great scene, really, and we use it now on our *Wide World of Sports* opening billboard as evidence of "the thrill of victory." But it wasn't what Chet really wanted at that moment, and it certainly wasn't what Jim Spence of ABC Sports wanted either. Jim, one of Arledge's key assistants, wanted pictures of me talking to the fighters.

I didn't know about all this while I was in the ring battling for my life, struggling to get the interviews. After the pandemonium had subsided and I had wrapped up the telecast from the ring, Chet told me about the pictures. "Get the fighters back in the ring," he said. "We don't have pictures."

I was thunderstruck, disbelieving and enraged all at once. Then I started to laugh. It was so absurd. The fighters were already in their dressing rooms being questioned by scores of reporters from all over the world. Outside those dressing rooms were thousands of islanders waiting for the fighters to come out, surging forward, but being pushed back by desperate members of the Jamaican Police.

And they wanted me to get the fighters back. . . .

I got my wife and we went back to the facilities truck where Forte was studying the tapes of the ring scene. He realized that it was damned good television, that it revealed one of the wildest ring scenes we had ever gone through. On top of that, the audio of the interviews was good. It was television true to life. But Jim Spence still wanted the fighters back in the ring. The three of us, Forte, Spence and I, shouted at one another for about 15 minutes. Forte was now in total agreement with me, and the whole argument was academic. There was no way I could get those fighters back. God didn't make the world for people to live and perform at the whim and fancy of a television executive. And the whole mood of the remarkable footage we already had would be lost, even if I *could* get the fighters back into an empty ring in an empty arena. In addition, Frazier was battered beyond repair. There was no way that he could be asked to go on television again.

We resolved the dispute by going back to Foreman's hotel. This was now an hour and a half after the fight had ended. George was under close guard and seeing nobody. But he let me in and agreed to come to New York several days later and view the fight with me, commenting on it in our studios.

It was only a little less hectic after the Forman-Norton fight in Caracas, Venezuela. I leave these scenes with a vague memory of faces, some of them snarling and ugly, some of them joyous, all of them aroused by the brutality and violence they've just witnessed; all of them pushing at me, hitting at me, oblivious to what they might be doing to me in their eagerness to get to the gladiators. It's a scary thing.

It becomes a sticky business, too, when fans mob you for autographs. Once, at the R.F.K. Stadium after a Redskins' Monday night game, my wife and I finally got to our car, but we couldn't pull away. Fans surrounded the car, some tried to get up on it, others tried to open the doors; they even pounded on the windows until we thought they would break them. There was no way our driver could leave the scene. You hope that you can reason with them, but that's all you can do—hope. That night we finally did escape. But certainly, during the incident, I feared for my wife and myself.

We have had many similar scenes at other stadiums in the country. The same kind of thing has happened at the Cotton Bowl, the Orange Bowl, the Sugar Bowl, Schaefer Stadium, and, after the final game of the 1973 season, it seemed to take forever to get away from Memorial Coliseum.

The thing you must remember is that when you are in public life, you must endeavor to take it all in stride no matter how much abuse, physical or verbal, you might be receiving. One harsh word from you, uttered in exasperation, one autograph refused, and you can wind up reading horrible things about yourself in the papers during the next few days. You're a sitting duck, a target for everybody. So that fear for yourself is often intensified by the awareness that you are helpless in every way.

Here is a vivid illustration of what I mean. The night before the first Ali-Norton fight in San Diego, I did a favor for a broadcasting colleague named Jerry Gross. He does a radio show on Friday nights before a live audience at a San Diego hotel. I had only arrived in San Diego with Emmy that afternoon and I was committed to appear at a benefit for sickle-cell anemia that night. But Jerry pressed me, and so Emmy and I went over to the hotel and I was on the air with Jerry answering questions from the audience and from callers for about 45 minutes. When the program ended I was besieged for autographs, and then, finally, Emmy and I started out for the lobby of the hotel to leave for the sickle-cell benefit. As we approached the lobby, two teen-agers came up to me and one jammed a piece of paper into me, lightly grazing my upper chest, and saying—no, really ordering—"Sign here, and sign your real name, Howie Cohen."

I couldn't believe what I had heard. Three thoughts occurred to me simultaneously. One, the remark was anti-

Semitic. Two, the lad looked Jewish, and he was implying that I was ashamed of being Jewish. Three, I thought of how I had angered millions of people by calling Muhammad Ali by his chosen name rather than by Cassius Clay and how important, as a matter of principle, that whole fight had been to me. I turned to the lad and his friend and said, "You despicable brat, I'll not sign. If your parents heard what you just said to me, your father would take his hand like this (and I lifted up my right hand), and slap you in the face. I can't do it."

Emmy, who was just a couple of feet away, asked the young man, "What did you say to my husband?"

He leered at her and said, "It wasn't so terrible. Ask him."

With that I took Emmy by the arm and left the hotel.

In the car I explained to Emmy what the young man had done, and then we forgot all about it. A number of weeks later, to my amazement, I got a letter from a San Diego attorney advising me that I had slapped his client in the face, had behaved, as a public figure whom young people looked up to, in an intolerable manner, had destroyed the young man's nervous system. Various other allegations were also detailed. His client demanded a written apology from me.

My wife and I were aghast. We agreed that as long as we lived, we would never submit to this sort of thing. I refused to apologize for something I had not done and the net result is that I am being sued for $100,000.

The reason for telling this story here and now relates to the subject of the dangers inherent in being in my business. Fear for your physical safety is not necessarily as troublesome as fear of what somebody you never say in your life can do to you in the way of harassment.

"There are a lot of kooks out there," Don Meredith was wont to say. I know something about that.

In 1973, for the first time in the history of *Monday Night Football*, we originated from the city of Buffalo. A few days before I was to go to Buffalo, I got a call from the FBI regional office in that city. The agent who called me told me that their office had intercepted a letter threatening my life. I was not disposed to take it seriously because I have seen many athletic figures receive just such threats. The FBI felt differently.

They had to take precautions, they said, because, after all, we were living in a society where anything could happen, where two Kennedys and Martin Luther King, Jr. had been assassinated.

What the agent said made sense and made me uneasy. "We want to assign an agent to meet you on arrival, and be with you throughout your stay in Buffalo," he told me. At this point I was delighted, and the treatment I got from the FBI in Buffalo is something I will always remember with heartfelt gratitude. They were wonderful to Emmy and me from beginning to end. At the Monday night game, three of them stayed in the booth with "Dandy" and me and "Giff."

Nothing happened in Buffalo except that, as I've already noted, O. J. Simpson set an NFL record for number of carries in a game as the Bills beat the Chiefs. Some months later, the FBI found the guy who had written the letter.

In 1973, we had a fantastically dramatic finish to our Dallas-Washington game in Washington. But, as we were in the final two minutes of the game, my concentration became divided. Our production assistant in the booth, Dick Buffington, was being handed phone messages from the stadium operators. They were about my wife, who had come to the stadium with me, and about my older daughter. Several were to the effect that Emmy had been involved in a serious automobile accident and had been rushed to a Washington hospital. One said that my older daughter had been involved in a severe accident.

The minute the telecast ended, I ran to the Stadium Club and called my daughter in Connecticut. There was no answer, which made no sense because of my two small grandsons. I knew my son-in-law was away on business. I was terrified, When Emmy arrived at the club, I quickly told her of the sick calls I had received about her, and then I told her about Jill and the failure to get an answer at her house. She calmed me down and told me that at that hour of the night, Jill often turned off the upstairs phone so as not to be awakened. We spoke to Jill the first thing the next morning. Everything was fine.

If I have fears, maybe now you can understand why.

But fear isn't the greatest drawback to my lifestyle, travel is. I get sick of it. So sick and tired of it, I sometimes wish that I would never see a plane again. My broadcast schedule is overwhelming. Recently I was in Panama City, Panama, on a Saturday. On Sunday I was in Miami and Houston. On Monday I was in Toronto, on Tuesday in South Bend, Indiana, on Wednesday in Akron, on Thursday in New York and on Friday in Caracas, Venezuela. This is not unusual. In fact, it has become routine, and the only thing that keeps me going is the fact that my wife makes virtually every trip with me.

I have recounted elsewhere the unnerving departure from Caracas when the plane failed to take off and braked just in time to avoid going into the Caribbean. But I have had a number of other harrowing moments, particularly on chartered planes which I must frequently use for the sake of time.

One such instance occurred in Jamestown, New York, in January 1961. Jamestown is a pleasant little furniture-manufacturing town in the northwestern part of New York State, about 60 miles south of Buffalo. It is in a valley, and by November clouds slip in and hover unceasingly, or so it seems, until April. During that time, it does nothing but snow.

There is a little fellow in Jamestown named Si Goldman who owns a radio station that is affiliated with ABC Radio. He puts together a sports banquet every year that attracts the outstanding stars in the world of sports. He does it on sheer hustle and indefatigable effort. I have always been astonished to see the Jim Browns and John Unitases of the world land via Allegheny (otherwise known as Agony) Airlines, in blizzard-like conditions, relieved to be alive and to be greeted by Si.

In the late 1950s Si hooked me. In fact, he got me three years in a row. And every time I went to Jamestown it was an adventure. Once, I flew Allegheny with Kyle Rote and Jimmy Piersall. We stopped at Scranton—Wilkes-Barre and we stopped at Olean. It was snowing, of course. The winds were violent, the visibility was poor. With each landing we prayed. Finally, we got to Jamestown. As we got off the plane, Piersall, who once had a mental breakdown, muttered, "They were right all along. I'm crazy. I've got to be to go through this just to be at a goddamned banquet."

But the biggest trouble with going to Jamestown was that you never knew whether or not you could get out the next day. The odds were that you couldn't because of the weather. This was why, in January 1961, I seized upon the opportunity to fly a private plane back to New York immediately after the banquet.

I was the emcee that year, and among the guests who had come up from New York were Roger Maris, the American League's most valuable player, Andy Robustelli, defensive captain of the New York Giants, Bill Fugazy, promoter of the then upcoming third Patterson-Johannson fight, and Dick Young, sports columnist for *The New York Daily News.* Fugazy had his own plane and had flown up in it. He offered me a lift back and said he was landing at Westchester County Airport, only 20 minutes from my home. I accepted immediately. Maris overheard the conversation and asked to be included. He was to be honored the next day at a luncheon in New York. Fugazy was delighted to accommodate him. Dick Young wanted to go too. Fugazy said he had room.

This left only Robustelli to be accounted for. Andy is deeply religious and a deeply devoted family man. He's got nine kids and lot of superstitions, including a horror of private planes. But he didn't want to be left behind. So, he became the final member of our traveling troupe. We all got into a limousine—Andy growling that he hadn't called his wife, Jeanie—and set off for the airport. The weather was horrible, nothing but snow and the roads were icy. Suddenly, about halfway to the airport, we smelled smoke. "The car's on fire," Maris said. "Stop the car." We all jumped out and, sure enough, when we lifted up the car seat, there was a lighted cigarette that someone had carelessly allowed to slip under the seat. We extinguished the cigarette, made sure the upholstery was no longer burning and started to climb back into the car.

But not Robustelli. To him the incident was a warning: Don't fly in that plane. But we couldn't leave him there on the road, and we didn't want to go back to the hotel. So Andy agreed to go on to the airport with us. Then he could be driven back to the hotel. We got to the airport and Robustelli, still grousing, decided he would take the ultimate risk. He would board with us. Maris, impervious to fear, sat up front next to the pilot. "I want to see how this thing operates," he explained. "If something happens to the pilot, I'll bring the damned thing down."

The plane was freezing. The heater wasn't working. And then the pilot quietly acquainted us with two problems: There was ice on the wings, and we were overweight by about 250 pounds. "That does it for me," Robustelli said. "Let me off and you'll be down to weight." But by now the limousine had gone, the airport was deserted, and there was no way Andy could go back to the hotel. The pilot assured Andy that the excess weight was not that much of a problem, and he also said that in a matter of moments he could get the ice off the wings. Andy had no choice but to stay. Nor did the rest of us. In about 20 minutes the pilot taxied to the runway and off we went. Never in my life have I been so cold. The only thing that made the situation bearable for me was that, for the first and only time in my life, I saw that Robustelli was cold, too. Andy has always been one of those rugged ones—proud of his physique, and determined to show that he is not vulnerable, like mortal men, to illness, cold or any of the ordinary vicissitudes of life that beset most of us. He would rarely, if ever, wear an overcoat in the winter, and he has never had any hesitancy in crowing about his superior body. But now he was reduced to a shivering shell. With the four of us huddling together and Maris up front next to the pilot, we had a calm, uneventful flight to Westchester County. All the worry was for naught.

Fugazy, who is also in the limousine-service business, had a car waiting for Andy and me. The others were going on to New York, but Andy lives in Stamford, Connecticut, not far from my home.

It was now about 2:30 in the morning. We left the airport, got to the Merritt Parkway and the car broke down. This was the last straw. The whole thing had become absurd. Somehow, the driver limped into a service station (the car needed only minor surgery), and at 3:15 I was banging on the front door, waking up my family, and trying to explain to my wife why I was home and what we had gone through.

"I told you not to go to Jamestown," she said.

I have never gone again.

But I have gone to Brainard, Minnesota. And therein lies another story. I made that trip with Herb Granath, head of ABC Sports Sales. Herb is an old and good friend, a delightful fellow with a fine sense of humor. He's attractive, dresses well, has a lot of personal style and class, but is afflicted with an apparent determination to get us both killed prematurely. Brainard, Minnesota, is a beautiful summer resort area, set on a picturesque lake which provides a positive mecca for boating enthusiasts. It was in this scene that the AMF Leisure Craft Division was holding its annual sales convention. They had requested that I address the convention, and since AMF is a major sponsor of ABC Sports, I found myself on the way to Brainard.

We flew to Minneapolis and were met by a pilot with a plane that looked too small to seat the three of us. But Herb and I scrambled in, belted up and off we went. It was a clear, beautiful day, and we had a marvelous view of a part of the country I had never seen before. I had forgotten, for instance, that the Mississippi River comes to its end in Minnesota. I have always regarded the state as a snow belt, and had neither realized that it had so many beautiful lakes, nor that there were so many people who would come from as far away as the East to spend their summer vacations there. But they do, and many of them go to Brainard.

I don't know how the hell they get there. That little plane of ours approached Brainard and I kept looking for a landing strip. I couldn't find one, but the pilot kept telling me not to worry. Finally, he pointed it out to me. It wasn't a landing strip at all! It was an open grass area, not too long, surrounded on every side by huge trees. As we started to descend, I began to rail at Granath. "Enough is enough," I shouted. "I'm not ending my life for ABC. There's no way we can land on that grass." I still can't figure out how we missed the trees. Nor do I understand how the plane failed to turn over on that bumpy terrain. But we did land, and the plane remained upright. For the moment, life was beautiful again. . . . Until the cocktail party before the dinner that night.

I was to speak at the dinner, and then we were to fly right back to Minneapolis. At the cocktail party I suddenly saw our pilot drinking from a martini glass. I grabbed hold of Herb and together we, tremblingly, watched him put away the whole drink. That was only the beginning. Herb and I saw him put away three more, and we couldn't take it any longer. We charged up to him and demanded to know how in hell he expected to fly us back to Minneapolis. We had no intention of flying with a drunken pilot. It turned out the fellow had a unique sense of humor. He was drinking Frescas from a martini glass—a studied routine he practices for his clientele to suitably unnerve them before take-off. It worked with us.

After the dinner and the speech, we joined the pilot and drove back to the "landing strip." It was pitch dark. Only then did Herb and I realize that there were no lights. Nothing. "How the hell do we take off?" Granath asked.

"It's simple," came the answer. "There's a guy parked in a car at the end of the strip. He puts on his headlights, and we head for them. At the start, they look like two little flashlights in the distance. As you approach them, they get bigger and bigger. Then, when they look about this big and this far apart (and he made appropriate motions), you take off. If I make a mistake of judgment I jump, and it's every man for himself."

Don't ask me why we got into that plane. All I know is that we missed the car, missed the trees behind it and in 40 minutes we were in Minneapolis.

One thing about Herb Granath. His clients hold their conventions in the damnedest places. The Mennen Company had one on Marco Island, Florida. Again, I had to make a speech. And again, we had to go down in the morning and come back the same night. So we flew to Fort Myers, drove to Marco Island, and were finished there at about 8:00 P.M. The only way we could get back to New York that night was to fly a charter from Marco to Miami where we could connect with a late plane. Our charter was a one-engine Cessna flown by a Cuban who spoke no English. I look back at the flight now as an all-time high in personal idiocy. I don't know why or how we ever did it. There we were, flying over the Everglades, in the hands of a total stranger with whom we could not even communicate. I began to have dreadful fantasies about crashing, about being eaten by an alligator or being bitten by a poisonous snake. I looked desperately for lights, for signs of a town and could see nothing—only darkness. After an hour that seemed like a decade, we got to Miami.

I could tell you about many more such incidents: about an airstrip at Kingston, New York, where you swoop in between a bridge and a telephone pole, and if you're lucky you make it; or about a search for Yoakum, Texas, or a landing at Carlisle, Pennsylvania. Try landing at Modesto, California, in the fog nearly scraping the mountain tops to get there. Or falling into air pockets over the French Alps on a flight from Nice to Paris. Or landing at Heathrow Airport in London in a fog so thick that the land is upon you—or you upon it—so abruptly that you almost snap your safety belt in two because you are so enmeshed with the tension.

But that's the television business, and Herb Granath will get me yet.

PART II

The chapters which follow are comprised of questions which I have been asked most often, either in the mail I received or during my speaking engagements throughout the country, and the answers which they engendered. They cover a fairly broad spectrum of subjects, and to deal with them has always been a most stimulating, challenging and satisfying facet of my life as a public figure.

The questions are by no means limited to the subject of sports alone. Even those that do are refreshing in that they intimate a public awareness that there are underlying sociological, political and economic elements that prohibit a thinking person from the religious acceptance of the doctrine of purity which had previously enshrouded the world of sport. This, of course, has been my primary preachment through all of my years in sports.

There are questions which deal with my private life, with personal experiences and philosophies and, as always, with the people who have made it all a trip worth taking.

CHAPTER 8

MORE THAN A GAME

Q. Why are you so critical of baseball?

A. I am asked this all the time, usually by people over 50 years of age. And when I am asked it, the question usually presupposes an attitude that baseball is the eighth holy sacrament. This attitude, I suspect, stems from many years of propaganda, duly parceled out by baseball announcers and baseball writers, to the effect that baseball is *the* American game, a slice of the country, something pure and noble like the American flag, motherhood and apple pie. Indeed, certain splendid writers, like Roger Ansell, have written articles and books which, in near magical words, bring to the game a sense of cultural art. They can find beauty in the precise timing required for the execution of a double play, exude excitement and suspense in the inning-by-inning development of a game, utter contentment in the leisurely pace of the contest, and near ecstasy in a stolen base or a game-winning hit. This is their right, and I respect their view. Often I find myself nodding in agreement with them as I read what they have written, so beautifully do they express themselves.

But for myself, I do not agree with what I consider to be a romantic notion that is passé. I am not as concerned with the game itself, as I am with what I consider the larger matters that are related to the conduct of the business of baseball.

And make no mistake about it, baseball is a business. As a matter of fact, it is the most favored business in the United States. It is the only business in this country which is, on the one hand, free of the antitrust laws, and, on the other hand, not subject to government regulation. What sense does this make? What justification is there for it? Professional football, hockey and basketball are all subject to the antitrust laws. Why not baseball? In the now famous Curt Flood case, the Supreme Court of the United States admitted that baseball's favored position is an anachronism, but the Court, by a five to four vote, said that it was the function of the Congress to enact legislation to rectify the situation. The Congress has done nothing! Why not?

Prior to the Flood case, the legal position of baseball has always been that it is a unique business, in legal phraseology, "tinged with and affected by the public interest." In other words, it is, inherently, a public utility; it represents a central part of Americana. All right, I'll accept that, on the condition that, like all other public utilities—the phone companies, the power companies, the broadcast companies, etc.—baseball becomes subject to federal regulation. But this has not happened. Baseball has to be one or the other, in simple logic. Either it is a business like all the other sports (and like General Motors, Ford and Chrysler), or it is a public utility. But why on God's earth is it neither? Why is it something separate and apart from all else, in effect, a sacred rite that has been sanctified by Heaven?

This all becomes even more relevant when one looks at the actions of the baseball owners; actions which continually defy the public interest and reject the very spirit of democracy that is the presumed hard core of American beliefs. One has only to examine the history of the crass and ugly carpetbagging of franchises which has dotted the recent history of baseball: the removal of the immensely profitable and traditional Brooklyn Dodgers to Los Angeles for the sake of a personal land grab by the owner; the removal of the Milwaukee Braves to Atlanta for the sake of a better television contract after Milwaukee had established attendance records for the National League. Indeed, when the Brooklyn owner moved to Los Angeles, he said he had to do it in order to compete with Milwaukee. Consider, also, the treatment of Washington, the capital city of the nation. For many years the fans there endured the worst team in baseball. Remember the old slogan,

"Washington, first in war, first in peace, last in the American League"? But nothing is forever, and after years of suffering, the Washington fans could see daylight. The Senators had come upon young players like Harmon Killebrew and Bob Allison. Better times were at hand. So, in 1961, team owner Calvin Griffith moved his team to Minneapolis, where the newly named Minnesota Twins won a pennant.

What did the Washington fans get? A new team, an expansion team and more years of last place. And then, for the second time, baseball, the great American game, deserted the nation's capital. The Washington franchise was moved to, of all places, Arlington, Texas. But it did not end there. Some people in Washington still wanted major-league baseball, including a millionaire named Joseph Danzansky. He thought he had a deal. He thought he had bought the San Diego Padres, a supposedly failing franchise that could be moved to Washington, where, for the first time ever, Washington could be "first in war, first in peace, and last in the National League." But no. First Danzansky had the franchise, then he didn't, as the National League owners played cops and robbers with him (and, in effect, with the people of Washington). Finally, San Diego got new ownership, and the Padres remained in California.

All of this happened before the very eyes of Congress, sitting right there in Washington, but still baseball is not subject to the antitrust laws. Again, I asked, why not?

In 1972, one man in the Senate tried to do something about it. His name is Marlow Cook, a Republican from the state of Kentucky. He introduced a bill, The Federal Sports Commission Act of 1972. Cook, an attractive, prematurely gray-haired man who is a walking replica of the Kentucky Colonel, was intimately aware of the abuses imposed upon an unsuspecting public by some sports operators. His bill would have established a Federal Sports Commission, and the bill contained a provision that would have prevented sports franchise owners from moving to another city without the approval of the commission, said approval not to be unreasonably withheld. The Senate Commerce Committee conducted hearings on the bill but, in the face of opposition lobbies and adverse sporting press, the bill died. And the abuses continue.

One could be amused by the situation in Seattle if it were not so sad. Major-league baseball expanded into Seattle a number of years back—the Seattle Pilots, they were called—and stayed in Seattle for all of one year. Then they jumped the town, and the principal owner, an old baseball man named Dewey Soriano, sold the club and escaped with a substantial capital gain. The citizens of that great city of the Pacific Northwest were enraged, and so were the municipal authorities. Baseball, they said, had raped them. A law suit was filed by the city against the American League and organized baseball. But, in the meantime, Seattle is in quest of a National Football League franchise, and the city is building a domed stadium to house both football and baseball. Under assurances from Baseball Commissioner Bowie Kuhn that Seattle might get an expansion franchise (or a transferred one), the city authorities have deferred their legal action. In a magnificent gesture of absolute hypocrisy, Kuhn duly noted his satisfaction with the city's decision. He even had the audacity to speak of the good that baseball could do for the community. How long are people in this country—adult people—going to stand for this kind of double talk and double dealing? Not too much longer, I suspect. Everywhere I go throughout the country, every-place I speak, I find a growing disillusionment with sports, and especially with baseball. And this disillusionment is finding its way into print. Not stories by the baseball writers, of course. Their principal concern is self-protection, prolonga-tion of their tiny little sinecures. The distinguished satirist, Russell Baker of *The New York Times,* in April 1974, wrote a column entitled, "Turn the Sports Off," in which he stated that he was no longer a sports fan, that he had become disen-chanted and emphasized the carpetbagging of baseball own-ers as one of the chief causes. He reflected, I believe, the feelings of increasing numbers of people.

It is, in my opinion, almost obscene that baseball still seeks to cloak itself in Americanism and patriotism. And, as I have emphasized many times, I deem it obscene that we still do not have black managers in baseball. It is 27 years since Jackie Roosevelt Robinson gave the business its appearance of democracy. Today the game is populated with great black ballplayers. Henry Aaron has made baseball history. Willie Mays became a legend. Bob Gibson will be a Hall of Famer. Dick Allen is baseball's highest paid player. One can go on and on. And yet, they are engulfed by frustration as they see the pattern of musical chairs continue in the hiring and firing of white managers.

In a recent *Magazine* show that I did on this subject called *Managing: For Whites Only?*, three eminently qualified men spoke out. Bill White, the former Cardinal and Philadelphia star, said, "In order to manage, you have to be white and you have to have failed somewhere else. This doesn't say much for baseball." Maury Wills, the old Dodger standout, said, "Once I stopped playing, they only knew the color of my skin." And Frank Robinson of the California Angels said, "I've given up. They said you have to have experience, even though men like Berra and Dark went straight from playing to managing in the big leagues. So I got the experience, managing in the winter leagues. Now they say that's not experience. They just don't want a black man."

I agree with them.

So I will leave it to others to regale us about baseball, to ponder (romantically) the exquisite beauty of the diamond, the niceties of the distances between bases, the electric excitement of the throw to first that arrives just before the runner. As long as I am in sports journalism, I will continue to dedicate myself to the task of bringing to the public attention the things in baseball that are antithetical to the public interest. And, above all, I shall work to bring baseball within the purview of the antitrust laws.

One more thing. At the advent of the 1974 season, the Atlanta Braves indicated that they would not play Hank Aaron in the opening series in Cincinnati. They wanted Hank to break Babe Ruth's career home-run record before the hometown fans in Atlanta. What an outcry this produced! The "integrity" of baseball was being challenged. Reams of copy appeared. "Put your best team on the field, you must try to win every game. That means Aaron must play." This was the chant. Bowie Kuhn, unparalleled as a man of expedient principle, responded. He ordered that Aaron play in Cincinnati. The "integrity" of the grand old game was thus maintained.

Nonsense! *Webster's Unabridged Dictionary* defines integrity as "moral soundness; freedom from corruption . . ." Where is the moral soundness and freedom from corruption in the carpetbagging, and in the studious avoidance of black managers? And why, instead of only a very occasional article, aren't there reams of copy on these two issues?

My criticism of baseball will continue.

Q. I saw you on *Monday Night Baseball* with Curt Gowdy and Tony Kubek. You told Kubek that professional race-car drivers have greater athletic ability than baseball players. How can a man who sits in a car be a greater athlete than a man who uses his entire body in a sport?

A. First, let's go back to the circumstances which led to my comment. Kubek, a man whose entire life has been devoted to baseball both as a player and as an announcer, was regaling the viewers about the game and the players to the point of ecstasy. He came up with a statement so simplistic that I could not believe it. The three hardest things to do in sports, he indicated, were to hit a baseball, to catch a baseball and to throw a baseball. Gowdy then said that Tony was right, that studies had revealed that baseball players were, indeed, the greatest athletes in the world.

At that moment I gulped with disbelief, took another look at the pitcher on the mound with the beer belly, and gazed at the slow-footed catcher who was finding it difficult to rise from his crouching position. I had just returned from Monaco where they had held the annual Grand Prix, and where I had had the opportunity to spend time with Jackie Stewart and the two late greats François Cevert and Peter Revson. I had watched them prepare for the race, work out in practice runs. I had studied the way they prepared; how every muscle, every sinew came into play; how the body and mind had to coordinate instantly in every respect; how, at the same time, they had to think about their competitors, know what those others had by way of strengths and of weaknesses; how they had to mesh their own efforts with those of the others on the course, always recognizing that one mistake, by them or one of the others, could produce death.

I saw that they didn't just sit in a car, that the body is extended and controlled and used on the hairpin turns and on the straightaways in a manner that gets the utmost out of the car, and demands the utmost of a man's body and mind. The wrists, the arms, the legs, the eyes, the mind—they are all as one. My admiration for the athletic skills of these men, always great, actually increased.

Thus, when Kubek said what he did, I simply mentioned racing drivers because of what I had just experienced in Monaco, and because I knew that both Tony and Curt were not familiar with motor racing.

I submit that Kubek's comment was openly ridiculous. I do not imply that baseball players are not, generally speaking, athletes. Of course they are, and their sport does require precision, timing and coordination of eye, mind and body. But the sport is sedentary; the action occasional. It is not like basketball, where the demands upon the players are incessant; where what a man does when he does not possess the basketball is as important as what he does when he has it; where the body contact is frequent, and where the drain upon a man's energy is total.

It is not like hockey where the action is continuing, and continuously violent, and where the instancy of teamwork is necessary, that is, having your eye on your opponent but at the same time looking for an open teammate to pass to. The opponent in hockey not only harasses you, he physically beats you on many occasions, jolting you into the boards with a fearsome impact. Then, too, the hockey player performs with what, in effect, are artificial legs and an artificial arm.

It is not like football, a game of crunching, almost terrifying contact, or violence, if you will. Remember, above all, that in football, basketball and hockey, even as men clash with one another physically, they must continue to coalesce in a team sense, to have an unending awareness of what the others are doing, and to have an instancy of reaction to what they, themselves, are doing.

It is clearly different in baseball, which emphasizes the individual. At infrequent moments there is the coordination of the double play which does command exceptional skills. And there is no question that hitting a baseball does command exceptional skills. When a ball is fired in your direction at a speed of 90 miles an hour there can be no doubt as to the courage and skill required to hit it. Neither can one underestimate the necessity for precision of the relay from the outfield to the infield, or to home plate to retire the runner; nor of the courage needed to execute a tag in the face of flying spikes. But, on balance, I do not believe one can possibly support the notion that a baseball player must show the same constancy of skill and effort, under the same trying conditions, that are required in the other sports, including motor racing.

Q. Who is the greater home-run hitter, Babe Ruth or Hank Aaron?

A. I think the question is unanswerable, irrelevant and juvenile. It's like asking one to compare apples and oranges. On bare statistics, Aaron has hit more home runs in his playing lifetime than Babe Ruth did. On bare statistics, Ruth hit more home runs in a given season—and he did this for a number of seasons—than Hank Aaron ever did. On bare statistics, Aaron had been to bat 3000 times more than Ruth when Hank eclipsed the Babe's career home-run mark. So what?

When I took a college course in elementary statistics, the first words of my professor were, "Statistics lie." And so they do, if you seek to apply statistics related to different eras, and to different circumstances and to different human conditions.

That's why any comparison of Ruth and Aaron is preposterous. When the Babe played, there was no night baseball, no jet transportation, no jet lag to cause diminished efficiency, no specialization in the game such as the pronounced use of left-handed pitchers against left-handed hitters and right-handed pitchers against right-handed hitters, no specialization in terms of relief pitchers with one after another ready to be thrown into the breach.

Thus, for the hitter, the game today is much more difficult to play and to excel at. On the average, and this is another reason why comparative statistics are meaningless, the athletes of today are bigger, faster and stronger than those of the past. Physical conditioning procedures are far better, dietary conditions are infinitely superior, the human body is better and even the equipment is better. The way of life is completely different, swifter, more debilitating. Mental attitudes and mental pressures are different, and certainly the pressures are greater because of the increased emphasis upon winning, the greater place that sports has achieved in the society, and all of the other sociological changes that have made the world a more complex place to live in than when the Babe was playing.

When Ruth was a star, baseball's westernmost point was St. Louis. The teams would travel by rail—a symbol of the good old leisurely days. They would get a day off every time they went on a road trip, sometimes two days.

For a time when the Babe played, if a ball bounced into the stands, it was a home run, not a double. Nobody can really certify, to this day, how many home runs Babe got in this manner.

Again, so what? Does all this mean that Aaron is a better home-run hitter than Ruth was? Nonsense. Who can say how many home runs Ruth would have hit were he playing at the same time as Aaron? He would have been a product of the time, conditioned to, and by, the times, enjoying all the benefits of the contemporary age and grappling with all of its hardships. He was a superstar, a superathlete who, almost by himself, saved the game of baseball after the Black Sox scandal. Ruth changed the nature of the game by his home-run efforts. His career record was good enough to have lasted until 1974, and the man's playing days ended in the 1930s. Mark him down as the most exciting and memorable player in the history of the game, apart from Jackie Robinson whose memorability is historic because of sociology.

As for Hank Aaron, mark him down as one of the greatest to have ever played, the man who surpassed Ruth's record and who did it under circumstances that were difficult, if not onerous. He did it with diffidence, with the quiet determination that lay within him from the day, in 1954, that he first joined the Braves. He did it with dignity, and he never said that he was the Babe, better than the Babe or anything like it. But he did it.

They were superstars of different times. Let it go at that, and put the silly argument to rest.

Q. Would you want a child of yours to play Little League baseball?

A. No, I would not. Originally, I was a staunch believer in Little League baseball. I was influenced by a remarkably dedicated man, Mickey McConnell, who worked out of national Little League headquarters in Williamsport, Pennsylvania. I had known Mickey for a number of years in his role as chief scout for the Brooklyn Dodgers during the time of the late Mr. Branch Rickey. McConnell is a gentle man, a thoughtful man, and he gives of himself completely in seeking to render service to young people. Little League baseball became the whole of his occupational life. I watched him work closely with the Springfield College of Physical Education and initiate studies to be conducted by national leaders in physical education and in mental health; all with a view toward realistically determining the values and the disadvantages of Little League baseball for youngsters and for their parents.

But this was in the beginning, before Little League baseball became the vast, sprawling movement that it is now, embracing virtually every community in the country and even extending as far as foreign nations. I wonder now, today, if Mickey McConnell ever thought it would become this big.

While bigness alone is not necessarily inherently wrong, it does create problems. And one of the major problems is that there is simply no way to be able to insure that, at the local level, the lofty standards and aims that were attached to the beginning of the program are being adhered to. On the contrary, at the local level this is what I have generally discovered:

As a matter of human nature, many parents become involved to the point where the youngster becomes a mere extension of the parent. Frustrated fathers view themselves as coaches and engage in heated rivalries with one another as to whose youngster should be on the team. It becomes a fiercely competitive thing, and the youngsters are the unwitting butts of this kind of competition. No longer are they playing for the fun of it, but rather they are being pressured to achieve to the extent that much of the fun goes out of it for them. Often they are pressured out of all proportion to their natural abilities. The inevitable result is emotional damage. In addition to this, there is the insensitive and insistently implicit pressure to win at any cost. The parents, the coaches and the managers are all involved in creating these pressures on the young people because, by the very nature of the way in which they have grown up, in a society afflicted with a big-time sports syndrome, it is all they know when it comes to sports.

I have seen managers tell a ten-year-old that he "stinks" because he struck out, and I have seen the youngster walk away tearfully, crushed by treatment he doesn't remotely understand. I have seen neighborhood strife over the selection of the starting team. I have seen banners and all of the trappings that go with big-time college and professional sports. I have seen adult excesses at playoff games that make one wonder about the intelligence quotient of American society. All of these things that I have seen envelop youngsters from the ages of 8 to 12 in an atmosphere which I am convinced can cause real harm to the sound development of a youngster's mental and emotional growth. I have seen Little League baseball produce not fun, but agony.

I have been to Williamsport, Pennsylvania, for the Little League World Series. I have watched these youngsters treated as if they were a group of Tom Seavers. I have seen them in a pressure cooker the likes of which could undo professional athletes in their thirties. I have seen them exposed to national television, and as one whose professional life is in that medium, I know how unequipped these kids are for the tensions that accompany this exposure.

No, I wouldn't want my youngster playing in this kind of national and even international competition. I wouldn't want my child ever to be subjected to unqualified leaders who have absolutely nothing in their backgrounds to warrant my allowing them to take my offspring into situations and conditions that are far beyond his ability to cope.

Now all of this does not mean that there are *no* qualified

leaders at the local level in the Little League program. Of course there are some. But they are exceptions. The physical education and psychological studies that helped kick off the program, that lent it authenticity, are, in my judgment, no longer applicable. They have been drowned in an ocean of bigness. Little League is "big league," and it's not for kids only 8 to 12.

Q. If your son were a professional athlete, what sport would you want to see him playing? What coach would you want him playing under?

A. Since I never had a son, I never faced the problem. But I do have two grandsons, and if they have a bent for athletics and are good enough to become professionals, I would hope that they would achieve in tennis and golf. These are sports in which one can participate in later years when physical fitness is of increasing importance and when one's leisure time is likely to be greater. These are essentially safe sports in the physical sense, absent of contact and violence, and I would naturally be concerned about the well-being of my grandchildren. And finally, in the current economics of sports, professional tennis players and golfers have the opportunity of making vast sums of money.

In tennis and golf, teaching is far more important than coaching. I would want my grandsons, if possible, to be taught golf by Claude Harmon, the club professional at Winged Foot. I consider him the finest teacher of golf in the world. He is understanding and sensitive with youngsters, and equally impressive with pros. On the professional golf touring trail, they come to him time and again when they are having difficulties with their games.

I would want them to be taught tennis by Bill Talbert, not because he was once a Davis Cup star, but because he is a superb teacher with a deep feeling for young people. Bill is a diabetic who once wrote a moving book about himself called, *Playing for Life*. If you could see Bill Talbert at Camp NYDA (New York Diabetics Association) on a summer day working with diabetic youngsters, teaching them to play, you would want him, and nobody else, to teach your son tennis.

Q. Can you justify an athlete receiving $500,000 a year just for throwing a basketball through a hoop? Aren't athletes' salaries ridiculous now?

A. The answer to both questions is yes. And there is no contradiction in that statement. In the abstract sense, of course athletes are overpaid. They don't make the contribution to society that teachers do, that scientists do, that medical researchers do or that individuals in literally dozens of other classifications of occupations and professions do. If ever a man was underpaid, it was Dr. Jonas Salk.

But the society in which we now live dictates the salaries that the athletes are receiving. It is a free-enterprise society, and the people of this country have created a spectator-sports boom. There are more and more leagues, more and more teams, and while, sooner or later, an oversaturation seems inevitable, at the present time there is no clear evidence of it. The net result is that in the free and open competition that exists between leagues, bidding wars for players' services are inevitable, and salaries go up.

To contain salaries would require some form of government legislation, and that would be highly unlikely. The only other way to contain salaries would be to obtain congressional approval for mergers (the NBA with the ABA, the NHL with the WHA, for instance). The precedent was set by the NFL-AFL merger which did receive congressional approval. But the temper of the Congress is different now, and it is not likely that such mergers will be countenanced in the foreseeable future. Indeed, the Senate has already blocked one attempt at merger between the NBA and the ABA. Merger, of course, produces monopoly, and when a player cannot bargain his services between and among two or more prospective employers, a more static or even reduced salary base seems a likely consequence. Certainly the salary escalations that we are now witnessing would be diminished.

I do not think that sports should get favored treatment in the form of special-purpose legislation. No one puts a gun to a person's head and says, "Go buy yourself a team." An owner goes into the sports business voluntarily, and is, or should be, aware of the economic risks involved.

On the players' behalf, there are a number of points to be made. First, they are responsible for the large-scale attendance at the arenas around the country. People don't pay to see owners. They pay to see John Havlicek, Hank Aaron, Joe Namath, Bernie Parent and all the other stars of the various sports. Since it is the players who produce the revenues, why shouldn't they get the lion's share of the income? Most economic studies that have been conducted on the subject of athletes' salaries seem to indicate that the owners will not be forced out of business by the current salary escalation, and, indeed, the players do not get an unreasonable proportion of the gross income.

Second, the media has a tendency, even if unwittingly, to stir up public indignation over salaries paid to athletes by their emphasis upon those monies paid to the superstars of sports. Kareem Abdul-Jabbar is not typical; he is atypical. So is Bill Walton, who, by himself, figures to make the Portland franchise of the NBA a profitable one. The same is true of the extraordinary players in the other sports, the ones getting $100,000 or more per year. Relatively, they constitute only a handful of the total playing personnel in all sports. The average salary in the NFL, for instance, is in the area of $27,000 to $30,000 per year. In major-league baseball, it is about $30,000 per year. It is higher in basketball and hockey.

Then there is the question of longevity, the most serious question of all as far as the athletes are concerned. In professional football, the average playing life is four and one-half years. In major-league baseball it is five years. Basketball and hockey are in the same general area. And in each of the sports, a performer's career is subject to peremptory termination by injury, most notably in professional football. And when an athlete's career ends, the average player has to pick up a whole new life; he needs a whole new start. So the salaries paid to the average players are not overwhelmingly high. They are illusory because of the few years during which the players are paid for their athletic performances.

Lastly, athletes are not the only ones who are overpaid in the sense that others who do more for the society are paid far less. I, myself, on such a measuring stick, am overpaid. So are many others in different lines of work. But this is the way it is in the peculiar and complex workings of the capitalist system, and no one that I know of has recommended a change in that.

Besides, who would promulgate the notion that the owners should get profits out of all proportion to the players' take? I have never read anywhere that Wellington Mara of the New York Giants is overpaid, and yet he got $10 million for "territorial rights to New York" from the American Football League and then proceeded to abscond to New Jersey. And the same goes for all those owners in sports who have made exorbitant profits while defying the public interest through their franchise removals, capital-gain deals and all the rest.

In summary, I like the way Larry Csonka put it on April 26, 1974, at the Dolphins' annual banquet: "If I could be twenty five for the rest of my life, I would play for Coach Shula for the rest of my life. But I am not twenty five anymore, and I will never be again. My years in football will now be few, very few. I owe it to my wife and to my children to provide as much security for them as I possibly can. The World Football League has given me that security."

What thinking person can argue with that?

Q. Do you think it is morally and ethically right for a player to jump from one league to another, the way so many stars have jumped from the National Football League to the World Football League?

A. Yes, I do. I think the athletes, like anyone else in the society, have every right to better themselves as long as, in so doing, they do not violate any legal obligation and do not fail to discharge those legal obligations to the fullest. It has yet to be shown, for example, that Larry Csonka, Paul Warfield and Jim Kiick will play with less intensity for the Dolphins in the 1974 season than they have in the past, despite the fact that they will be in the World Football League the following year. And how in the world can anyone blame Csonka, who is married and has children, who is the best fullback in football but only made $58,000 last year, for seizing the chance to become a near millionaire, when, if fortunate, he will be playing only four more years.

You must remember that owners jump in the sense that they carpetbag profitable franchises at the expense of the public they piously proclaim to be serving. Now *that* is truly an absence of ethics and morality.

You must remember, too, that the very coach for whom the three Dolphins play, Don Shula, jumped from the Baltimore Colts to the Miami Dolphins. It was at that time that Carroll Rosenbloom, then the Colts' owner, told NFL Commissioner Pete Rozelle, "You must not allow this. If coaches can jump existing contracts, what's to stop players?" Rosenbloom was exactly right, but Shula was allowed to go, and all the Colts got in return was a first-round draft choice.

By contrast, no football player has yet sought to jump an existing contract. They are only contracting for future services at better pay.

Q. What do you think of the World Football League's practice of stealing players from the National Football League?

A. The World Football League is not "stealing" anything. In a free-enterprise society, they have the legal right to hire employees for future services at better pay, as long as they do not interfere with that employee's existing contractual obligations. Similarly, as I explained before, an employee has a right to contract out his future services for better pay as long as he does not breach any existing contractual obligation. This is basic in the American system. The only exception to this freedom in our country is in the business of baseball where the reserve clause binds an employee to an employer forevermore. And, as I have indicated elsewhere in this book, Congress will sooner or later have to do away with that absurd anachronism.

The National Football League does not even have a legitimate complaint about the ethics of what the World Football League is doing. The act of raiding the personnel of another team in a different league was first executed by Wellington Mara of the New York Giants when he signed kicker Pete Gogolak of Buffalo, which was a member team of the former American Football League. When the National Football League countenanced Mara's action, they were hoisted by their own petard. They had established an unwholesome precedent.

I feel badly for the fans in these "raiding" cases. In Miami, where the love of the Dolphins is at an unbelievable emotional level, the fans feel that Csonka, Kiick and Warfield have betrayed them. They talk about the support they have given the three players in the past, and how, in effect, they adopted them as heroes. I can understand this, but I must point out that they have victimized themselves by their juvenile adherence to the sports syndrome of our time: To wit, sports is something separate and apart from real life, where everything is pure and holy. Professional sports is business, big business, and adults should realize this. More and more are beginning to.

Q. Do you think the World Football League will succeed?

A. This depends on how you define success. They will succeed in damaging the National Football League. They have done this already by acquiring about 60 National Football League players, including some of the biggest stars of the game.

However, as to whether they can survive and prosper on a long-term basis, I have my doubts. The World Football League has two basic problems: The first is the absence of sufficient investment capital in a number of franchises. The second is the absence of a big-money national television contract such as the American Football League had, and there is no visible prospect of getting one.

In a sense, the World Football League reminds me of the old All America Conference, which wound up with three of its franchises—Baltimore, Cleveland and San Francisco—being absorbed by the National Football League. I believe the World Football League will suffer a similar fate in the long run.

Q. Do you think the new rules will improve the National Football League? Are there any other rule changes you would like to see?

A. Generally speaking, I think the rule changes recently enacted will improve the NFL. The game had become stereotyped, with field goal after field goal being kicked, making for overwhelming domination by the defense. By moving the goal posts to the back of the end zone, and by returning the ball to the line of scrimmage after missed field-goal attempts from more than 20 yards out, the resort to the field goal should be diminished and the chance for the touchdown should accelerate.

Also, the kick-off return, one of football's most exciting plays, should be in greater evidence. It had become standard practice to see kick-offs sail into the end zone with no return. By moving the kick-off back to the 35-yard line, there should be some increase in kick-off returns.

I also like the new rule that bars continuing bump-and-run tactics by a pass defender against a potential pass receiver. Under the new rule, the defender can bump the would-be receiver just once as the receiver is passing the line of scrimmage. The receiver should now be able to get loose more frequently. At the same time, as a defensive compensation, the heralded zone defenses will come into greater prominence than ever. There is, on the other hand, the possibility that there will be a greater propensity by the quarterbacks to attempt to hit the downfield receiver rather than throw those short, side-line hitch passes that beef up the pass-completion percentages but bring little to the game in the way of excitement.

I like the rule that forbids crack-back blocking by a wide receiver. This practice was dangerous, and probably greatly responsible for many knee injuries.

I think that the new punt rule—wherein offensive linemen were to remain at the line of scrimmage until the kick returner had touched the football—was self-defeating. The rule was intended to increase the possibility of long punt returns, but it probably would have resulted in most kicks being directed out of bounds. Perhaps sensing this inherent difficulty, the NFL owners, at a meeting in the commissioner's office in New York in early June 1974, voted to amend the rule so that the outside receivers on the offensive formation of the punting unit may pursue downfield when the ball is snapped, but the remainder of the unit must wait until it has been touched, as the original rule stated. Though the intent of both the original and amended rule is good, I still think that it will result in the punter aiming for the distant sideline. I also think that the rule will create problems for the officials at the line of scrimmage.

The reduction of the offensive holding penalty from 15 yards to 10 yards is also subject to question. This rule change was enacted because it was felt that too many offensive drives were stifled by the length of the penalty. It may well be, however, that by lessening the punishment, it may only serve to compound the felony. Offensive holding, which already occurs with frequency, may increase due to the reduced penalty. The result would be a greater number of ten-yard assessments, thus posing the same disruptive effect on offensive drives, not to mention the increased pressure upon the officials who have to call these penalties. Therefore, the advantage of this rule change is questionable.

There are two additional rule changes that I would like to see take place. In order to bring even greater probability of kick-off return action, I would like to see the ball kicked off from the 30 rather than the 35-yard line. In this way, an even higher percentage of balls would fail to carry out of the end zone, or at least deep enough to render attempted return unwise.

I would also reinstate the old AFL two-point conversion option into the rule book. The coaches are against this one simply because its absence precludes the necessity of a key decision for which they could be second-guessed should they make the wrong choice. But in terms of excitement, it would bring a whole new dimension to the game.

Q. Who do you think is the best coach in professional football today? How does he compare with Vince Lombardi?

A. Don Shula of the Miami Dolphins. His record bespeaks the fact. He was a winning coach at Baltimore, but his accomplishments there were diluted in the public mind because of the Super Bowl loss to the Jets when the Colts had been favored to win by 17 points.

There can be no watering down his accomplishments at Miami, however. He took an expansion team and quickly molded it into a championship unit. The Dolphins have been

to the Super Bowl three years consecutively. They have won in
the past two years. Only Lombardi before him had been able
to win two Super Bowls in a row. And Shula has done something Vince was never able to do. In 1972, Don guided his
team to an unbeaten season; a record of 17–0, including the
playoff games and the Super Bowl victory over Washington.
In this day and age of professional football, where the competition is extreme and injuries a compelling factor, an unbeaten
season must be considered a phenomenal feat.

Shula's qualities as a coach are many. He is physically impressive, and his very being exudes leadership. He is a good-
looking man with a winning smile, but it is the cut of his face
that gets you. It is a strong, square-jawed face, and as quick as
he is to smile, that's how quickly the face will harden and set,
the lips will suddenly become taut and thin, the fire can be red
in the eyes, and you know that you are looking at Shula, the
disciplinarian. He is much like Lombardi in this regard. And
there is no question that Vince had a major impact on him.
Vince would fine his players and chastise them, but he had a
great sense of humor and understood his players as 40 different individuals. Shula is the same way, and this is particularly
evident in his relationships with Csonka and Kiick. They are
to Don what the wise, wide receiver, Max McGee, was to
Vince.

At Biscayne College where the Dolphins train, I had a long
talk with Shula in the summer of 1973. We spoke about his
basic problem as a coach in facing the forthcoming season. It
was: How do you keep a team's incentive up after an unbeaten
season and a Super Bowl victory? Shula had been thinking
about the question almost immediately after the Dolphins had
defeated Washington in the Super Bowl. His answer lay in the
history of Lombardi and the Green Bay Packers. Lombardi
had done it. And Shula met the problem by reminding his
players continually that they had a chance to do what only
Vince and the "Pack" had done—win two Super Bowls in a
row.

The philosophy worked because every player I spoke to on
the Dolphins' squad talked about Lombardi and the Packers.
Shula imbued his squad with the notion that, despite their
incredible 17–0 season, many people in the country still

tended to discount them, still thought that they had been lucky in escaping injuries and still believed that they had taken advantage of an easy schedule. As a result of this, in my opinion, the Dolphins embarked upon the 1973 season with an even fiercer pride and determination than had marked their efforts the year before.

I feel that Shula's greatest accomplishment to date has been his ability to repeat as champion; to keep his team emotionally peaked for a second long season of greatness. I also believe, even though it will be the last year for Csonka, Warfield and Kiick, that he will do it for an unprecedented third season, though that has yet to be proved. If he can do it, he will have surpassed Lombardi.

Not only am I believer in the way Shula handles his players, I am impressed by his wisdom in selecting his coaching assistants and in the manner in which he allows them to do their jobs. Shula wants top people around him, not flunkies. He wants men who are good enough to be head coaches. His defensive leader was Bill Arnsparger, now the head man for the Giants. Arnsparger is, in the opinion of the Dolphins' defensive players, a genius in devising defenses for a given opponent. Shula was of the same mind. He knew what Bill was doing, believed in it and left him strictly alone. Monty Clark, the offensive line coach, is another. Monty, in my judgment, is a born leader, certain to become a fine head coach; and he knows how to build an offensive line. The development of offensive guards such as Larry Little and Bob Kuechenberg does not occur by accident. It happens by design, and in these two cases, Monty Clark has been a critical planner and executor of the design.

It is an open secret that Shula and Dolphins' owner Joe Robbie no longer get along. But Don doesn't let that fact bother him in coaching his team. It upsets him personally and he doesn't disguise his distaste for Joe, but he simply won't permit Robbie to interfere with his relationship with his players. Neither will he allow the unwholesome situation with his owner to sift down to the assistant coaches.

Shula never has football out of his mind. Again, he is much like Lombardi in this respect. He knows every player in the league and he never forgets what they can do. His eyes are always focused on possible acquisitions and trades, and he is a shrewd trader. There was no other way he could have gotten Warfield and Nick Buoniconti, and those two acquisitions were vital to the construction of a championship team. In the 1973 College All-Star Game, a lad from Penn State named Bruce Bannon showed well for the collegians as a linebacker. He was a Jets' draft choice. Bannon never did get an opportunity with the Jets, who decided to let him go. Shula and Arnsparger remembered his play against the Dolphins, and picked him up. Bruce Bannon, in the not too distant future, will succeed Buoniconti and, I suspect, will be a Grade A talent.

As exceptional as Shula is, I believe he will shortly be facing a challenge from a young man who looms as the next great coach. I refer to Chuck Knox of the Los Angeles Rams, and the manner in which he got that job proves all over again that, in life, one must have the luck of opportunity no matter how talented one may be.

I first caught up with Chuck in the 1960s when Weeb Ewbank brought him to the Jets as offensive line coach. This was when Weeb was the old master at building a football team, and his choices for assistant coaching roles were superb. None was a shrewder nor more important selection than Knox.

Chuck was an unknown. He had attended Juniata College near Philadelphia, and that fact alone could have disqualified him in the minds of some; no big-time college football background, that sort of thing. It never bothered Chuck. He moved on as an assistant coach in the college ranks, and then got his shot with Weeb.

The way the Jets were constructed, Joe Namath was the whole ball of wax. He could lead them to a title, but without him they were nothing. Ergo, Namath, with those damaged knees, had to be protected from injury. The burden of protection was lodged in the offensive line. It was Chuck Knox who forged and developed that unit, and a large share of the credit for the Jets' Super Bowl year was due to that young man.

Subsequently, Knox moved on to become offensive line coach for the Detroit Lions. Ewbank has never been exalted for his generosity in the area of salaries for either his players or his coaches—except for Namath. Knox proceeded to build a fine offensive line at Detroit.

By then Chuck had established a long tenure in the National Football League. He knew the teams, their strengths and weaknesses. He knew the players. Intelligent and understandably ambitious, he knew above all else that he was ready, that he had matured sufficiently to become a head coach. But he was stymied at Detroit. Joe Schmidt had the job, and even if Joe were fired, Chuck had reason to know he wouldn't get it.

One day late in the 1972 season, I got a phone call. It was from Chuck Knox in Detroit. He told me that he had no opportunity to move up in the Lions' organization, but that he felt he merited the chance to become a head coach, if only he could get the chance. I told him I would make some calls on his behalf. I immediately called Phil Iselin, the president of the Jets. The Jets were a declining ball club, in disarray, and the feeling was that Weeb Ewbank would be leaving as head coach, but staying on as general manager. Since the Jets' owners were familiar with the calibre of Knox because of his prior coaching duties with the Jets, I thought the situation would be ideal for all concerned. Iselin told me that he was well aware of Chuck's availability and qualifications. "He is number one on our list," Phil said. I called Knox and told him.

To my astonishment, it was not long after my talk with Iselin that the Jets called a press conference to announce that Ewbank would coach one more year, and would then be succeeded by his son-in-law, Charley Winner, a past head coach with the St. Louis Cardinals and, at the time, one of George Allen's assistants at Washington. I was thunderstruck at the announcement. It made no sense to me any more than it did to the sportswriters. The action was assailed as "pure nepotism."

But in this case, after still another link in the chain of circumstances, things were to work out for Chuck Knox.

Carroll Rosenbloom, the owner of the Rams, called me. He said that he wanted to get rid of his coach, Tommy Prothro. "Tommy's a good guy," he said, "but we'll never win with him. I'm convinced of that. The man I want is Bart Starr. You're a good friend of his. Would you contact him and have him get in touch with me?"

My occupation had suddenly become that of a liaison man for potential head coaches in the National Football League. But I am a close friend of Bart Starr, and I believed he was qualified. He had done a wonderful job at Green Bay as an assistant to Dan Devine. So I called Bart, gave him Rosenbloom's number, and he and his wife went out to meet Carroll. They stayed at the Rosenblooms' for a couple of days. Then I got still another phone call. This time it was from Bart. Gentleman that he is, he called to advise me that he had turned down the job because his wife wanted him to leave football. He had spent too much time away from the children in their very important formative years. Besides, he was getting a second automobile dealership in Birmingham, Alabama. He added that he was tremendously impressed with Rosenbloom. "If I had a choice of any coaching job in the league, this would be the one I'd want," he said.

The next day I spoke with Rosenbloom, who had been very much taken with Starr but who understood completely why Bart had turned down the offer. The he asked me who else I might recommend. That's when I made a pitch for Chuck Knox. Carroll didn't know much about Chuck, but the Rams' general manager Don Klosterman knew him and his reputation. Several weeks passed as the Rams interviewed a number of candidates, including Knox and Monty Clark of the Dolphins. Finally, Carroll called and said, "We're going with your man."

So Chuck Knox became a head coach. The Los Angeles sports pages applied some heat to Rosenbloom. "Who's Chuck Knox?" was their question. The inference was that Carroll had signed a nobody, and that he could have done much better.

By the end of the season, Chuck was the kingpin of Los Angeles, acclaimed everywhere, and elected Coach of the Year by the football writers of America. The Rams won 12 and lost two; lost to Dallas in the playoffs because of one bad play by a defensive back. Overall they had a tremendous season in the wake of a disastrous one in which they had failed to make the playoffs. And, during the course of the season, Chuck developed some fine young players.

For Chuck Knox it was only the beginning. He is the equal of Shula in dedication. His players admire him and would do anything for him. His selection of assistants was as sound as Shula's. He is, at the moment, lacking in Shula's experience, but when it comes to coaching, Knox is a quick study. I repeat: He will be the next great coach, and the Rams will be up there for years to come.

But look at the sequence of events before he finally got the shot he deserved.

Q. You work on professional football telecasts. What do you think of the college game?

A. I like it very much, and I think it has many advantages over the professional game. In the first place, many more plays are executed during a college game than in a pro game. This is because less time is officially allowed between plays in a college game. Thus there is more action, better opportunities for the trailing team to catch up and, generally more excitement.

In the second place, the quarterback is an integral part of the running game in college football. In the pro game, while some quarterbacks scramble, no quarterback in pro football, with the possible exception of Bobby Douglass of the Bears, can be called a planned factor in a team's ground attack. I agree with John McKay, the head coach at the University of Southern California, when he says: "As long as the colleges use the quarterback as a running back as well as a passer, the college game will have more deception, more action and more excitement than the pro game."

I do not pretend for a moment that the collegians execute with the excellence of the professionals. The average college team does not compare in size, speed or experience with a professional team. But nobody expects that. Even so, the degree of efficiency of execution at the college level is outstanding.

The people in professional football know all about the college game and its inherent advantages. They are not fools. This is one reason why so many rule changes have been instituted this year, in the hope of bringing more excitement to their contests.

But they are also realists. They are convinced that no quarterback in pro football can physically survive, long term, if he is used as a runner. This is why they do not employ the exciting wishbone-T formation. The defensive linemen and linebackers in pro football are so big and so quick that they might physically demolish the running quarterback.

They also ask: Why have the quaterbacks risked running with the football when, in the pro game, every team has outstanding running backs, people like Simpson, Csonka, Mercury Morris, Floyd Little, John Brockington, McArthur Lane, Larry McCutcheon, Calvin Hill, Joh Riggins and Ron Johnson. The pure drop-back passer, they will argue, is the most effective passer. Locked in the protection pocket, he has an infinitely better view of the downfield; his passing is bound to be more accurate than when he is on the run, and his potential receivers can adhere to their carefully constructed pass patterns. Thus the synchronization between passer and receiver is more precise.

Stripped to the nub, what they are really saying is: We have the best football players in the world at each and every position. Each player is a specialist doing what he does better than anyone else, and the end result is the most professionally excellent product of its type to be found anywhere. They are right when they say this. The only drawback is, it is not necessarily the most exciting product of its type.

Give the pro-football people credit, though. Their sports is in its golden age. They could stand pat on their present popularity. Yet they have enacted rule changes to intensify interest in their game. Compare that with the baseball people and their resistance to change.

Q. The new leadership of Madison Square Garden has threatened to drop boxing. What is your view?

A. I don't think the Garden should drop boxing, nor do I think it will. I do think the end has come for the Madison Square Garden Boxing Department as we now know it, and I think it's long overdue.

The new president of Madison Square Garden, Alan N. Cohen, issued the threat after Malcolm Wilson, the governor of New York State, vetoed a bill that would have given state tax relief to fighters. You may remember that Muhammad Ali and Joe Frazier were socked with a $348,000 state-tax levy for their first bout at the Garden. The way the law reads, non-resident boxers, fighting in New York State, must pay taxes not only on income earned within the state, but on income derived from outside the state if their efforts within the state have produced the income. Thus, closed-circuit television receipts from all over the country are subject to New York State tax, and it is obviously undesirable, from the fighter's point of view, to fight in New York.

I think the governor was dead wrong in his veto, because a bout like the Ali-Frazier fight brings literally millions of dollars worth of business to the state, and as a natural concomitant, tax revenues with it.

But there was a lot more to Mr. Cohen's threat to drop boxing than Governor Wilson's veto. The Garden Boxing Department, formerly headed by Harry Markson, is now run by Teddy Brenner. Both are relics of the boxing past. Neither has ever done anything to build up the faith of the public in boxing, nor have they had the business acumen to get the Garden into the one area of boxing where the big money is—closed-circuit television. As a result, state tax or no state tax, the Garden Boxing Department has been an economically struggling operation, with a less than desirable image.

Garden officials knew this long before Mr. Cohen issued his statement. On different occasions in recent months, Michael Burke, president of Madison Square Garden Center and president of the New York Knicks, has had conversations with me in which he reflected upon the advisability of eliminating the department.

When Mr. Cohen uttered his threat to drop boxing, Harry Markson, now the Garden's consultant on boxing, said, "At the risk of being fired, I disagree with Mr. Cohen. I'm a boxing man, not a bottom-line man." Harry has always enjoyed a favorable press. He became, in his own way, a boxing institution. He had the history dating all the way back to Mike Jacobs, and he had been a sportswriter before that.

But favorable publicity does not alter the need to ask questions. What is a boxing man? Is it a man, for instance, who worked for the I.B.C. and the late Jim Norris? Is it a man who interrupted me in the middle of a telecast and tried to get me to say what he wanted me to say for the sake of his promotion? Is it Teddy Brenner, who apparently is deeply concerned that old-line boxing promoters like Herman Taylor of Philadelphia get favored theater franchises so they can make money out of the closed-circuit telecasts of big fights? Robert Arum, who runs the closed circuit corporation, Top Rank, Incorporated, and who does business with the Garden Boxing Department, has complained of this Brenner attitude many times.

Is a boxing man one who can't get along with many of the key managers and fighters because of the deals he tries to put over on them? George Foreman, for instance, doesn't want to have much to do with Brenner. Is a boxing man one who puts together a series of summer matches for television, and then labels some "championship bouts," bouts for a mythical "American Championship"? Is a boxing man one who brings in Joe Louis, at age 60, to referee a presumed major bout: the Quarry-Frazier affair in June 1974? Joe Louis is an American legend and he doesn't deserve abuse. But he was grossly unqualified for the assignment, and he proved it in the ring. He couldn't handle a low-blow situation, and he didn't stop the fight when it should have been stopped. He seemed hopelessly confused throughout the encounter. But don't blame Joe. Blame the cynical man who spent the weeks before the fight building up "the new Quarry," and the alleged importance of the fight. If the fight were really significant, how in the world could he have brought in Joe Louis to referee it? Is this a boxing man, and does he provide a good image for the most famous sports arena in the entire world?

Garden officials know all about Brenner's failings. This is why, sometime past, Michael Burke took over the negotiations of fights for the Garden. Garden officials also know that the real money in boxing comes from theater-television revenues on big fights. Why didn't the Garden Boxing Department get into the business? How could a young lawyer like Robert Arum have teamed up with Michael Malitz, a closed-circuit television executive, back in 1966 and gone on to become what he is now, the head of Top Rank, Inc., and a major figure in closed-circuit telecasts of the big bouts? Where was the Garden Boxing Department?

From my talks with Garden officials, I think they're aware that they can rent out the arena to a legitimate promoter who has negotiated an attractive bout. They don't need a boxing department for that. If they want to continue to run nothing bouts in the Felt Forum, an area with a smaller seating capacity that is part of the Garden complex, they can do that with new, young and vigorous people who can capture public attention and improve the image. They don't have to do it with Teddy Brenner and old-world boxing hangers-on who are the day-in, day-out tenants of the Garden Boxing Department offices, some of whom go back to the days of Jim Norris and the I.B.C.

What the Garden will probably do is take a look, in light of all of the above, at the broad boxing picture. They will rehabilitate their boxing structure, and doubtless seek to find a way to get into the theater-television business for the big fights. Boxing will not die at the Garden. Only the old guard will.

Finally, and on a different tack, when Mr. Alan Cohen said, "If you ask me whether I'd rather have a Stanley Cup and a basketball championship at the expense of a profit, I'd say no," he was being foolish. First he was alienating the fans to whom he has a fundamental obligation of trying to produce a championship team. Second, the statement is financially fallacious. In the long run in sports, you make money by spending money. Losers don't draw.

But they are right to review their boxing situation, for the reasons already stated. And they will bend every effort to get a new bill enacted into state law that will ease the state tax burden on fighters. That issue is not yet dead, despite the governor's veto. In fact, that's why Alan Cohen fired his verbal salvo.

Q. Which sport do you think has the most intelligent athletes?

A. It is a hard thing to generalize about, because every sport has athletes who are intelligent. The dictionary defines intelligence as, "the capacity to apprehend facts and proportions in their relations and to reason about them." By itself, that is a complex definition and it seems to me that education has to be involved in the development of what *Webster's* calls "capacity to apprehend facts and proportions. . . ." While it may be true that we're all born with a certain degree of intellectual aptitude, it would seem clear that that aptitude must be developed by way of education.

If one accepts this as a premise, then one would have to say that fighters are the least intelligent of all athletes. This is primarily because they spring from the ranks of the disadvantaged and have little or no education. Yet I have discovered in my many interviews over the years that fighters have perhaps the deepest feelings about life: fear and courage, discrimination, poverty and struggle and avarice among those who surround them. I know, too, that regardless of the fact that they have had little or no education, they can be well equipped with boxing intelligence. Boxers have those quick, automatic, reflexive insights that enable them to decipher an opponent's vulnerabilities and to strike at them with immediacy. They can amaze you with their perception, and, even though they're in a brutal sport, with their sensitivity and concern for others.

And I will tell you this: I have never met a more naturally acute man than Muhammad Ali. He can hold his own with anyone, yet he is virtually without education. Somehow, the things he says wind up making sense, a lot of sense, and his arguments in debate can be amazingly perceptive.

I have found wisdom in Archie Moore; thoughtful sensitivity immersed in confusion in Floyd Patterson; the horror of reality and understanding of the lethal nature of his business in Emile Griffith, after he killed Benny Paret; a natural gift for the one-liner in Joe Louis.

So I am not sure that education is the whole measuring stick of intelligence, any more than I believe that mere flashes of surprising insight constitute real intelligence.

I have found most baseball players to be afflicted with tobacco-chewing minds. The general run of conversation in the clubhouse and the dugout is a slovenly descent into boastfully profane and vivid recitals of the sexual conquest of the night before. It seems to be almost a psychological compulsion to reestablish one's manhood every day on the ignorant premise that the ability to conquer someone sexually is the all of manhood. And yet, even in the clubhouse and the dugout I have found intelligence. Wally Moon, the old Cardinal and Dodger, who is now teaching at John Brown College in Arkansas, was one of the brightest men I have ever known in sports. The old Dodgers, as a group, were an outstanding group of men: Carl Erskine, Pee Wee Reese, Ralph Branca and, of course Jackie Robinson, who was one of a kind. As I have thought back to those men through the years, I have to think that they were a reflection of Mr. Branch Rickey, who I believe was one of the few truly great men I have ever met.

Like boxers, a preponderant majority of major leaguers have baseball intelligence, good instincts for what they do. Men like Hank Aaron and Willie Mays are prime examples. Neither had an education. Neither is articulate. But, on the base paths, these two men have revealed native gifts that translated into an instinctive art form. Each knew every move, every habit of the pitchers on the mound; each knew, instinctively, exactly when to break for the next base. This is why Hank Aaron—perhaps the most unrecognized base-stealer of all time—has had an absolutely phenomenal percentage of successful steals. Nobody, but nobody, knows more about pitching habits than Willie Mays. Early in the 1974 season, when Tom Seaver was going badly, Willie knew what Seaver was doing wrong. At the right time, and in the right way, he finally got to Seaver and explained to him that he had forsaken his normal crouch toward the batter, that he was releasing the ball from an almost straight, upright position and that the ball, therefore, was hanging high and home runs were the result. Seaver took the advice, went out and fanned 11 batters and seemed to be back in form for a while—until he suffered an injury. But baseball intelligence does not constitute a questing mind and hardly falls within the dictionary's definition of the word, *intelligence.*

A step up the intelligence ladder are the basketball and football players. Nearly all of them are college graduates. They have learned, on the average, to think, to use their mental processes, to discuss more than just the games they perform in. Bill Bradley is not one I am alluding to here. He is a rare bird, a Rhodes Scholar. But men like Oscar Robertson, John Havlicek, Willis Reed, Walt Frazier, Bart Starr, Merlin Olson, Len Dawson, O. J. Simpson and countless others, impress me with their intelligence and their capacity for growth. Articulate, vitally interested in the world around them, they show more, far more of "the capacity to apprehend facts and proportions. . . ." Not that these athletes are not absorbed with women and sex. They are. They just are a little more subtle about it.

I rate track and field athletes at the same level as the professional football and basketball players.

At the top level I would put tennis players, professional golfers and racing drivers on the Grand Prix circuit. I really believe that their international travel has something to do with it. They get a sense of the breadth of the world, the nature of peoples, an understanding of what people and countries are all about and a sense of proper proportion as to their own individual importance in the whole vastness of the civilization.

There was, by the way, a time when the tennis and golf stars were affected with snobism. In my judgment, that is long past.

I have never spoken with a more fascinating man than Jackie Stewart. He left school when he was 15. He is a self-taught man, yet he is positively brilliant, literate and cultured. He has learned as he has come along, moving easily through the most sophisticated circles of people. He thinks often about life because, until he retired, he lived on the precipice of death. He understands reality, the beauty of nature, the beauty of words, the beauty of living. Somehow he is as one with the fair country of Monaco. His eyes grow warm and loving as he stands beside the magnificent harbor and looks up at the great cliffs of the principality; cliffs that are dotted with homes that seem part of the past, never to be recaptured. He will drive 2.5 kilometers into France, stop at *Le Chateau, Le Chevre D'Or* for a superb meal and sit out in the darkness and listen to the nightingales and quote Keats. He is, in a phrase, a man of enormous capacity. If you could spend a couple of hours with Jackie Steward you would understand.

I also wish you could have spent a couple of hours with the late Peter Revson, whom Stewart described as the perfect prototype of the open-road racing driver. Men like these can converse with perfect ease about politics, government, war and peace, economics and all of the areas of existence that envelop us in our daily lives.

Revson spent two hours with me once discussing *apartheid* in South Africa and evidenced the deepest dismay and horror at that system. Revson was always talking about people. Everywhere he went in the world he wanted to meet people and learn about them. On the subject of *apartheid,* Revson really knew what he was talking about. He could recite the most detailed ugliness of the system. He had been to South Africa, and, in fact, he died there sometime later.

Stewart and Revson are representative. Stirling Moss, the late Jim Clark and most of the others were and are of the same ilk. These are the men, in my judgment, who have the fullest sense of where it's at.

In the long run, they destroy themselves by their irresistible impulse to do what they do—race the open roads at breakneck speeds. Thank God Jackie quit in time.

Q. Do you ever root for a team or an individual?
A. Generally speaking, no, but there have been exceptions. One, of course, would be when I was growing up and I all but lived for the then Brooklyn Dodgers. They were the paramount interest in my life at that time. Naturally, too, I rooted for New York University when I was an undergraduate student there and at the law school. But ever since I became a professional broadcaster, I have been very careful not to become emotionally involved with who wins and who loses.

I rooted for Jackie Robinson, Roy Campanella, Willie Mays principle because I was sympathetic to the efforts of a group of men to engage, under the free enterprise system, in legitimate competition with the establishment, the National Football League. Knowing that the American Football League had to make it in New York in order for the league to survive, I rooted for Sonny Werblin in his efforts to build the Jets, and, in that sense, I suppose you could say I rooted for the Jets.

I rooted for Jackie Robinson, Roy Campella, Willie Mays and Hank Aaron, and all the black players who formed part of the brigade determined to sink prejudice in big-league baseball.

I am rooting for a black manager right now, and for black quarterbacks in the National Football League and for black head coaches. I will not stop rooting for these goals until real democracy in sports has been achieved, or put another way, until hypocrisy in sport has been materially diminished.

You better believe I rooted for quarterback Joe Gilliam of the Pittsburgh Steelers when he started against the Miami Dolphins on a *Monday Night* game in 1973. I didn't care who won or lost, but I wanted Gilliam to do well.

I rooted for Bill Toomey to win the decathlon in the 1968 Olympics because I felt his victory could inspire young people all over the world. Knowing the way Bill had grown up, knowing the multiple physical handicaps he had surmounted and knowing that he was almost 30 years of age yet competing in the most grueling athletic test in the world, I felt his victory could serve as an index for people everywhere of what the human spirit can achieve. It had nothing to do with the fact that he was an American.

So you see the kinds of things I root for.

CHAPTER 9

ALWAYS, IT'S THE PEOPLE

Q. On *The Emmy Awards Show,* Johnny Carson called you a legend in his own mind. Did you resent it? Do you think you are a legend?

A. I didn't resent it at all. I laughed along with everyone else. The first time Johnny used the line was when he was emceeing the Don Rickles Roast in New York City. I was one of the "roasters," and when Johnny introduced me, he used the line for the first time, and it brought down the house.

What you must understand is that the best comedy in the entertainment business often emerges when people needle one another. Carson is a past master at it. So is Don Rickles. I like to think I'm pretty good at it too, and, given equal time as was the case at the Rickles Roast, I got my own shots in at Johnny.

I can't tell you how much I admire Carson as an entertainer. I think he is the absolute best, quick as lightning with his quips, incomparably poised, possessed of a marvelous personality and always giving the impression that he is having fun with what he is doing. His sarcasm is superb, his ways of using his face—the expressions, the wryness, the nuances—are exactly right. There's a reason why Johnny Carson has been on top all these years. He's an extraordinary talent, and when he acknowledges me by having good clean fun at my expense, I am the opposite of resentful. I am gratified.

As to whether I think I am a legend, that's just silly. I have performance confidence, I believe in what I do, I do it as well as I can and I leave it at that.

165

Q. What television show have you enjoyed doing most?

A. This question breaks down into several answers. The show I most enjoyed producing was *Run to Daylight,* the story of the late Vince Lombardi and the Green Bay Packers. The reason is because I was fascinated by the impact Lombardi had upon his players, and I was equally taken by the actual love they felt for him. Also, as a journalist, I highlight that show because it was a first, an exclusive. Lombardi had never permitted anyone to film his training camp activities before.

The show I most enjoy performing in, as a continuing series is *The Howard Cosell Sports Magazine,* because it is adult sports television. By this I mean that it deals with issues, with people and with breaking news stories. For example, it provided the forum for examining the new pro-football war between the World Football League and the National Football League; it was on this show that Larry Csonka, Jim Kiick and Paul Warfield of the Miami Dolphins announced that they were jumping to the World Football League. It was on this show that I could speak in-depth with Billie Jean King, film O. J. Simpson in Oroville, California, while he was making a movie with Richard Burton and Lee Marvin, and broadcast live from Madison Square Garden with George Foreman at the Ali-Frazier weigh-in.

This was the series that gave me the opportunity to do "Managing: For Whites Only?" And this was the series that enabled me to pinpoint the possible death of the National Summer Youth Sports Program, a terribly critical and efficiently run summertime service for disadvantaged youngsters throughout the nation which had been earmarked for extinction by the Nixon Administration. Dealing with subjects like these is far more challenging for me than merely transmitting a sports event. After all, the events come and go, here today, forgotten tomorrow. On the other hand, issues must be met and, hopefully, resolved for the public good. And people are the whole of life, enduring yet forever changing.

The television show that I most enjoyed guesting was *The Odd Couple.* I like to think that I have some acting ability and I was given a major role in this show. And I enjoyed the atmosphere of the show, including the show's basic story line. Nor do I know of an easier, more engaging man to work with than Jack Klugman.

Next to *The Odd Couple,* I liked *The Dean Martin Show.* Greg Garrison, the producer, is a smooth, delightful man who is, I think, the most relaxed fellow I have ever worked with. And Dean Martin gives you the same feeling. Neither man ever manifests tension. The show was fun to do.

Q. What television show did you least enjoy doing?

A. That's easy. *The Sonny and Cher Comedy Hour,* and the reason was Cher. I found Sonny Bono a warm, pleasant fellow, interested in his guests and anxious to put them at ease. I think that the show's producers, Chris Beard and Allen Blye, are top professionals, and so is the director, Art Fisher. But I want no part of Cher.

I guested on the premiere show of the series for the 1973–1974 season. So did Chuck Conners, who happens to be an old friend. Chuck, like me, had grown up in Brooklyn, and he had played professional baseball in the Brooklyn Dodgers' farm system and later in the National League. We go back a long way together.

From the time Chuck and I arrived at the CBS studios, Cher never even had the courtesy to acknowledge us. Not one word. This hardly puts one at ease, and the temptation was to tell her to go to hell and walk out on the show. But we're professionals and we didn't do it. A group of fine and talented young men were in the show's troupe, and they told Chuck and me that Cher behaved this way with everyone. It was an open secret that she and Sonny were, to put it mildly, at odds with one another. So the atmosphere on the set was heavy, very heavy.

Finally, on the last day of my shooting schedule, I had the honor of being spoken to by Cher. "Howard, get your ass over here and do some promos for us," she said. I suppressed the rage I felt, did the promos and then advised the producers that I would not do the final sketch I was slated to do with her. I told Chris Beard they didn't have to pay me my fee. And I left.

I will say this. Cher is an authentic talent. But quite obviously she has personal problems. I didn't ask to go on her show; they asked me. It was a disgusting experience.

I wish Sonny luck in his new show, *The Sonny Comedy Revue.*

Q. At half-time during the San Francisco-Green Bay game last November, George Foreman called you a "racist." What do you say to that?

A. I say it was an unfortunate attempt on George's part to be funny, and it didn't come off. As Milton Berle, who was in the broadcast booth at the time, put it, "The guy's a fighter, not a comedian. He shouldn't try to be Muhammad Ali."

I think you should know—if you already don't—my relationship with George Foreman. It began in Mexico City in 1968 when he won a gold medal in the Olympic boxing competition. I believed in him as a fighter immediately because I was awed by his punching power. I also took to him personally. I liked his courtesy, his humility and his positive joy at being a part of the 19th Olympiad. As a result, I followed his professional career closely, stayed in touch with him, and even had him with me at ringside in Munich in the role of a guest commentator.

In Kingston, Jamaica, before his fight against Frazier, I spent a lot of time with him, and told him that I picked him to knock Joe out within two rounds. This is why, in the ring after the fight, Foreman dedicated the victory to me. Subsequently, George has been a visitor to my home, has done many shows with me and I consider him a friend.

On the night to which the question relates, George visited me in the broadcast booth before the game, and I invited him to come on at half-time. Then he left me to join my wife for a cup of coffee in the Stadium Club at Candlestick Park. He came back at half-time and, based upon all the dialogues he has seen me engage in with Muhammad Ali, he tried the same tack. It didn't work. Frank Gifford was stunned. He said, after Foreman left the booth, "What the hell was wrong with him? He sounded like he meant it." I was upset, too, for myself and for George. Much of my track record in sports broadcasting has been one of support for the causes of minority athletes: the way I backed Muhammad Ali, my fight to get black managers in baseball and a lot of other cases. And then I began to think about George, about the bad publicity he had been getting because he had not been fighting in defense of his crown, about all of his other problems, marital and financial, and about how his statement to me on the air would certainly be misunderstood and cause him new grief.

The next day I got many calls from broadcasters and writers asking me for a reply to what George had said. I told them that George was only trying to be funny. And then I got a call from George. He was beside himself. He, too, had been besieged by broadcasters and writers. "Don't they know how I respect you?" he asked. "How you've backed me from the beginning? How kind you and your wife have been to me? How we always kid around?"

And then he really astonished me. "You know what else? I'm even getting calls from Republicans in Congress asking me about you. I got mad and hung up a couple of times." I told George to forget the whole thing.

Unfortunately for George, some of the black press did not. They really scorched him in editorials that pointed out my whole history of support for black athletes. Yet, incredibly, some white writers, only a handful, picked up George's statement and hinted at the notion that I am, indeed, a racist. None of this has changed our relationship. When George is in New York I see him, and when I'm in California I usually see him.

Q. Have you ever been embarrassed on the air?

A. Of course I've been embarrassed. When a guest says to you, "Let's see, do I bullshit you or do you bullshit me," you better believe it's embarrassing. That's exactly what a pitcher named Tracy Stallard said to me, live, on a local television show a number of years ago. Tracy was a journeyman pitcher with the New York Mets during their early, comic-clown years; his previous fame derived chiefly from the fact that he had thrown the 61st home-run ball to Roger Maris.

The incident occurred on the night before Christmas Eve, a night when I wanted desperately to get home to Pound Ridge to be with my family. My reason for having Stallard on as my guest was because he was serving as a Santa Claus on behalf of the Mets; delivering gifts from the ball club to needy young-sters to help brighten up many Christmases. Tracy did abso-lutely nothing to brighten mine. I came on the air jovially that night, identified Stallard as my guest and then broke for a commercial. Just as the commercial ended and we came back on live, Tracy elected to ask me his now-famous question. I gulped, pretended it had never been said and plunged into the interview. His image as a Santa Claus was punctured, however, and as I left the studio, our newsman, Bill Beutel, shouted, "Howard, you've disgraced us all. You put a drunk on the air." That was all Stallard had to hear. He was, in fact, not drunk or anything like it. He had simply pulled an on-the-air blooper. I tried to mollify Stallard, who was threaten-ing to go back and punch Beutel. Then the chief telephone operator got hold of me, and told me the switchboard was flooded with calls. I went into the telephone room to answer as many as I could while Stallard stormed off in a rage.

I never did get home to Pound Ridge that night. I was in the phone room for three hours listening to irate parents tell me that I had destroyed the morals and dreams of their children. To each of them I apologized, even as I wondered about the potential hypocrisy lodged in every complaint. I find it hard to believe that in the average home, young people never hear profanities uttered by their parents. That didn't make Tracy's verbal miscue right. It should not have gone out over the air.

I didn't just have the parents on my back. Suddenly I got a call from Roosevelt Hospital. It was from Dr. Peter La Motte, the Mets' physician. Tracy Stallard was with him, he told me, and Tracy had just taken the test for intoxication. According to the good doctor, Stallard was stone sober, and any implica-tions to the contrary by anybody at ABC would result in a law-suit. That was all I needed. I got hold of Beutel and filled him in. Then I contacted John Gilbert, the station manager, and reported on the whole chain of events. Then I called my wife and told her I couldn't possibly get home that night.

I then called Roger Kahn, the writer, and arranged to have dinner with him and his wife that night. At midnight I went back to the Kahns' apartment to spend the night there. At two in the morning I was still awake. I quietly got up, dressed, walked a block to the Park Sheraton Hotel and spent the rest of the night there. At eight in the morning I met John Gilbert at his office and we reviewed the whole matter. We agreed that all of the parents and children who heard Stallard's remark would somehow survive. We agreed that Tracy had not been drinking. And for the next month, everywhere I went, people would ask, "Does Stallard bullshit you or do you bullshit him?" Neither—and there'll never be another chance.

Q. Why do the NFL players have such strong feelings against Commissioner Pete Rozelle?

A. I am not at all sure that very many of the players do have stong emotions against Pete Rozelle personally. But I do believe that many of them feel that he is endowed with too much power and authority and, as a matter of principle, they fear the abuse of both.

There can be no question that Rozelle is the most powerful of all commissioners. He has two areas of authority which the players most strongly object to. He is the sole arbiter in grievance disputes arising between players and owners under contracts executed between them, and under the rules governing professional football. This is not true of baseball or basketball. Impartial arbitration is the procedure by which such disputes are handled in those sports. It should be noted that on matters involving "the integrity of the game," the other commissioners appear to have the same total authority that is entrusted to Rozelle.

Rozelle also has a special authority under the so-called Rozelle Rule. This term covers the procedure that is applied when a player plays out his contract. The man is bound, under the contracted "option clause," to play for that team for one more year after the term of the agreement has expired. Then the player may, if he desires, sign with another team. However, if the player does sign with another team, Rozelle—and this is the essence of the Rozelle Rule—forces the other team to pay compensation to the team from which the player is departing. This compensation is in the form of player personnel and/or future draft choices. There is always the possibility that a team will be deterred from signing a player who has played out his option for fear that Rozelle will invoke compensation that exceeds the value of the player sought. This is the specter that haunts the NFL Players Association, and so their cry is that the Rozelle Rule hinders freedom of movement by a player. There is also, they point out, the possibility of collusion between owners; a collusion which would preclude any other offers to the player who has played out his option. In point of fact, many players have played out their options and have been signed elsewhere; some of them have been outstanding players, like Verlon Biggs, who went from the Jets to Washington, and Dave Parks, who went from San Francisco to New Orleans. According to the Players Association, however, this has nothing to do with the dangers inherent in the principle involved.

In his role as sole arbiter of grievance disputes, Rozelle has decided more times in favor of the players than against them, but once again the players say that it is a matter of principle. Basically, they feel that since the owners pay Pete's salary, he is the owners' man, and that grievance disputes should be resolved by impartial arbitration as is the procedure in other sports. In other words, even if Rozelle has proved to be a benevolent despot, what if the next commissioner did not?

The NFL Players Association also objects to Rozelle's utilization of power in other cases. The Lance Rentzel matter comes to mind. When Rentzel was found guilty of an indecent exposure charge, Rozelle took no action against him. When Rentzel subsequently pleaded guilty to a drug charge, Rozelle suspended him from football indefinitely. But after a one-year layoff, Rozelle reinstated him. At the time of the suspension, Ed Garvey, executive director of the Players Association, charged that Rozelle had no right to strip Rentzel of his livelihood without due process of law. Rozelle, on the other hand, was concerned with the public image of professional football. There are arguments in favor of both sides here, but naturally the Players Association sees the matter in its own way.

Not too long ago, Rozelle fined eight members of the San Diego Chargers for "drug related abuses." Garvey once again decried the action as being in violation of due process. What he did not point out was that the general manager, Harland Svare, and the owner, Gene Klein, were also fined.

Now, there very well may be legal ramifications to both the San Diego and Rentzel cases. But the point is, they are legal questions that relate to the extent of Rozelle's powers as commissioner, and should not necessarily relate to the commissioner as a person. And that goes back to the heart of the question. I don't think legitimate collective bargaining on legal issues should be confused with personal animus.

At the moment of this writing, the players and the owners are locked in a confrontation, and bargaining is not taking place. The key issues are the so-called freedom issues, that is, Rozelle's powers as described above, which, according to the Players' Association, are depriving the players of their freedom.

Q. How do you compare Pete Rozelle and Bowie Kuhn as commissioners? How do you think the public views them?

A. In comparing the two men, one must look at the kind of person each is; whether he is strong or weak, whether he is afraid or not afraid of losing his job, whether he will take stands and do battle for what he thinks is right. According to the way the two men have reacted to those tests in the conduct of their jobs, different images have resulted for the two. And I believe it is fair to say that Rozelle's image is that of a strong leader, controlling the NFL owners; or, if not controlling them, guiding them and not lying down before them. On the other hand, I think it is fair to say that the image of Bowie Kuhn, the baseball commissioner, is that of an administrator, not a leader; a man preoccupied with detail, not with scope; a man subservient to the owners and always looking to them for guidance and for approval.

I think that a fundamental difference between Kuhn and Rozelle is not only in personal makeup, but in outlook. Rozelle is a much more contemporary-minded man than Kuhn. He understands change and the need for it. Kuhn does not, or if he does, he gives no visible evidence of the fact. Instead, he likes to adopt the tired litany of the owners, that baseball is the only game, that its traditions must stand forever.

Each man is deeply aware of the importance of personal public relations and the consequent image that derives from it. But even here there are sharp differences. Rozelle's public relations are slick and subtle. Somehow the illusion has grown that Pete has been responsible for the tremendous growth and prosperity of professional football. Rozelle and the "Golden Age" of football seem as one, inextricably interwoven. Don't ask me how this impression has developed because Rozelle is not a ceremonial man. He doesn't appear on TV for opening games, he doesn't want everyone to see him, he is careful about his interviews. He is, indeed, subtle.

Not Kuhn. Bowie wants to be on television, wants everyone to see him, is absorbed with personal publicity. Ask NBC Sports. They carry major-league baseball, and they know all about it. Somehow, though, for Bowie the exposure doesn't prove beneficial. While he is ceremonial, he has little impact.

Kuhn is a decent man who, above all, wants to be liked. He is not a forceful personality, nor is he a particularly shrewd man. He is easy to read. Rozelle has a pleasing personality and is an attractive man who keeps his youth—how I don't know. He is a student of open cordiality, but there is little that is open about him. He is a terribly difficult man to penetrate and he rarely, if ever, gives of himself in conversation about the business of the National Football League. This is part of his shrewdness, and if there is one thing Pete Rozelle is, it is shrewd. His growth in his position fooled everybody, including the NFL owners. During the course of Rozelle's stewardship, they have, in a way so subtle that they probably didn't even realize it, turned to Pete more and more for leadership. And they admire enormously his ability to achieve compromise among them for what he deems to be good for professional football.

Rozelle did not get his job the way Kuhn did. Rozelle was an accident, the only commissioner in history to be elected unanimously on the 23rd ballot. He was a virtual anonymity at the time, a young man most remembered as sports publicity director for the University of San Francisco, and only mildly known for his work in the front office of the Los Angeles Rams. Once, back in 1956, he was in his own public-relations business. His key client was the government of Australia during the Olympic Games in Melbourne. Thus he was an astonishing selection as commissioner, and he hardly seemed qualified to succeed the ruggedly aggresive leadership of Bert Bell. The owner who officially advised Rozelle that he had been elected commissioner was Carroll Rosenbloom. Carroll is an absolutely brilliant man who likes to assume the role of the "Godfather," and even he was fooled. As of now, Rosenbloom wonders how Pete ever got so powerful in the job, and the two have a number of differences. But Rozelle reigns, as he established when Rosenbloom's coach, Don Shula, jumped from Baltimore to Miami. Carroll will never forgive Rozelle for allowing that to happen.

Kuhn came to his job in a much simpler manner than Rozelle, in a much more predictable manner. He had no public recognition, but he was intimately known by the baseball owners as the attorney who handled many of baseball's legal problems. The owners knew him to be their man—no worry about that—and they knew him to be an old-line baseball traditionalist. They didn't have to be concerned about any intransigeances on his part. Besides, Bowie could provide the right front. He is a big man, about 6-feet 4-inches tall, has a fine voice and speaks impressively. Physically, he conveys authority and strength.

The media people were immediately taken with Bowie. His self-assurance was magnetic, his knowledgeability apparent and he succeeded an obscure, nonbaseball man who was a palpable puppet for the owners. So there was a honeymoon period for Kuhn. The image was good and getting better.

The Dennis McLain case produced a radical change in that image. When it was disclosed that the Tigers' pitcher was helping to finance a bookmaking operation, Kuhn merely slapped him on the wrist. He suspended Denny for only three months. At the massive press conference wherein he announced the suspension, Bowie defied his own legal background, indulged in some meandering phraseology and wound up saying, in effect, that a bookie is not a bookie if he gets no return on his investment. One can only wonder what Judge Kenesaw Mountain Landis would have done. That stern gentleman, with a granite face and character to match, restored credibility to baseball in the public mind after the Black Sox Scandal. Integrity became baseball's watchword. Where was the integrity of Kuhn's action, or was he more concerned about the box-office effect if baseball were to lose one of its greatest stars indefinitely? Most understandably, the media asked these very questions. Bowie's image has never recovered.

By way of contrast, look at the Paul Hornung and Alex Karras cases. Both men were superstars in the National Football League. Both were suspended indefinitely by Rozell when it was learned that each was betting, though never against his own team. Certainly neither was ever involved in bookmaking operations. After one year Pete lifted the suspension.

And then Rozelle, at the very peak of Joe Namath's career—after Namath had led the Jets to their Super Bowl victory over Baltimore, when he was by far the biggest draw in the game—ordered Namath to divest himself of his ownership interest in Bachelor's III, a New York restaurant and bar that was being populated by gambling types. Purportedly, gamblers were using phones in the place to conduct business. Namath, who said that he was being victimized by guilt by association, declared that he would not have his freedom impinged upon and stated that he would not give up his interest in the restaurant. He announced his retirement from football. Rozelle never budged. Finally, and reluctantly, Namath knuckled under.

When one looks at these matters in retrospect, along with the Rentzel and San Diego cases, one must, it seems to me, admit that Rozelle showed strength and, concomitantly, reflected an image of integrity for his sport, while baseball showed much less of one.

From the beginning, Rozelle has had a top-flight security department to safeguard his sport against gambling influences. Kuhn put one in only after the McLain affair.

Major-league baseball now has an interesting innovation, the "designated hitter" rule—but only in the American League. And the rule does not apply when the World Series is played. This is manifestly absurd and Kuhn should use his authority under baseball's general-welfare clause to force the National League to adopt the rule. Can you imagine the American Football Conference having one set of rules, and the National Football Conference another under Pete Rozelle? Fat chance.

Rozelle has a problem Kuhn doesn't have—a very big problem. Professional football is subject to the antitrust laws. Major-league baseball is not. Thus, when the NFL and AFL merged in 1966, that merger could take place only if Congress enacted legislation that freed the merger from antitrust laws. This was where Rozelle was at his very best. Working smoothly, steadfastly, behind the scenes, he lined up the necessary votes to get the merger approved. While I, personally, disagreed with the merger and fought it, I have to respect the job that Pete did.

Rozelle took over as commissioner in January 1960. At that time, CBS had individual television contracts with many of the teams in the NFL. Obviously, because of the size of the different markets, teams like New York, Chicago and Los Angeles would receive much greater sums for television rights than would those of smaller cities like Pittsburgh. A little town like Green Bay could get almost nothing. NBC, which then had a few teams signed up, had a deal, for instance, with Pittsburgh and Baltimore whereby they might carry a Baltimore game one week and a Pittsburgh game the next week. Clearly, an enormous financial advantage lay with the big-city teams who could translate their monies into acquiring top players, or by making trades with monetarily less fortunate teams. They could, in effect, buy key players to fill holes in their clubs. Thus, there was always the threat of imbalance in the league.

Rozelle took quick action to alleviate this situation. He had every team clear—or terminate, if you will—its existing television contract. His aim was to make one big-money contract for television rights to the NFL with one network, and then divide the total television monies equally among all teams. This would enable the small-city teams to be more competitive with the big-city teams.

But once again there was the problem of the antitrust laws to which professional football was subject, and to which baseball was not. The Justice Department, relating back to a court decision of the 1950s that seemed to indicate that Rozelle's plan would be in violation of the antitrust laws, took the position that the NFL could not execute the plan.

Rozelle went to work and by September 1961, Congress passed legislation which freed the NFL to make a deal with one network and pool its television monies. If any one thing has contributed to the prosperity of the NFL, this has been it. And, of course, all television monies are pooled to this day. Denver and Buffalo get what New York and Los Angeles get.

In all of the foregoing, I do not intend to convey the idea that everything Rozelle does is good, and everything Kuhn does is bad. In all fairness to Bowie, he stood up to Charles O. Finley, the owner of the Oakland As, when Finley sought to oust Mike Andrews from the team during the World Series. Kuhn ordered Andrews back on the team, and subsequently fined Finley for his actions.

And I know that Bowie would like to modernize the televised presentation of baseball contests. This is why he supported Carl Lindemann, head of NBC Sports, when Carl initiated the idea of using guests on *Monday Night Baseball*.

As Marvin Miller, executive director of the Major League Baseball Players' Association, told me, "It's not that Kuhn has done anything very bad, it's just that he doesn't do much of anything unless the owners want him to. We were talking about him the other day, and we agreed that it all goes back to the Dennis McLain case."

In my opinion, Rozelle has an Achilles' heel in Wellington Mara, president of the New York Giants. If the NFL isn't careful, Mara will destroy it and the record proves it.

It was Mara who initiated "raiding" when, during the NFL-AFL football war, he was the first to raid the other league. He signed kicker Pete Gogolak of the Buffalo Bills. Having permitted this, Rozelle and the NFL owners shouldn't kick when the WFL raids their personnel.

I think Rozelle should have stopped Mara from abandoning New York City. The record proves Mara had standing-room-only crowds for every game. The record also shows that Mara got $10 million from AFL owners for territorial rights and that the intent and spirit of that payment was for the rights to New York City, not East Rutherford, New Jersey.

As a prelude to moving to New Jersey, Mara went to the Yale Bowl in New Haven, Connecticut, and the Giants' games were televised into neighboring Hartford, only 35 miles away. This broke the NFL's 75-mile blackout rule, and thus left Rozelle and the NFL owners without any real beef when Congress passed legislation lifting the blackout rule under certain conditions. Rozelle should not have allowed Mara to be an exception at the expense of everybody else.

Even more important, Mara's leaving will provide an opening in the biggest market in the world for the New York Stars of the WFL. They will have a brand-new Yankee Stadium, be part of a great municipal renewal program and will probably be adopted by New York City in the way that the Mets and Jets were. I cannot understand why Rozelle has permitted all of this to come about.

Rozelle also blew a big one early in his career when he allowed the NFL to play its scheduled games on the Sunday of the week when John F. Kennedy was assassinated.

It may be, too, that Pete could have exercised greater leadership than he did to stop the incursions of the WFL. But that is doubtful because of professional football's susceptibility to the federal antitrust laws. He dare not say or do anything that might later be construed in a court of law as having been an effort to hinder an independent group from setting up business in a free-enterprise system.

In light of all of the above, and considering how Kuhn started personally strong and Rozelle personally weak, I rate Rozelle a strong commissioner who has presided over the continuing growth of his sport, who has seen it rise to unparalleled prosperity; a commissioner who has survived one pro-football war and emerged secure as the commissioner; one who has shown an unending determination to preserve public confidence in his sport.

I rate Bowie Kuhn a decent man who has done little, if anything, to enhance his sport, to innovate, to lead the way with creative ideas for change that would restore a sense of rebirth to baseball instead of a sense, at best, of standing still.

Bowie seems a caretaker of the past, rather than a forger of the future.

There is one thing more. Rozelle's greatest challenges are, at this writing, yet to come. The confrontation with the Players Association as well as the new war with the WFL will try him, and the NFL, to the utmost.

Q. Do you think that Commissioner Pete Rozelle has too much power?

A. I do not think he should be the sole arbiter of grievance disputes. I think such disputes should be handled by impartial arbitration. As a matter of fact, I don't think Rozelle much cares about whether or not he should have the power to be sole arbiter. I think the only reason he would want to retain that authority at this time would be because of ego. He might not want to be reduced back to the level of the other commissioners.

I do not believe that the Rozelle Rule should exist. I think it gives him too much power. But, in fairness, the Rozelle Rule doesn't represent the utterly excessive power that baseball has in restricting freedom of job movement. Baseball has the odious reserve clause which binds one man to one team, forever, and which was curiously sustained by the United States Supreme Court in the Curt Flood Case, despite the fact that the Court admitted the clause was an anachronism. The Court suggested that Congress could enact legislation obviating the reserve clause or modifying it. So the football players have more freedom of movement than the baseball players. I would like to see the reserve clause legislated out, the Rozelle Rule collectively bargained out, and the free market of supply and demand control sports as it does all other businesses. I do not believe that anarchy would result as baseball and football owners have stated, because owners would still have two fundamental protections: 1. They can negotiate long-term contracts with their key players. 2. They can insist upon the right of first refusal when the player's contract has expired. In other words, if a player is given a better offer by another team, the owner should have the right to match that offer.

It may be that Rozelle has too much power in matters like those concerning Rentzel, Namath, Hornung and Karras, and the San Diego drug cases. However, professional sport is quasi-public; it lives on public confidence and professional sport will die, or at least will be savagely hurt, when that confidence declines. Rozelle's actions in the above matters were probably good for the sports and, more important, necessary for the sport.

The problem that arises from the possession of the power to take the actions that Rozelle did in the above cases is a legal one, and what you must always remember is that any such action taken by Rozelle is subject to legal challange. The questions that arise when he invokes such actions are: Is he not sentencing a man before a trial has been held and guilt has been established? Is he not, therefore, violating a man's constitutional rights? Even if a man has been found guilty, or pleaded guilty, as in the case of Rentzel, should he, nevertheless, be deprived of his right to earn a living?

These are hard questions to answer in a legal sense, and they must be weighed against the question of public confidence in the integrity of the sport. Without that confidence, the sport will not survive. That is exactly what Judge David A. Thomas, Superior Court Judge, County of Los Angeles, decided on August 23, 1973. The NFL Players Association and Lance Rentzel had sought a preliminary injunction against Rozelle and NFL to prevent Rentzel's suspension. The claim was that Rentzel had been denied due process. Judge Thomas's opinion, in part, said that:

> *The Court concludes otherwise. It is clear that the defendants have sought for years to establish a standard of public conduct for professional football participants, including players. This standard (which might be better termed "image") includes the portrayal of players as high type, admirable young men who are worthy of the respect and emulation of the young (Rozell Decl., particularly paragraphys 10 and 11). (Or, to borrow from another segment of the entertainment industry, football seeks to present itself under a "G" rating.) This is understandable, for professional football is a privately owned and operated entertainment enterprise pursued by those in it for their own gain, and they have determined that it is to their best interest to promote an image (that is, maintained a standard of public conduct) of a*

kind described above. Thus, conduct which injures said standard (image) is considered by the NFL to be detrimental to it. It is not up to the Court to criticize this standard or attempt to change it unless it impinges on the rights of plaintiff.

Incidentally, the powers employed by Rozelle in the above cases do not belong exclusively to Rozelle. The other commissioners have the same powers under a clause that relates to maintaining the integrity of the game. And if it is ever determined, legally, that commissioners cannot take the kind of action that Rozelle took, certainly some new procedure will have to be found that will enable professional sports, on the one hand, to preserve public confidence in its integrity, and, on the other, to insure that the individual rights of players are safeguarded.

Q. Who do you think is the smartest general manager in professional football, and why?

A. I think the smartest general manager in professional football was Jim Finks of the Minnesota Vikings, and he is no longer in the job, which is par for the course. Finks operated with a limited seating capacity at Metropolitan Stadium in Bloomington, Minnesota. Thus the Vikings don't have the gross-receipts potential that many other clubs have. Despite this handicap, Finks had drafted consistently well, made some excellent trades and contained salaries within reasonable bounds (so that the problem of the small stadium became surmountable). And the Vikings have been perennial contenders, twice going to the Super Bowl in the last five years.

He built the Vikings by himself, player by player, from the time they were an expansion team until the time he left. Bud Grant was his coaching selection. His only failure was the failure to win the Super Bowl, and inevitably that victory would probably have come to the Vikings had Finks stayed on.

Why then did Finks leave? He left because he felt that the Vikings' owners had betrayed him. He had worked dedicatedly for them from the time the ball club was born. After the 1973 season he took a look at himself and his life Now in his late forties, he felt that he wanted a piece of the ownership—which he wanted to buy—and thus create an equity position for himself in what had been his lifetime effort. So he sought to buy 100 shares of *nonvoting* stock, which would have given him a measure of equity, but not an ownership operating voice. The five owners voted him down by a margin of three to two. In the wake of all he had done for the ball club, he was utterly disconsolate. At the winter-league expansion meetings in New York, when Tampa was announced as the newest franchise, it was Jim's hope that he could syndicate a group to become the owners of that franchise with him included. Right now, his job is "consultant to the National Football League," whatever that may mean. It is an indignity to Jim Finks, and to professional football, that all of this has been allowed to come to pass.

There are two other general managers for whom I have vast respect. One is Don Klosterman of the Los Angeles Rams, who is probably the very best at evaluating player personnel. Nobody works harder at his job than Don.

The other general manager I respect is Jack Steadman of the Kansas City Chiefs. An accountant type, Jack has had the brains and the vision to realize the limitations of profits from professional football. And with the multimillionaire Lamar Hunt as his boss, he is diversifying the organization. For example, the Chiefs are now in the amusement complex business. Someday, with costs rising the way they are, you may see every front office seeking to diversify its operation. But Steadman has led the way.

Al Davis of Oakland might be the smartest football man of them all, but I exclude him from this answer because he is a principal owner of the Raiders even though he, in effect, serves as general manager, too.

Q. Do you socialize with athletes?
A. Only rarely because of the obvious fact that the athletes of today are not in my age group. They are contemporaries of my two daughters and my son-in-law. There are exceptions, of course. We do see Marguerite and O. J. Simpson occasionally, but we really don't want to spend our social time discussing zone blocks and odd-man fronts, anymore than we're

interested in the pick and roll or in whether Gaylord Perry has given up the grease ball.

This was not always the case. While Jackie Robinson was alive, we did socialize with him and Rachel, and we still see Jeanie and Andy Robustelli reasonably often. Apart from them, we were very close with the old New York Giants, the Y. A. Tittles, the Del Shofners, the Don Chandlers, the Tom Scotts and others. But, of course, they were our contemporaries then. Naturally, too, Emmy and I do see Frank and Maxine Gifford, and we used to spend time with Suzie and Don Meredith.

The people who we most often see are ABC executives and their wives, not athletes. This is understandable because our lives are in the same flow. We have common problems and common interests. We also socialize a good deal with people who are involved in sports, but who are not athletes. Marion and Walter Kennedy—he is the outgoing commissioner of the NBA—are among our closest friends. Don Klosterman is another and so are the Al Davises and the Hank Stramms and Lamar Hunts. Sonny and Leah Ray Werblin are two more. So are Georgia and Carroll Rosenbloom, the owner of the Rams. Among our writer friends are the Jim Murrays and the Mel Durslags and the Mickey Herskowitzes.

We are also close to Michael Burke, who now runs Madison Square Garden. And there are many others too numerous to mention.

But there is a danger inherent in all of these friendships. You can never let them affect your reporting and commentating on matters they're involved in or which affect them. If you find yourself holding back because you don't want to hurt them, you are no longer a reporter. But if you fail to hold back, you risk the loss of their friendship. I have grappled with this problem many times, and I honestly believe that I have met the test. On occasion, it has cost me friendships.

By way of illustration, Phil Iselin and Leon Hess, and their wives, have in the past been very good friends of ours. Leon Hess is even a member of the board of directors of the American Broadcasting Companies. Iselin and Hess are two of the four owners of the New York Jets. I have been unremitting in my criticism of the Jets' ownership. Ever since Sonny Werblin left the Jets, the team has declined. In my judgment, Phil and Leon became absentee owners and deeded the team over to Weeb Ewbank. Ewbank was once a great coach who deserves a place in the Pro Football Hall of Fame. But as a general manager, he practices 17th-Century economics. As a result, the Jets, in my opinion, are on the verge of becoming the worst team in professional football. In addition, Phil and Leon allowed Weeb to name his son-in-law, Charley Winner, as the new head coach. This is an unhealthy situation, smacking, as it does, of nepotism. I have been outspoken about all of the foregoing on the air.

As a consequence, Emmy and I no longer see the Iselins socially, the way we used to. The relationship is clearly strained. On those occasions when we are together, there is never an overt word that would indicate that this is the case. Betty is too much of a lady and Phil too much of a gentleman. But the atmosphere is heavy. We're sorry about it, but that's the price we have to pay.

Carroll Rosenbloom's friendship means a lot to me. I enjoy being with him. He is an incisive man, a satirical man, a clever man and, I think, a brilliant man. He has a deliciously sardonic sense of humor. He is also a generous and a caring man, and his players will tell you that he is the finest owner in American sports because of the way he treats them.

But if Carroll is ever crossed, or thinks he is being crossed, he can become an implacable enemy. He never forgets, and he carries a grudge the way Lancelot carried a shield. The Don Shula case is an example. Once Shula left the Colts for the Dolphins, Carroll was *personna non grata* to the Dolphins' principal owner, Joe Robbie, for what seemed an eternity. Rosenbloom didn't mince words. He told everybody what he thought of Shula because of what Don had done, and or Robbie, whom he accused of tampering.

In the summer of 1973, I went to Biscayne College to do two one-and-a-half hour shows on the Dolphins. I asked both Shula and Robbie to state their side of the case vis-à-vis Rosenbloom's. Their answers played on the air and Carroll saw the shows. Word came to me from Don Klosterman, his general manager, and Ed Hookstratten, his lawyer, that Carroll was upset with me for playing the Shula and Robbie statements. I had had no choice. As a reporter, I had to let them have their say. Carroll had had his many times, with me and other reporters. Carroll and I are still good friends, but for a while there was a coolness in the air.

When Andy Robustelli was named director of operations for the New York Giants not too long ago, I was startled. Remembering the way he had left the Giants, disappointed in the ownership and the way he felt he had been mistreated, I never dreamed that Wellington Mara would offer him the job. And I was even more surprised that he took the job. But pro football is in Andy's blood, it's his life's dream, so back he went to the Giants. I wasn't even at the press conference when the announcement was made.

But as soon as the announcement was made, Dick Young of *The New York Daily News* wrote a column which was headlined, "How'll Howie Let Andy Run the Giants?" The thesis of the column was that Andy and I were long-term friends, and that oddly, Andy listened closely to my football opinions, inexpert though they were. Thus the implication was drawn that I might become the invisible head of the Giants, and that their football fortunes might become even worse. And, of course, Dick knew that Mara and I don't talk because of my unstinting opposition to his abandonment of New York.

The column got some attention in New York City. I immediately called Andy, congratulated him on his new job, wished him luck and told him that I would understand if he and Jeanie decided that it was in their best interests not to see Emmy and me any more. It would not affect our underlying friendship. Andy scoffed at the notion, and said he didn't give a damn about the column.

I also wrote a letter to Wellington Mara expressing my confidence that the column would in no way hurt Andy since Wellington had seen fit to hire him and had known Andy's character over a span of 20 years.

In point of fact, when Andy and I are together now, we rarely discuss football, and then, only cursorily. After he first got the job, he did ask me, as he asked many others, whom I thought would make a good head coach. I gave him two names, Bill Arnsparger and Monty Clark of the Miami Dolphins. I recommended Monty Clark because I felt he had better leadership qualities than Arnsparger. But I felt that either would be an exceptional choice. Andy picked Bill, which is a reflection of how completely my influence dominates him.

Yes, indeed, it's a sticky wicket to be a sports reporter, to have friends in the field and to remain your own man. But you have to do it, no matter what the cost. That is, if you want to live with yourself.

Q. Who are the most courageous men you have known in sports?

A. Courage takes many forms. There is physical courage, there is moral courage. Then there is a still higher type of courage—the courage to brave pain, to live with it, to never let others know of it and to still find joy in life; to wake up in the morning with an enthusiasm for the day ahead.

Using these measuring rods, I would have to say that Jackie Robinson was the most courageous man I have ever known in sports. The other two I think of may surprise you. One is Don Klosterman; the other is Walter Kennedy.

In his younger years, Don Klosterman was a good athlete. He was a quarterback at Loyola of Los Angeles, matriculated to the National Football League, did stints with the Browns and Rams, did a very brief turn with Dallas and then wound up in the Canadian Football League with Calgary. Although primarily a football player, Klosterman loved all sports and, among other things, liked to ski. One day, in Banff, Canada, as he was coming down the slope, a woman suddenly moved directly in his path. Don instinctively swerved to avoid her. When he woke up he was in a hospital in Calgary. They didn't really expect him to wake up. The last rites had already been pronounced.

In avoiding the woman, Klosterman had lost his balance, gone over a cliff and, horrifyingly, become impaled on the limb of a tree. Paralysis was immediate because of damage to the spine, and recovery seemed impossible. He underwent eight major operations, during which time the last rites were once again administered.

Somehow, Don survived. His will was indomitable. But he could not walk, and the doctors said he would never be able to. He has no feeling at all in his legs to this day.

For Don Klosterman, the thought of being a paraplegic was too horrible to endure. Always a physical man with a positive zest for living and a craving to be active, on the go all the time, there was simply no way he could accept the prognosis of permanent paralysis of the legs. Once out of the hospital he began his own recuperative process. It took week upon week, it seemed endless, but, unbelievably, he began to make false prophets of the medical pessimists. He forced himself to crawl. And he vowed that he would walk down the aisle at his wedding.

He succeeded in doing it. He gradually converted his crawl to an upright position and slowly began to walk—well, not to walk, really, but to negotiate one leg in front of the other slowly, painfully, in the manner of a robot. And that's the way he walked down the aisle. He doesn't walk much, if any, better today. He maneuvers with a curious kind of shuffle and, indeed, some of his closest friends call him "Shuffles." He is never without pain, though you would not know this because he is almost never without a smile on his face, laughter in his eyes and a ready quip on the tip of his tongue.

The man plays golf, and it is incredible to see. He uses a golf cart, of course, to get around the course, but he is a good golfer. His upper body and hand strength are enormous.

He lives with a near-permanet kidney infection, a result of the accident. He has to take pills for this every day of his life. You can put a pin in his legs and there will be no reaction. Dr. Robert Kerlan, the brilliant Los Angeles orthopedic surgeon who is retained by the Rams, has called him the most extraordinary medical case he has ever seen. But nothing, absolutely nothing, can dull Don Klosterman's enjoyment of life and gratitude for the fact that, miraculously, he is still alive.

Often, when I am with him, I find myself complaining about the way I feel, how tired I am or some other trivial annoyance. Then I look at Don smiling at me, his handsome face unlined by the physical tragedy that befell him, and I feel ashamed.

Every day that he lives is a testimony to courage.

Walter Kennedy is in his sixties now. He doesn't look it, although he has permitted himself to develop a stomach. He has been in sports a long, long time. It began for him when he was a freshman at Notre Dame. He walked over to the athletic office one day and tremblingly asked a secretary if he could see Knute Rockne. The young lady asked him if he had an appointment and he said no. "Mr. Rockne can't see you now," she said, "but leave me your name and dormitory and I will tell him that you came by."

At that very moment the door behind her opened and out came the great coach. "What do you want, young man?" he boomed. Kennedy told him he wanted a job. Rockne asked him what he wanted to do and Walter stammered, "Anything, sir, I'll sweep out the press box." Rockne turned to an assistant and said, "Get this young fellow a broom and put him to work. He's assigned to sweep out the press box."

Kennedy has come a long way and done many things since then. For a time he was a broadcaster, working with the incomparable Ted Husing. He has been in public relations, representing industrial companies. He has been in politics, as the mayor of Stamford, Connecticut, and as the campaign manager for Senator Abraham Ribicoff of that state. And he has been the publicity man for the Harlem Globetrotters during the era of the late Abe Saperstein. It was his basketball background, together with his political stature, that led to his getting the job as commissioner of the NBA.

Despite his successes, life has been physically difficult for Walter. He has a club foot. He has lost a kidney, and the remaining kidney causes him trouble. He is frequently in the hospital because of it. He has lost hearing in his left ear. And very recently he suffered a stroke, leaving him blind in his right eye. I doubt that anyone knows this latter fact, but Walter has given me permission to disclose it.

The point is that, notwithstanding all of these handicaps, Walter's personality, like Klosterman's, has never changed. He is a man of high humor, unendingly good spirits, incapable of complaint and concerned not with himself, but with helping his friends.

One ear, one eye, one kidney and a club foot—all ignored. That's courage.

Q. Do you foresee the continuing emergence of women in sports?

A. You bet I do. We have only just begun, and, quite apart from Billie Jean King's victory over Bobby Riggs, 1973 was a year for laying the cornerstone of their emergence.

In 1973, a woman named Helen "Penny" Tweedy came into national prominence. As aristocratic in bearing as her thoroughbred Secretariat, with her manner, charm, grace and knowledge, she brought a new look to thoroughbred racing. People identified with her, as they did with the great horse. Warm and friendly, her appearances on television endeared her to many Americans, and made them aware of the fact that women are involved in the sport.

That fact was certainly embellished by the rise of Robyn Smith and Mary Bacon as jockeys. Miss Smith is an attractive women who once thought of a career in Hollywood. But she had an overriding love of animals, particularly horses. She had lost none of her femininity by becoming a jockey, and as far as her riding ability is concerned, give her the good mounts and she'll win her share of races. Riding under the silks of Alfred Gwynne Vanderbilt, Jr., she has already won several stakes races. Her problem is to get the mounts. One morning, early, I interviewed her at the Vanderbilt Stables at Belmont Park. She thinks jockey, talks jockey, lives jockey. Her only concession to femininity was that, instead of getting her own orange juice, Mr. Vanderbilt brought it to her. Then I watched her work a couple of horses, and I was caught up with they way she handled them—with assurance and total control. Thoroughbred racing is one sport where women can compete with men on equal terms.

Mary Bacon, like Robyn Smith, is attractive and absorbed with her job. She may be an even better jockey than Robyn. But the point is, she is there, and so are some others, and there will be more and more. Now the task of media people, like myself, is to keep the pressure on owners through public information, so that women jockeys get their fair share of good mounts.

Ellie Brown of Louisville, Kentucky, is the wife of John Y. Brown, the man who made Kentucky Fried Chicken a household name, and then sold the company to become a multimillionaire. John Y. began the Kentucky Colonels franchise in the American Basketball Association. He turned it over to Ellie, who serves as chairman of the board, and has an all-women board of directors. The job Ellie has done is simply incredible. She and her fellow directors have made the Colonels a community happening. They have actually gone door-to-door selling season tickets. They have made themselves a part of every community gathering. They run a dinner for their season ticket holders. They make the fans a part of the team and will talk to each and every one of them about the problems of the team. In their first year, 1973, under Ellie's leadership, the gate attendance of the Colonels went up 75 percent.

Ellie, not incidentally, is a beautiful brown-haired, hazel-eyes, young woman. The mother of three, she is the Southern belle personified, brimming over with cordiality and appeal. I can't think of anyone who could resist buying a season ticket from her.

1974 was the year of the fight for girls in Little League baseball. If there must be Little League baseball, why in the world should girls being part of it ever have become an issue? Up to the age where strength matters, girls have always played with boys, and you will find many girls between the ages of 8 and 12 who are equal to and, in some cases, superior to their male counterparts in terms of ability.

Under pressure from the federal government, girls are in the beginning stages of getting their fair share of the athletic budgets in colleges and universities. If physical fitness is so important in life—and it is—and if athletic endeavor is one key to physical fitness—which it is—why should all of the athletic budgets be allocated to men only? This antiquated notion is now in the early process of change, and you will see college after college devoting more time and money to women's sports. St. Johns University recently named a woman athletic director. Watch many others follow suit.

Was Billie Jean King a factor in at least some of this, if not all? Yes, because of the sense of pride she brought to all women, and the sense of awareness that there is a very real place for women in sports.

Q. Who is your best friend among the other sports announcers?

A. Curt Gowdy of NBC. We go back a lot of years together. On camera Curt is all seriousness, but off camera Curt is a hot dog. He is a man of dry wit, a good storyteller, a man who loves to sit up into the wee hours of the morning talking, who is not averse to lifting a cup of cheer and who relishes the flavor of his cowboy background in the good old days in his native state of Wyoming. I have had many memorable times with Curt.

One I'll never forget. It began on the way to Cheyenne. The governor of Wyoming had proclaimed a "Curt Gowdy Day" thoughout the state, and to mark the occasion, had gone so far as to name a new state park after him. Gowdy and his wife and children were understandably thrilled. From small beginnings, Curt has spent a lifetime in working his way to the top of his profession. He's done it the hard way, step by step, working at small radio stations in the hinterlands until he finally got to New York and had the opportunity to work with Mel Allen on the Yankee broadcasts. He never envisioned the day when he would go back to Cheyenne to be celebrated as one of Wyoming's most illustrious sons. But it had happened, and the governor had set up a big dinner to honor him, and to announce that the new state park would be called "Curt Gowdy Park."

I was invited to speak at the affair on behalf of Curt's colleagues. I had never been to Wyoming before, nor had Emmy. We caught up with Curt in Los Angeles. Together with Carl Lindemann, head of NBC Sports, Carl's wife, Cissy, and Phil Harris, the entertainer and an old friend of Curt's, we all flew to Denver. We were to fly a chartered plane from Denver to Cheyenne. The plane was a two-engine job, with tight seating capacity. The six of us were jammed in together,

Curt, Carl and I sitting side by side, with Phil, Emmy and Cissy facing us.

The flight from Denver to Cheyenne is a short one, but we were buffeted by heavy winds. Phil Harris is terrified of flying, especially in a charter. As we were rocking about in the wind currents, Phil became ashen pale. I was talking with Curt when I looked toward Phil and noticed that he had a strong clasp on my wife's knee. My instant reaction was to tell him to take his hand the hell off. But I knew Phil Harris and I knew his wife, Alice Faye, and I suspected that his days of sexual lust are long past, so I stilled my impulse even as I realized that, in some strange way, Emmy's knee was affording Phil a sense of security. It was like a baby sucking his thumb.

When we landed in Cheyenne, Phil was off the plane before the rest of us could even move.

A festive scene awaited us at the airport, a colorful replica of frontier days. A cowboy band was strumming country music and half the town, with banners and pennants waving, appeared to be on hand, including, of course, Curt's wife, Gerry, and his three children. The old cowboy-turned-broadcaster was beaming. "You're in my country now," he chortled. "They do things right out here. Just look at that." And he pointed to an ancient stagecoach, which looked authentic enough to have been used in the John Ford movie of the same name.

Even as Gowdy motioned to the stagecoach, he, Carl and I were ushered into it. We were getting the royal treatment, a stagecoach ride through town to The Hitching Post, the motel where we were to stay and where the dinner was to be held. As we drove off, Carl and I began to remonstrate with Curt. "What about the girls?" we asked. "They'll get lost in the crowd."

"Don't worry about them," he answered in that flat tone of his, with just a trace of annoyance in his voice. "I told you, you're in my country now. We take care of our women here."

Thus reassured, Carl and I sat back to take in the scene and enjoy the ride. I'll probably never see anything like it again. I felt like I did when I was a kid, at the movies on a Saturday afternoon watching Tom Mix or Buck Jones being welcomed into town. Only this time it was Curt Gowdy, as people in the streets waved to Curt and store windows had signs of welcome. It was a heart-warming experience, and I felt very proud for Curt.

When we got to The Hitching Post, however, and 20 minutes elapsed with no sign of Emmy and Cissy, I began to get edgy. So did Carl. "What are you worried about?" Gowdy growled. "What's going to happen to them in Cheyenne?" Damned if I knew, but when another 15 minutes passed, I sure was going to find out. Carl and I went out in front of the motel to get a car to take us back to the airport to look for them, when a car drove up and out came Emmy and Cissy. They had been left stranded at the airport, had walked for about eight blocks and had finally hitched a ride to the motel.

I spun around toward Gowdy and spat out, "We're in your country now, huh. Hell of a way to treat our women." Curt flushed and stuttered, "I'll find out who blew this thing." The image of the big man from the West had crashed. To this day, whenever Curt starts telling us about Western courtesy, and how he's king when he goes back home, Lindemann and I shut him up with a reminder of how our wives were abandoned at the Cheyenne airport.

By the way, after the dinner the next night we drove back to Denver. Phil Harris didn't want to risk the chartered plane again. And I didn't want his hand on Emmy's knee. . . .

Then there was the night of the great blackout in the Northeast. On that night, Mel Allen was being feted at a dinner in a temple in Norwalk, Connecticut, where Mel had always commanded a booming popularity. Many of Mel's sportscaster colleagues were joining in for the occasion because Mel had been fired by the Yankees and it was a most difficult time for him. Among those who were to be present were Chris Schenkel, Lindsey Nelson, Phil Rizzuto, Jerry Coleman, Bob Murphy, Curt Gowdy and I—all men who had known Mel and worked with him for many years.

The trip to Norwalk started innocently enough. Schenkel, Gowdy and I were to meet Sonney Werblin and drive up in his limousine. Sonny was then running the New York Jets, but in his earlier days as an agent with the Music Corporation of America, he had represented Mel. We got into Werblin's car at Madison Avenue and 57th Street, where the Jets' offices are, and proceeded northward up Madison Avenue. When we hit 65th Street, the city suddenly became dark. No street lights, no office lights, no lights anywhere. None of us gave a remote thought at the time to the idea that we had been struck by a mass blackout that would envelop much of the northeastern area of the nation. We did suppose that something had gone wrong with some local power units of Consolidated Edison, but we expected that the breakdown would be repaired in short order. So, at a reduced speed we wended our way northward, out of New York City, through Westchester County and on into Connecticut. But the darkness persisted and we virtually inched our way. The car radio kept us informed as to what was going on, and only through this means did we learn of the massive nature of the blackout. We grew more and more concerned, first as to whether we should continue on the trip and then, more importantly, about our families. Sonny grabbed the phone in the car, called home and got no answer. He was disturbed. Then the phone line was jammed, so that none of the rest of us could reach our families. We all began to worry, but we kept going. It was a hairy drive, with a mutual sense of unease controlling the atmosphere. After what seemed forever, we snaked our way into the driveway of the temple. I don't know how we ever found it. Unbelievably, the place was packed with cars. We went inside and witnessed a truly remarkable scene. The ballroom was brilliant with candlelight, and more than 1000 people had braved the blackout to honor Mel. These were Connecticut people, Mel's home folk, and they loved him. Nothing could deter their enthusiasm.

Amazingly, too, all the other announcers were already there. I had never seen Mel look happier. But he had to know we would all be there. Mel had been a giant in our profession and had, in one way or another, helped each and every one of us.

We had all chipped in for a gift for Mel. We decided to give him—it was Chris's idea—one of those old, big, round, 1920s style radio microphones. And Chris had had it gold plated. It was a beautiful thing, a unique gift and one that Mel would be certain to treasure.

I was the emcee that evening and, in view of the blackout,

our abiding concern was to get the affair moving swiftly and over as quickly as possible. One by one I called on Mel's past associates. Each was warm, brief, to the point. There were some tears shed that night as old times were recalled. But the blackout hovered in all of our minds. During the course of the evening, Chris sneaked out momentarily to try to reach his wife on the phone. He still couldn't, and his worry grew. The same was true of nearly all of us.

Finally I got to Werblin who was to make the presentation to Allen. The way he had it figured out, we would be done and on our way by 10:30 P.M. It was all up to Mel.

The "Voice of the Yankees" got up in front of that audience and began this way:

Folks, this occasion reminds me of a time at Yankee Stadium. Tommy Henrich was coming up to bat. It was to be his last trip to the plate before entering the military service in World War II. Dizzy Trout was on the mound against him. The public-address announcer told the crowd that it would be Tommy's last at bat for the duration. The fans stood as one and gave Henrich an ovation. They wouldn't stop cheering, but "Old Reliable" stayed right there in the batter's box. He wouldn't budge. Trout stepped off the mound and said, "Get the hell out of there, Tom. You'll never have a moment like this again." So Henrich finally stepped out of the box, doffed his cap and the crowd cheered and cheered. Gentlemen, that's the way I felt tonight.

Everyone in that Norwalk, Connecticut temple stood up and clapped. It was a moving, tender moment. Curt Gowdy, who had been sitting on my left, slapped me on the back as we sat down and said, "He did it. What a tag line. What a way to go out."

One hour later, Curt was still at the dais, his head drooping in slumber, moving only when he snored lazily. Mel Allen was still speaking. He was delivering a discourse on the dangers of communism. I kept waking Gowdy up, but he would lapse back immediately into the quiet comfort of his dreams. Schenkel, Werblin and the others fidgeted to a point of total exasperation. Chris muttered to me under his breath, "Dammit, you've got to close this thing out." "How do I do it?" I asked. "Do I grab him by the shoulders and sit him down?" It was interminable, but finally it was over and everyone fled. Curt and I got a lift from a neighbor who drove us to my home in Pound Ridge.

The lights were on. Pound Ridge had had electricity restored at about 11:00 P.M. Emmy was waiting up for us—it was well after midnight—and she told us that New York City was still dark. Curt called his wife at their home in Wellsley Hills and learned that everyone was fine there. Now he was alive again. Bed was not for him. At about three in the morning he was still telling Emmy about Mel Allen's speech, about how he had blown the best tag line Gowdy had ever heard and how we all could have gotten home hours earlier. "What the hell has communism got to do with a sports banquet?" he complained. "That Henrich story, that was great."

At three-thirty "The Cowboy" was spinning tales of Ted Williams.

At four I persuaded him to go to bed.

At four-fifteen I could hear him talking to himself about Tommy Henrich.

At four-thirty he was snoring—again

CHAPTER 10

THE BOOTH AND THE BOX: SPORTS JOURNALISM

Q. You always seem to be at odds with sportswriters. Are there any you respect?

A. I respect a great many, particularly among the columnists. I think that Mel Durslag of *The Los Angeles Herald Examiner,* a syndicated columnist, is probably the soundest, most knowledgeable sportswriter in the country. He works very hard, is dedicated, and he gets inside the issues of sports much more than most and with a much greater wisdom and insight than most. For instance, the man understands a balance sheet. As simple as that may sound, many sportswriters have never even looked at a balance sheet. They don't know what it's all about; don't know the economics of the sports they cover; aren't concerned with all the factors that surround the sports they cover other than what happens on the diamond, or gridiron, or basketball court or hockey rink itself. Durslag does. He is well placed, well connected.

I think that Jim Murray, another syndicated columnist with *The Los Angeles Times,* is a brilliant satirist, one of the very few who understands the difference between satire and sarcasm—and it is a very fine line. Murray has the intellect to keep sports in its proper perspective, which means that he never solemnizes it.

I think that Jerry Izenberg of *The Newark Star-Ledger* and the *Newhouse Press* is an exceptional writer. There is a tendency toward redundancy in his style, but he is a dead-honest writer and he does have a great way with words. I also have great regard for Cooper Rollow of *The Chicago Tribune* and Rick Talley of *Chicago Today* and *The Chicago Tribune*. Jack Murphy of *The San Diego Union* is a fine columnist who is unafraid to put the finger on anybody, and who also has the capacity to combine humor with insight. Blackie Sherrod of *The Dallas Times Herald* is another I respect. Mickey Herskowitz in Houston, who worked on my first book with me, has exceptional humor, exceptional wit and is one of the truly fine sportswriters in the country. Ed Pople of *The Miami Herald* is still another.

Red Smith of *The New York Times* was my original hero when I went into sports. I think he is one of the finest writers I have ever read, in terms of drollery, wit, wryness and a perspective about life and about the role of sports in life.

Robert Lipsyte, who used to write for *The Times,* is an outstanding writer, with a great sensitivity, whose only problem, it seems to me, is that sometimes he can be a trifle obsure. Dan Jenkins of *Sports Illustrated* and Pete Axthelm of *Newsweek* are gifted men. There are many others I could name.

Q. I read that in a speech in Orlando, Florida, you called all sportswriters dishonest. Do you really believe that?

A. No, and I never said it. The question refers to a November 1973 talk I gave to the Managing Editors Association of American Newspapers. I was invited to speak before this august group by Wick Temple, the sports editor of the Associated Press, and Will Grimsley, the Associated Press's sports columnist. I know of three columnists who took an abbreviated wire-copy story on my speech and then wrote columns about it. That wire-copy story made it appear that I had called all sportswriters dishonest. The three columnists to whom I allude were Shirley Povich of *The Washington Post,* Bob Lancaster of *The Knight Press* and Dave Condon of *The Chicago Tribune.* Not one of these three was present at my speech. Not one of them called me to discover what I had actually said. So what they wrote about me, and what I had presumably said, was the shabbiest kind of journalism. In fact, it was no journalism at all.

As everyone who was present knows, and they represented
the top people in the newspaper industry, the thrust of my
talk related to the whole of sports journalism, both broadcast
and print. I decried the absence of journalism in the sports-
broadcast profession. I pointed out that at the local level,
broadcasters were paid by teams, not by the stations which
transmitted the games. I emphasized that this was a failure of
my industry and a forfeiture of obligation and responsibility.

I made it clear that the airwaves are publicly owned and that
stations are publicly licensed and subject to the jurisdiction of
the Federal Communications Commission. I pointed out that
when station operators seek to have their licenses renewed,
they are the ones who must go before the FCC, not owners of
sports franchises. They are the ones who are responsible for
what is transmitted through their facilities over the airwaves,
not owners of sports franchises.

And so, I asked, how dare the station operators allow the
owners to hire the announcers?

And how, I further asked, could we possibly get any journalism into the verbal transmission of a contest? How could an
announcer tell some truths about the game he is witnessing,
about the performances of the respective players, about pau-
city of attendance and about many other things that his boss,
the *franchise owner,* might find unpleasant? The answer, I
stated, was that he couldn't. He would be fired, the way Red
Barber was fired by the Yankees!

I did not stop there. I moved on to the network level and
accentuated the fact that fear dominates the television industry when it comes to sports—fear of sponsors, fear of advertising agencies, fear of commissioners, fear of owners, fear of
offending any of them. And, finally, the biggest fear of all:
The fear of losing the right to telecast the event to a competitor because your announcer has offended one or more of
the foregoing groups.

Out of this fear there has developed some unholy procedures in network television sports such as allowing sponsors
or commissioners or owners to have a right of approval over
the announcers assigned to cover the events. And then the
announcer himself is riddled with fear, fear of saying any-

thing that might cost him his job. The net result is the inhibition of journalism. Say only the nice things. Say only the right things, not from the public point of view, not in terms of truth, but in terms of the selfish interests of the parties involved.

I also pointed out that I had been fortunate in having a boss like Roone Arledge, who placed no restriction on me and who, when he signed a contract with the NFL for *Monday Night Football,* refused to give Commissioner Pete Rozell announcer approval.

I then added that I was wholeheartedly in favor of the FCC investigation of sports announcers, which was taking place at that time. The investigation had been initiated because of a series of articles in *The Washington Star News,* citing chapter and verse on the ills of sports broadcasting, and the absence of journalism therein.

Then, and only then, did I get to the subject of sportswriters.

Having stated the evils inherent within my own profession, I commented that the sportswriting profession was not without sin. But even before I did that, I established that sports-print journalism had one prepossessing advantage over sports-broadcast journalism. This advantage lay in columnization, opinion and commentary in written form. This is an integral and significant part of journalism in any area. Because of limitations of broadcast time and the absence of courage, there is almost none of it in sports broadcasting. I made careful note of the fact that I was there in Orlando because of my respect for Will Grimsley, and I mentioned my admiration of others like Red Smith.

Then I dealt with what I consider to be two major failures in the sportswriting business, and laid the blame for one of those failures on certain publishers. The first failure, I indicated, was that some newspapers in this country still permit writers who are assigned to cover teams to travel, eat and live on the road at club expense. This creates a clear conflict of interest and is a practice that should be dispensed with immediately. I told the audience, by way of illustration, that there was a newspaper in New York and one in Boston that continued to adhere to this practice. Because I did not want to embarrass anyone in that room, I did not name the papers.

I also took issue with the fact that many sportswriters write promotional films for teams they cover, and get paid by the ball club for it. Also, they write articles for club programs. I suggested that this, too, could be construed as conflict of interest and that a sportswriter's responsibility was solely to his newspaper and to its readers.

I then launched into the philosophy of sportswriting, the problem of attracting as many readers as possible, a problem which is much like that in the television industry where we must attract as many viewers as possible. I drew the analogy that, in general, the majority readership is in the young-adult age bracket, just as the majority viewership is. I said that, in my opinion, too many sportswriters were "old world," and that this was reflected in their incessant attack upon *Monday Night Football* because its presentation is a marked departure from traditional game presentations of the past. I suggested that there should be a marked departure in current sportswriting as well. Too many sportswriters merely use press releases and rewrite them. I added that the daily AP "Sportwhirl" began almost without exception with baseball items, no matter what else had happened in the world of sports. This, I said, was a religious adherence to the past.

I wound up by saying that I thought that sportswriters, in general, were neglecting the great issues in sports on the grounds that the fans were not interested. I pointed to matters like the frustration of our young athletes by the AAU and the NCAA, the malfeasances of the U.S. Olympic Committee, legislation in connection with both, carpetbagging of franchises, projections concerning the future of sports and all of the other problems that now draw the sports arena into the economics, politics, law and sociology of this country. And I submitted that my own success in my profession related to my dealing in depth with these subjects.

Therefore, I concluded, the fans—especially the young adults—are interested. But even if they weren't, such matters should be treated within the sports pages more than they are because it is right to do so, it is the function of journalism to do so. That was what I actually said, and it needed saying.

But David Condon wrote, among other things, that the managing editors should know better than to ask a sports announcer to address them on any area of the newspaper business. Such thinking might have enjoyed a place in medieval times, but not now. Norman Miller of *The New York Daily News* wrote a letter to Wick Temple assailing me and expressing his disgust with the fact that I was asked to talk before a newspaper assemblage.

Unwittingly, Condon, Miller, Povich and Lancaster were making my very point. Nobody outside of their own little fraternity could offer his own observations of their profession. But they could vilify me without ever calling me, going to the source to see what I had really said, or for that matter, calling Wick Temple or Will Grimsley to discover what the real content of my speech had been. No, in their minds, the sportswriting fraternity is sacrosanct, a holy little group of self-appointed experts. Temple and Grimsley are of another ilk. They have an abiding concern about improving the journalistic standards of their profession, as I have about mine. And the three of us agreed that there would be retaliation against me by any number of sportswriters. But Wick didn't give a damn, and neither did I. The speech was so well received that the association committee, charged with the continuing study of sports-print journalism, grew in number on the spot from 2 to 16, the first time the association had shown a major interest in sportswriting.

In the question-and-answer period after the speech, somebody told me that he had read that I had been silenced by the NFL because of statements I had made on *Monday Night Football* concerning the dullness of the game due to an overabundance of field goals. The questioner was from Florida, and I knew exactly where he had read it. My sister-in-law had sent my wife a column by John Crittendon of *The Mami News*. Crittendon quoted a source in the commissioner's office with the statement that I had been silenced. I told the questioner that Crittendon had never called me; that nobody from Rozelle's office had ever called me on the subject, and that if the commissioner, himself, called me to try to tell me what to say or how to say it, I would expose him. And then I told the questioner that what Crittendon had done was exactly the kind of failure in sports journalism that I had been talking about, and that I thought the association members should be concerned with.

Give me a guy like Red Smith. While I was in Caracas for the Foreman-Norton fight, I was in the hotel bar with Terry Jastrow, the producer of the fight telecast. Red Smith walked in, I waved to him and he shot right toward me, his usually whimsical brow now furrowed. "Did you say that all sportswriters were dishonest in a speech you made?"

I sat back and told him in essence what I have just said here. Then we had a drink. I toasted him because like a true reporter, he had gone to the source.

By the way, those sportswriters who don't want criticism from broadcasters now have much more than just Howard Cosell to worry about. CBS's *Sixty Minutes* devoted a section of one show to so-called free rides for the journalists, both in broadcast and in print. Sportswriters were singled out as perhaps the worst offenders. WNET did a show on journalism called *Behind the Lines.* It made the very points I had made in my speech at Orlando, devoted abut five minutes to sportswriters and stated that, "nowhere have ethics been more of a problem than on the sports pages."

Q. Why do so many sportswriters knock sports announcers and, in particular, you?

A. In the first place, no one is above being knocked. In the second place, many sportswriters have a built-in antipathy toward television as a medium. The medium, itself, has stolen much of their thunder. People see the event as it happens, know for themselves what did happen and often, by way of post-event interviews, get the inside of what happened right on the spot. For those writers who are assigned to cover the event, it has changed the whole nature of their job. They have to be more thoughtful, more creative. A mere recital of what happened in the game on the day after most people have seen it constitutes a redundancy. The sportswriter is materially reduced not just in his function, but in his importance. This has caused many a sportswriter to feel bitterness and envy: Bitterness over the fact that he has a declining significance, envy in the fact that his pay scale is far less than that of the average announcer.

As to why I so often seem to be the object of their disaffection, one reason is that I am not afraid to criticize them, to take them on. Another is that I am more competitive with them in the sense that I engage in commentary and am more concerned with breaking news stories than my colleagues are. They also resent my close connections with many of the athletes and front-office people, which produce scoops.

Once, for instance, I did a show on a split screen with Vida Blue, the Oakland pitcher, and his lawyer. Blue announced that he was ending his holdout and would fly to Boston that night to join his team.

A couple of days later, Dick Young of *The New York Daily News* wrote that some of his colleagues were upset about my alleged scoop with Vida Blue. It was no scoop at all, he indicated. There was a rumor, he wrote, that ABC had paid $7500 to Blue for the interview. This only *proved*, he added, that Blue and I were just a couple of paid employees working for television.

Vida Blue was never paid one cent for the interview.

Then there was the time that I recounted earlier in this book when Joe Frazier and Muhammad Ali wrestled to the floor in an ABC studio while I was doing a prefight *Wide World of Sports* show with them. The story made front-page news. Young wrote that the whole thing was a phony, a buildup for a fight. He wasn't even there! What he wrote so incensed a colleague, Rick Talley of *The Chicago Tribune*, that Talley publicly rebuked Dick in Talley's own column. Talley had been in the studio and had written the truth—that the incident was no put-on.

None of this is to say that I don't deserve some of the raps I get. I'm a constant needler, especially where certain writers are concerned, and thus induce resentment as a natural consequence of my own actions.

I will say this, however. When a writer engages in a personal vendetta against an announcer—any announcer—over a long span of years, he does two things. He lowers his own credibility and lowers the standards of his profession, thus embarrassing his colleagues.

Q. Do you mind having to promote forthcoming ABC shows on *Monday Night Football?*

A. Yes, I mind. I wish I didn't have to do it, but I resent being singled out and criticized by some sportswriters for doing it. All announcers do it under company orders, yet some columnists have labeled me a "company prostitute" for doing it. This is a cheap shot of the lowest order, and people in glass houses shouldn't throw stones.

The whole issue of on-air promotion on *Monday Night Football* reached its peak toward the end of the 1973 season. The issue arose because the number of on-air promotions materially increased at that time. There was a business reason for it. ABC Sports had lost NBA basketball to CBS. We were embarking upon a whole new program structure on Sundays to make up for that loss which would begin in January. Our new lineup would include, for the first time, a Sunday *Wide World of Sports* as well as the Saturday presentation. It would include an expanded *Superstars,* and it would also have my *Magazine* show. In addition, we had the Sugar Bowl Game coming up on New Year's Eve between Notre Dame and Alabama, both unbeaten, for the National Collegiate Championship.

Roone Arledge put out a memorandum pointing out that we had whole new competitive problems with CBS because that network now had the NBA. He emphasized that we had to impress upon our viewers the nature of our new shows for January and that, in his words, "On-air promotion is the lifeblood" of our battle. Thus, under his orders, the number of promotions was escalated. He had every right to do this. In fact, it was necessary for him to do this, in his everlasting struggle to stay ahead of his business rivals. No man has a death wish. And it is my responsibility and obligation when my employer tells me to do something to do it, unless by doing it I am defying a principle so important that I couldn't keep my self-respect. Such a principle is not remotely involved in on-the-air promotion.

When I promote an upcoming program it is to help attract viewers which we need in order to present future programs. In our business, without viewers you're out of business. When I broadcast the game itself, if the contest stinks, I say so. I don't shill, and never have during any broadcast I have done, with regard to the event I am covering. Joe Falls of the *Detroit Free Press* last season quoted Bob Cochran, head of TV and radio in the NFL commissioner's office, as saying, "It takes us a week after a game to repair the damage Cosell does." Cochran was presumably talking about statements I had made characterizing the dullness of Detroit's 31–6 victory over Atlanta. And that to me is the test of a shill: Does a man tell the truth about what he is seeing, or does he color it honey because his company is carrying it? I don't. Quite the contrary, remember the uproar I created the first year of *Monday Night Football* just by telling a few simple truths of a type not told before in the transmission of a contest?

So as far as I am concerned, I violated no personal principle in reading on-air promotions but was, instead, fulfilling my obligation to my boss and to my company. I don't know how much good those promotions did for our new shows. I do know that the returns are now all in and, for the period January 1–March 31, 1974, of 15 weekend sports series, the top eight rated shows were ABC presentations. The NBA on CBS was clobbered. The NHL on NBC was almost invisible. And so next year, we will have the advertisers necessary to insure the continuing presentation of programs that the public has indicated it likes and wants.

I have said that I don't like doing the promotions. I don't like doing them because they interrupt the continuity of a telecast, and they do make a reporter sound like a promoter. But as I have pointed out, there is no other choice and there is no relationship between that which I say about the contest I am reporting upon and the promotion of an upcoming program.

I could ask these questions of all those who have written calling me a "company prostitute" for reading on-air promotions: why have you not criticized Roone Arledge for ordering them to be read? Why have you not singled out other sports announcers—because all of us read them—and labeled them "company prostitutes"?

And then I would ask another question of these writers —who do you think you're kidding? When you write for the sports page, all around you on that page, in most cases, are commercial advertisements. Without those ads, your papers couldn't live, wouldn't survive. Your advertising department takes care of those ads. They go out and sell them, but your industry is as necessarily commercial as ours. Yet, my industry is always chewed out for commerical interruptions. Also, when it comes to promotion, time after time, I read promotional blurbs in the sports pages as to what the writers will be covering in the future, and which writers will be covering what games and where. I'll read blurbs about how good the writers are, what their special insights are.

But more than that. *The Chicago Tribune,* for instance, sponsors the annual Collegiate Football Allstar-NFL Champion Game. It is played for charity, for a good cause. *The Tribune* spends weeks in advance of the game promoting it, assigns a writer to the Allstars' camp for daily reports and also has daily reports out of the NFL champions' training camp (except for this season when the players' strike canceled the game). *The New York Daily News* sponsors the New York Golden Gloves. They engage in weeks of promotion for that event. I repeat the question: Who are they kidding?

Q. You always talk about truth in sports. What makes you think the public wants it, and who says you tell it?

A. Not everybody does want to hear the truth, especially in the closely guarded ivory tower that the world of sports has become. But that is not the question. The question is: What is right, and what are the duties and obligations of a journalist? Many people to this day do not want to hear the truth about Watergate, and the truth about the corruption that has been disclosed in their government. Nonetheless, two young reporters on *The Washington Post,* Bob Woodward and Carl Bernstein, have performed an historic role in journalism, and an historic service to the American people by a steadfast and remarkable pursuit of truth in the Watergate case. What they did was right, and what they did was in conformance with their duties and obligations to a total society. It should be no different in reporting and commenting about sports.

As to the question of whether or not I tell the truth, the answer is that I tell it as I see it. I can do no more than that, and certainly I have no monopoly on truth or anything else. Katherine Fullerton Gerould in her classic essay, "What Then, Is Culture?", began by quoting Sir Francis Bacon, "What is truth, said jesting Pilate, and would not stay for an answer." The question is well taken. Truth on any matter is always subject to interpretation. This is why, in law, we have a built-in system of evidentiary safeguards. Before testimony can be admitted into evidence, a foundation must be laid, corroborating testimony provided and so on. You don't often have this kind of situation in sports, but what you do have are owner groups and player groups issuing self-serving statements, plus the problems I enumerated in my Orlando speech: sports announcers employed by teams so that these announcers lose credibility; pressures upon network announcers from sponsors, advertising agencies, networks, commissioners and owners. And all too often, sportswriters identify with given teams and given sports for a wide variety of reasons. Thus the credibility of such writers can be impaired.

I do not pretend that in my career I have not been subjected to pressures similar to those placed on my colleagues, but I have been fortunate, in the main, in escaping them. As examples, ABC Sports carries NCAA football, yet I have never let this deter me in my assault upon the evils of big-time college recruitment, nor have I weakened, at all, in my attacks upon the NCAA for their continuing jurisdictional hassle with the AAU that results in injustices to young athletes. Neither have I ever refrained from calling a game or a fight dull; nor an athlete something less than sensational in his performance; nor the fans something less than seemly in their behavior. Nor have I hesitated in excoriating the U.S. Olympic Committee for its mistakes, or in exposing individual coaching mistakes.

These stands are not always popular but, in my judgment, they are right. And that is telling the truth as I see it.

Q. You are always knocking sports. How can you bite the hand that feeds you?
A. This is a question that I am asked frequently, and I am always surprised to hear it because I believe it is based upon utterly false premises. In the first place, the hand that feeds

me is the American Broadcasting Company—not any commissioner of sport, not any league, not any owner, not the
NCAA, not the AAU and not any Olympic Committee. I am a
reporter-commentator and my obligation and responsibility is
to my employer and to the American public.

In the second place, you are not knocking sports when you
are dealing with defiances of the public interest by certain
sports operators, or laying bare injustices imposed upon individuals. To be specific, is it knocking sports to point out that an
owner is doing the wrong thing when he carpetbags his
franchise from one city to another even though he is making a
profit in the city from which he is departing? Walter O'Malley
did this with the Brooklyn Dodgers, and now Wellington
Mara is doing it with the New York Giants. Is it knocking
sports to point out that the U.S. Olympic Committee failed to
do its job and thus cost a 15-year-old California lad a gold
medal in the swimming competition at Munich? Is it knocking
sports to reveal that Chris Dunn of Colgate, the nation's
leading indoor high-jumper, can't leap against the Russians in
a meet at Richmond, Virginia, because of a power struggle
between the AAU and the NCAA? Is it knocking sports to
decry the action of a politically appointed boxing commissioner when he strips a heavyweight champion of his title and
his license to fight in violation of guarantees lodged in the
Fifth and Fourteenth Amendments to the Constitution?

I suggest that such stands do not knock sports but, rather,
help sports—help by protecting public and individual interests that deserve protection, and by bringing honesty to an
area of life that has its share of dishonesty, like any other part
of life. It must be realized, once and for all, that sports are not
separate and apart from life, a special "wonderland" where
everything is pure and sacred and above criticism. A football
game is not a holy sacrament, and baseball does not truly
equate with apple pie and motherhood and the American
flag. I suggest that in American society today, it is time to tell
it like it is—and that includes sports.

Q. Do you think sports is news or entertainment, and which
category do you think *Monday Night Football* falls into?

A. Sports is both news and entertainment, and there is absolutely no conflict in that statement. Certainly, who wins or loses a game is news. More significantly, player strikes, owner lockouts, the race for Ruth by Hank Aaron, the professional football war, the Olympic games are all news.

But the transmission of a contest is also entertainment, and if it fails in this regard then the likelihood is that games won't be transmitted the following year because of absence of sufficient viewers to attract an advertiser. This is especially true with respect to the transmission of a contest in prime-time television (the hours between 7:30 and 11 P.M.).

To make clear what I am saying, one must understand the basics of the broadcasting business. ABC is currently paying more than $18 million for the right to televise NFL *Monday Night Football* for the next four years. To make back that tidy outlay, we must get $100,000 per commercial minute during each game we televise; to make it back, that is, and show a profit. This means, in round numbers, that to be able to get advertisers to spend $100,000 for a one-minute commercial, we must attract an average of between 30- and 40-million viewers a game, which is no small order.

The difficulty in attracting this number of viewers, on the average, is complicated by a number of factors. Hard-core football fans do not exist in sufficient quantity to sustain the average. And, in prime time, the competition for viewership is fierce. The first year of *Monday Night Football*, for example, we had to go against Carol Burnett, a great performer with an enormously popular show, and Lucille Ball and Doris Day. They were opposite us on CBS. On NBC we had to face the *Monday Night Movie*, with one hit show after another going head-to-head against us. Try Liz Taylor in *Cat on a Hot Tin Roof* for size.

Now add to such competition the carefully researched fact that the audience composition in prime time consists substantially of women, who, in the past, were not considered to be football fans. How could you get them to tune in to football games?

The problems seemed weighty. All the betting odds in the television industry were against the success of *Monday Night*

Football. This is why CBS and NBC, both of which had had first crack at the package, turned it down. They were confident it would fail. Indeed, a couple of times in the past CBS had tried pro football in prime time—with Vince Lombardi's Green Bay Packers—and on one of those occasions, when the game was opposed by a *Miss America Contest,* professional football was a pitiful loser in the ratings.

ABC was aware of all this when it bought *Monday Night Football,* particularly Roone Arledge. He also knew what the other two networks knew—that with both CBS and NBC having professional football on the air on Sunday afternoons, there was the problem of oversaturation, or so it seemed.

In the light of all of the foregoing, Arledge decided that the presentation of *Monday Night Football* had to be different from other football presentations. He knew that not every game is exciting, and that not every game features teams competing for the playoffs and for the ultimate Super Bowl victory. He also believed that the time had come for a change from what he felt were the relatively static telecasts of the other two networks. Research revealed that the majority of viewers lay in the young-adult population, people who had been growing up in swiftly changing, severely trying, turbulent, even tormented times. Such people would not be likely, after a long day's work, to be responsive to a studiedly serious transmission of a football contest placed in the context of an event solemn enough to be originating from St. Patrick's Cathedral. Furthermore, technical excellence—pictures, isolation, dual isolation, slow motion and replays—would not be enough. Arledge, the great innovator in these areas, is smart enough to know that these techniques are no substitute for human communication, and even more, that the other networks now had the same technical skills.

The answer, he decided, lay in the verbal presentation. Be better in your technical presentation than the others, add more cameras, humanize the athletes with close-up face shots. Fine. Give all the information relative to the game. Let the play-by-play announcer, as a kind of public-address announcer, do that. But above all this, add insight and humor and frankness to the telecasts. If a game is bad, admit it, and

crack jokes. If a player lapses, say so. The solution as he hopefully saw it: "Dandy" Don and "Humble" Howard.

As the American public now knows, the whole thing
worked. Some nights we had great games, some nights we had
disasters. But we kept the audience, and steadily built it. We
were providing news and entertainment. *Monday Night Football* actually changed the social habits of millions of Americans. What was wrong with this? Nothing, except for the fact
that beginning with the second year of the package in 1971,
the two competitive networks began their attack upon us.
Neglecting the fact that they were now moving *The Carol
Burnett Show* to another night, CBS called us clowns, said we
were strictly show business and decried the fact that we were
"ignoring" the game. Hogwash. NBC said practically the same
thing. More hogwash.

But during that second year, and even during the third and
fourth years of *Monday Night Football,* many football writers
took up the chant. It's entertainment, they would write, not
football. Even more hogwash. Yet all of this probably prompted the basic question: Is sports news or entertainment?

I have already said it is *both,* and have indicated that serious
sports news should be dealt with soberly, and less serious
sports news should be treated more lightly. And the special
nature of *Monday Night Football,* with its unique problems,
required even different treatment.

This latter fact is not something football writers necessarily
understand, nor should they. But the public should. And the
public quite apparently does, as the ratings show. Television
—in this case sports television—does not program for the
tastes and wishes of a tiny body of writers, each of whom is
read by a relative handful of people. They do not have the
problem of attracting 30 million viewers, and more, at one
time. They don't have go get back $100,000 a minute for every
paragraph they write. If they did, they could not possibly keep
their jobs with their endless recitals of odd-man fronts, seams
in the zone and all the rest of their tired dictionary of football
clichés. I know one writer on a New York paper who sets
three carefully prepared charts in front of him. He works over
these charts during the course of a game and fills them with

detailed minutiae which almost requires a microscope to read. And when he gets it all done, nobody gives a damn. He is foremost among those who cry, when he writes of *Monday Night Football,* "It's entertainment, not football."

Wrong. It's both. And it's damned well going to stay that way until the public starts tuning out. Because there will be even more games for him to chart this year. The World Football League has been born, and the danger of oversaturation will be greater than ever. But ABC will not be like the others. We'll be number one because we make football entertaining.

Q. What do you think is your role on the *Monday Night Football* telecasts?

A. As I see it, I have a number of functions. First, I have to provide the pace for the telecast by serving as a catalyst for Frank Gifford and, in the past, for "Dandy" Don Meredith. I will have to do the same with Fred "The Hammer" Williamson. Second, I have to give the game a perspective, spotting the telecast with quick analytical recapitulations and analyses, highlighting the reasons for one team's dominance and the other team's failure. Third, I have to provide human insights into the players, anecdotal or otherwise, when it is timely to do so; that is to say, when a given player calls attention to himself by his performance, or when the absence of a given player has a relevance. We have found this human dimension to be very important in terms of attracting women viewers. Fourth, I have to do the highlights of the previous day's games for the half-time interlude, a phase of the total telecast that seems to have become as important to many viewers as the game itself. And fifth, I must always be prepared to amplify, clarify or embellish—when I deem it proper—something said by either of my colleagues.

I must be especially prepared for games that are not competitive, and we have had a number of these. We cannot afford loss of viewership and this is where personality becomes vital to the oral presentation. This, too, is where my company feels "Dandy" and I had maximum value. We would kid one another endlessly, and kid the game. Fortunately, the chemistry we engendered worked.

Q. What do you think of the trend of ex-athletes becoming sports commentators? Are they more knowledgeable because they have played the game?

A. I am really tired of answering this question. I have expressed my views on the matter many times, and they haven't changed. Yet I keep facing the question again and again, everywhere I go.

In general, I am against hiring ex-athletes as announcers, and I consider it a cheap concession by my industry to commercial expedience. In other words, it's an effort to make a quick sale to a sponsor based upon name value, and without regard to background, ability and qualifications.

In exploring the matter, one must distinguish between the different ways in which ex-athletes are used on the air. One must also look, subjectively, upon the individual backgrounds and training of ex-athletes who are employed as announcers.

It is a matter of fact that most ex-athletes, when placed on the air, have had little or no training or education in journalism, communications and verbal delivery. This being true, how in the world, at the local broadcast level can a station hire an ex-athlete and put him on the air as an all-purpose sports reporter? Journalism is a profession of the highest order. It has never been more important to this nation than now. Why debase journalism in the world of sports broadcasting? What does the ex-athlete know about the who, what, when, where, how and why of a story—the very nuts and bolts of journalism? How many stories has he been out on, and had to investigate and develop? What has been his training for this? How many people has he interviewed? Where has he learned how to pursue an answer to a question and develop an interview—which in itself is a form of journalistic art. All of these questions are truly rhetorical because, patently, the ex-athlete is unprepared in all of these areas.

Reporting sports today is no longer an easy matter, no longer is it just reciting scores or reading wire copy. It is uncovering stories, developing stories, getting inside of people, hitting issues head on. What qualifies an untrained ex-athlete to go to Washington to interview distinguished people like Senator Marlow Cook, Senator Lowell Weicker, Senator John

Tunney and dozens of others on projected legislation concerning the amateur and professional sports structures in America? Again the question is rhetorical because the ex-athlete, on the average, it totally unqualified to do this.

What makes a man who pitched a baseball qualified to talk about football, basketball, tennis, golf, track and field, soccer, Irish hurling or anything other than his diminutive world of the diamond? And, for that matter, what even qualifies him to talk about that? Based upon my experience, the ballplayer's intelligence does not extend to real curiosity about all of the members of all the other teams in both leagues and very often not even to the other members of his own team.

In a similar vein, the same is true when a football player, or a basketball player, or any other athlete, is put on the air as an all-purpose sports reporter. The whole practice is an indignity to professional standards. To top it all off, where is the training and background in on-the-air communication; the ability to deliver words fluidly, articulately, forcefully, meaningfully, so that maximum viewer attention and interest can be commanded?

Now, all this applies to making an ex-athlete, overnight, into an all-purpose sports reporter. Another way that an ex-athlete may be used on the air is as an analyst. The underlying theory is that because he has played the game, he can bring to his analysis nuances and insights not given to the average professional sportscaster who never played the game. This is nonsense on at least two grounds. First, on the average, the ex-player does not have the ability to translate, quickly and fluidly, that which he sees and that which he is attempting to analyze into the spoken word. Second, the theory implies a complexity to sport that simply doesn't exist. What do the ex-athletes really say, on the average? If it's a former baseball player, he will tell you that because the man is on first with none out or one out, the batter will try to hit to right, behind the runner, to avoid the double play. Isn't that startling? If he is an ex-football player he will tell you in every single game about the tight end hitting the seam of the zone up the middle, or isolating the set-back, one on one, against the linebacker, which means you're putting a fast kid against a slow kid.

There is a further disqualification for ex-athletes as analysts in most cases. They are tied to the game. They romanticize it. They're unwilling ever to criticize a player, an owner, the commissioner or the sport. They are bound to all by past allegiances.

There are exceptions, of course, and I have dealt with them elsewhere in this book. Bill Russell and Don Meredith don't give a damn. They're willing to tell it like it is, and constitute a happy relief from the stereotype of the ex-athlete sportscaster. But always remember, even they do it under leadership from a professional announcer. They don't do it on their own, and it remains to be seen if they ever could. Dick Button on the other hand, is an ex-athlete who has proven he can do it on his own.

Perhaps the worst thing of all in the practice of hiring ex-athletes as announcers—at least in my view—is the effect it has upon young people in this country. I have spoken at campus after campus all across the land. I have lectured at the Pulitzer Graduate School of Journalism at Columbia University, and always I am asked the same question by brilliant young people majoring in journalism and communications, people achieving outstanding grades, people being trained on the college and university newspapers and radio and television stations: "How can I get into your business, get your kind of job?"

What can you tell them? Can you tell them to throw a baseball, hit a baseball, throw a football, catch a football? No, you can't add to their frustration. You tell them that you still believe in the American system of free enterprise. You tell them about yourself and about luck and hope and opportunity and work. But deep inside, you don't feel clean about what you tell them. And so you tell them the truth about your industry, and how it debases journalism in the field of sports.

But you don't stop there. You question the many sportswriters who automatically praise and almost, on occasion, revere the jocks. As they do this—those who do—as they impart special knowledgeability to those who played the game, they are really indicting themselves. If the athletes know so much more, then, clearly, all sportswriters should be ex-athletes. But I've never heard a single sportswriter suggest that. In fact, they blow their tops when, at World Series time or Super Bowl time, their own editors debase sports-print journalism by using the by-line of an athlete participating in the event.

Why don't we carry the whole ugly practice to its logical conclusion? Why shouldn't a newspaper music critic have to be an ex-pianist? Why shouldn't a newspaper drama critic have to be an ex-actor? Because they don't have the professional observer's skill, that's why; because they don't have the perspective, the perception, the background of years of listening to the great performances, or watching them.

Writing is a profession, and so is broadcasting. Let the broadcast industry take hold of itself and deal with sports broadcasting as a profession. Let the ex-athletes vie in open competition with any young person getting out of college trained in communications and journalism. Then, let the real standards of the profession prevail. If the broadcast industry had done this in the very beginning, there would be some decent journalism in sports broadcasting today, instead of the orthodoxy and the tripe dispensed on a daily basis to a public that has been inundated with this mediocrity ever since television began.

That's telling it like I think it is.

Q. Who are some of the other broadcasters who you respect in the industry?

A. I have to answer this question at the national level since I am not sufficiently familiar with the work of local sportscasters around the country to form an opinion.

In terms of traditional play-by-play announcers, I most respect Keith Jackson of ABC and Curt Gowdy of NBC. Each works very hard. Each comes to every assignment very well prepared. Each is enormously versatile, that is, he can cover just about any kind of sporting event.

I respect Jim McKay of ABC very much. He has had the arduous task of broadcasting a wide variety of events not hitherto seen by the American public, from things so inane as demolition derbies to Irish hurling to surfing to cliff diving and all the rest of the many and varied competitions seen on the most enduring and popular show in the history of television sports, ABC's *Wide World of Sports*. He brings to his job a boyish enthusiasm. He brings dignity to the competitors, and he always brings dignity to himself. He is a man with an inquiring mind who wonders about the motivations of people and, in his own way, is a philosopher about life. He has traveled the world with more frequency than perhaps any statesman in history, including Henry Kissinger. And everywhere he goes, he takes something back with him, about the place and about the people.

Because he is a man of some intellectual depth, he had the capacity to perform, splendidly, as an international news reporter when tragedy struck the Olympic Village on September 6, 1972, in Munich.

In terms of color commentators, or analysts, if you prefer, the ones I most respect are Bill Russell, Dick Button and Don Meredith. These three men represent to me the best of the announcers "who played the game." Each is a definitive personality, not a "jock." Russell has rare humor, marvelous insight and total frankness. I really think he is an important person in our society, with the ability to do almost anything in almost any walk of life. His only hang-up that I know of is Wilt Chamberlain.

I have discussed Don Meredith at length in my first book and again in this book. He is a man with a flair, and he has helped to bring a new look to football.

Dick Button is exactly right for what he does. A former Olympic figure-skating champion, he probably knows more about a sport strange to most than anybody else in the nation. He has a magnificent ability to translate the nuances of that sport into instant, precise and superbly descriptive verbiage. And he, like Jim McKay, has an eternal enthusiasm.

I don't see anybody around doing editorial commentary other than myself. I blame the industry for this because the announcers are not given the opportunity to speak their minds.

Q. Why aren't there more black sportscasters?
A. That's like asking why there aren't more black managers in baseball, more black quarterbacks in professional football, more black anything in any walk of life.

They haven't been given the opportunity.

I will say, though, that an active effort is being made to employ more and more black announcers. At ABC, we had Bill Russell; we use O. J. Simpson wherever possible; we have used Wilt Chamberlain; we have employed Muhammad Ali even when it produced political repercussions to do so.

With the signing of Fred Williamson as the third man in the booth on *Monday Night Football*, a member of the black race has not only been made a sportscaster, but has been placed in the spotlight for three consecutive hours of prime-time television. It is by no means assured that he will be successful in this role. But, as I have already indicated, I believe that "The Hammer" will make it!

I note that NBC has used Willie Davis. WNBC has used Art Rusk and Bob Teague on the local level in sports.

CBS tried Elgin Baylor but, unfortunately, it didn't work. In football they use Irv Cross and several other black ex-players.

And ABC has used Timmy Brown on college football.

Bill White, the former St. Louis and Philadelphia baseball star, is one of the voices of the New York Yankees. This was a breakthrough by Mike Burke who was then running the ball club. I, myself, was involved in that. White was a sports announcer for ABC's affiliate station in Philadelphia. He called me one day, and said he would like to do baseball play-by-play. I put him together with Burke, and he got the job.

And now, Maury Wills does baseball at the national level for NBC.

I'm sure that there are others on the air whom I don't know about. So at least there is a beginning. But, in fairness to the broadcast operators, one must remember that sports broadcasting is a limited field with limited opportunities. There are only a relative handful of jobs.

Q. What, if any, changes do you see for sports broadcasting in the future?

A. Perhaps an increase in candid commentary at the local level. And certainly a large-scale increase in the number of women sports announcers. But not much more change than that.

In my travels I detect more and more young announcers—where ex-athletes are not employed—attempting to tell the truth about the local sports scene. It is not easy for them, because in the structure of sports, there is always the fear of reprisal—the fear that the sports operators will ban them from the clubhouses, or the fear that players will no longer talk to them. But they seem to be trying.

I do not foresee much, if any, change in the transmission of an event at the local level, as I have discussed elsewhere within these pages. Again, my industry is to blame for allowing team owners to name the announcers, or to veto the selection of an announcer they do not want. There is no better evidence of the farcical nature of local play-by-play announcing than the fact that Jack Brickhouse, a member of the board of directors of the Chicago Cubs, broadcasts the Cubs' games, and Chick Hearn, an officer of the Los Angeles Lakers organization, broadcasts the Lakers' games.

At the network level, I do see some relief from the "religionizing" of contests because of the success of the *Monday Night Football* approach—but not much.

Women will be getting more and more opportunities as sports announcers for two reasons: First, they deserve it. Second, broadcasting is a business that seeks the greatest possible audience. Women constitute a major part of that audience, and women sports announcers will help to cultivate the female audience, thus enhancing the total viewership and listenership. Male sportscasters will grumble and so will many sportswriters, some of whom have been so Neanderthal as to seek to bar women sportswriters from the press box. But the inevitable will prevail—and it should. God did not draw a diagram of the world, and carefully mark off broadcast booths and press boxes with the sacred words, "For Men Only "

CHAPTER 11

REACTIONS

Q. There is talk that you are going to run for the United States Senate. Why would you want to do this, and what makes you think you are qualified?

A. I have not said that I intend to run for the Senate. I have said that I am considering the possibility and whether or not I do so will be a family decision involving my wife, Emmy, my two daughters, Jill and Hilary, and my son-in-law, Peter.

There are two basic reasons why I am giving thought to the matter. First, I do not believe that sports has provided the ultimate intellectual challenge of my life. I an not at all sure that there is anything left for me to accomplish in sports, and I have an inner drive to do something more meaningful with my life before my string has run out. This does not mean that I deprecate the usefulness, indeed, the importance of sports in society. I think, as much as anyone, that I am strongly aware of how seriously the emotions of most Americans are aroused by the great events (and I am often disturbed by this fact, because I also believe that too many people emphasize spectator sports out of all proportion to what should be their real place) in American life. On a personal level, I cannot be of that ilk. I enjoy a Super Bowl game, a World Series, a heavyweight championship fight and many other events, but they are not the whole of my life. There are other, far more important things happening in the world today that occupy my attention.

The second reason I am considering a political effort is that I am discouraged by, and disgusted with, the caliber of the

222

Congress as we see it today. There are days, many of them, when I read carefully worded, self-protective quotes from our elected officials and I want to shout out, "Good God, isn't there anyone with the guts to speak up, take a stand? Are they all just concerned with staying in office, not rocking the boat?" I have watched Watergate, followed it from the beginning, seen highly placed men admit to crimes, read of the ex-president and his taxes, his two homes, the ITT deal, the dairy industry deal, the Ellsberg doctor's break-in, the Hughes-Rebozo affair and I have an irresistible urge to go to Washington and question, question and question. The hell with reelection. When will men emerge on the national political scene who are concerned with one thing and one thing alone—not with their own skins, but with the quest for truth. I think, therefore, the question should not be, "Why *I* would want to run for the Senate?" I think it should rather be, with so many decent, educated and caring people in the country, "Why don't more of *them* take a greater interest, and give thought, themselves, to public life so that we can begin the long task of uplifting standards of government?"

As to the issue of what makes me think that I am qualified, I would say simply this: I am qualified on the basis of my education, background and experience. I am a lawyer, and was scholastically able at law school to have achieved membership on the Editorial Board of the Law Review (the Phi Beta Kappa, in effect, of law schools). I practiced law for ten years. In the course of my legal education and practice of the profession, I developed an intimate knowledge of constitutional law, government and political science. I learned much about management, labor and labor relations. I represented both management and unions in my practice of the law. I am a journalist (and law training has helped in this regard) and, as such, I have an inbred concern for directness and for facts: The who, what, when, where, how and why of a story, that is, the search for truth.

I have been a prolific speaker in every part of the country, for management groups, legal groups, on campus, wherever. I have come to learn much about the problems that occupy the minds of people in every region of the country, and, especially, I have come to grips with the attitudes and thinking of the young people and the minority groups throughout the nation.

I had a distinguished military career in World War II, rising from buck private to the grade of major. During that career, I had the opportunity to grow in leadership capacity, to learn staff procedure and to develop skills in personnel analysis and the selection of qualified aides.

I am not a party hack, reared and shaped by the local political club, with ties and obligations that would bind me forevermore. In my judgment, today more than ever, this country cannot afford elected representatives who emerge from the mediocrity and political intrigue of such backgrounds. These are the very people who won't speak out, who stand for nothing, who, if they get to Washington, are more concerned with party and reelection than they are with trying to resolve the great issues besetting all of us in the current complex, turbulent and even tormented society of which we are all a part.

Finally, I have traveled much of the world, know something about other countries, their problems and how they feel about us.

You bet I think I'm qualified, and that is exactly why, in my address before the Association of Managing Editors of the American Newspapers at Orlando, Florida, when Wick Temple of the AP asked me the very questions I am now answering, I concluded my answers by jocularly saying, "I doubt that there are ten better qualified persons in the United States."

Ronald Reagan and George Murphy were movie stars. The former became the governor of California, the latter, a United States Senator. How is that for a pair of precedents?

Q. If you do run for the Senate, do you seriously think you could win?

A. I think I would win easily if I could get the nomination of the Democratic Party, and there's the rub. My opponent would be the Conservative-Republican incumbent, James Buckley, whose chief claim to fame is his anonymity. He was elected by a fluke, in my opinion, the result of a three-way split on the New York State ballot. His concern with the interests of the great majority of New York State residents seems to be almost nil. There will be no coattails for him to ride in 1976, no public fear of McGovern, no diminished inflation, only a hangover from the maladies of the Nixon Administration. I think he will be laid bare for what he is: A man deeply rooted in the philosophy of medieval times.

Q. I see that Jim McKay and Don Meredith have won Emmy Awards. I also see that Keith Jackson, Curt Gowdy, Chris Schenkel and Ray Scott have won awards as Sports Broadcaster of the Year. If you're so good, why didn't you win any?

A. In the first place, I think I am good and I don't apologize for it. Any man who performs before an audience has to think he's good. Otherwise, he couldn't possibly perform effectively.

As for awards received by my colleagues, they are to be congratulated for having attained them.

As for awards to me, I feel that I have been fortunate to receive my fair share, especially those awards I particularly wanted. For example, I received the first annual Jackie Robinson Award for my work in furthering the cause of minority athletes. I received what I believe is the highest award in my industry, the Broadcaster of the Year Award given by the International Radio and Television Society. This award has never been given to anyone else in the field of sports. It is a professional award that has gone, in the past, to people like Walter Cronkite, the late Chet Huntley, Arthur Godfrey, Jack Benny, etc. It is not an award based upon a popularity poll. I have received the Cine Golden Eagle Award for Journalism, an award given to me for the production, *Grambling College —One Hundred Yards to Glory*. I have also received numerous other awards, like the TV Bureau's Man of the Year Award for 1973; Radio Man of the Year for 1973; and the Detroit Advertising Agencies' First Annual "Tell It Like It Is" Award. This last honor meant much to me because the Detroit people didn't even want me on *Monday Night Football* when it began. It was their way of saying, "We were wrong."

With regard to winning an Emmy, I personally don't much care. I've got the one Emmy I ever wanted in life . . . my wife. The Emmy Award, as those in the trade know, is a popularity contest, nothing more, nothing less. This was never more clearly manifested than in May 1974 when Dwight Hemion won the Emmy as Best Director of the Year for a Barbra Streisand musical special over the man who directed *The Autobiography of Miss Jane Pittman.* It was a public embarrassment for the Emmy telecast and Dwight, who is a man of class and style, was the first to say so. In fact, Dwight confided that the Streisand musical was one of the weaker shows he has done in his career. And another point: As yet, Johnny Carson, the best and most durable entertainer in the television business, has never won an Emmy.

With respect to the Sports Broadcaster of the Year Award, which some of my colleagues have won, that refers to an organization in Salisbury, North Carolina. I have never belonged to that group. They set themselves up in what I considered a local promotion from the start. They also name a sportswriter of the year. They lump sports columnists together with on-the-beat sportswriters who cover teams. This is, *prima facie,* absurd. They do different work. They also lump play-by-play announcers together with commentators. This is equally absurd for the same reason. Then all writers and broadcasters vote and the thing becomes a popularity contest. So I don't feel I've missed anything. Under any circumstances, while we all like to enjoy approval for what we do, I think the ultimate approval has to lie within yourself. And the ultimate award for anyone should therefore lie in his or her own inner satisfaction with what he has done, and the knowledge that he has lived up to the standards he has set for himself.

Q. Have you had to possess the "killer instinct" to succeed in your business? How have you dealt with all of the infighting of the corporate situation?

A. No, not the "killer instinct." That implies hurting somebody else. I have never in my career hurt a colleague, politicized him out of an assignment or anything like that. Myron Cope, in his profile of me in *Sports Illustrated* in March 1967, made that very clear. The two things I have had to possess —apart from whatever brains and talent that I have—are perseverance and self-belief. It has taken me 18 years to reach wherever it is I have gotten; 18 years of scraping, scrambling, struggling and surviving. Above all, surviving, because obviously my type of sports reporting is totally different from all of what had gone before and which still, generally, dominates the industry.

There can be no doubt about the problems of corporate infighting. I am an expert on that. For 5 years of the 18 that I have been in the business, I was not permitted to perform on the television network. Two key executives of my company were in open contempt of my performance abilities, and one of them was responsible for ostracizing me. Fortunately, I survived them both.

And that leads to still another vital factor. You have to have somebody who believes in you and has the guts to give you the opportunity. Roone Arledge did. Not only that, he has backed me every step of the way. I owe much of my success to him.

But, in perfect candor, Arledge and ABC owe me something too. I've brought a lot of excitement and attention to ABC Sports.

Q. What role do you think luck plays in success, relating it to your own career?

A. The luck of opportunity, it seems to me, is a critical element in anyone's success, and this is certainly ture of mine. As I have indicated elsewhere, I languished for years until Arledge gave me my opportunity.

I have seen people of exceptional talent never get the chance to display it. I have seen it in the legal profession, I have seen it in business and I have seen it in entertainment. Timing is a factor correlated with luck. If the opportunity is presented to a person at a time when it is just right, when he will be most noticed, when he will have the most impact and effect, then, if he has the ability and the willingness to work hard, that opportunity can be translated into a lifetime career.

In my own case it was luck when I was offered a chance to perform on radio. It took some courage on my part, and my wife's part, to leave the law profession when I did and seek to start a new professional life in my mid-thirties. Then, it took work, more opportunity, more work, and it's an endless cycle. You can never sit back, never relax, never figure that you have it made.

I have learned, too, that in the business of reporting, luck can be a natural and probable consequence of endeavor. The first rule in sports reporting is to "be there," to get to know the people, to be on the scene when it happens and where it happens. If you do this, day in and day out, you will inevitably come upon stories that others who are not there will never get.

For example, I was in Los Angeles talking with George Foreman, when Daryl Lamonica jumped from the Oakland Raiders to the Southern California franchise of the World Football League. Literally within moments after I had heard the news, I was able to get Lamonica, WFL President Gary Davidson and the owner of the team on national television.

In the 1972 Olympics, I was present when Reynaud Robinson and Eddie Hart came back to Olympic Village after failing to be at the starting blocks in time for their heat in the 100-meter dash. I didn't have to be there. My own immediate assignment had been completed elsewhere. But by being there, I was able to bring the story to national television.

I could go on endlessly with stories like these throughout my broadcast career.

Mr. Branch Rickey once said, "Luck is the residue of design." I try to remember that.

Q. Looking back over the course that your life has followed, is there anything that you would change, that you regret in terms of your personal life, in terms of the progression of your career, or in terms of any stands that you have taken as a broadcaster and commentator?

A. In the first instance, circumstances made my life. I went to law school because my father wanted me to, and I certainly don't regret that. It gave me a diversified education; an education that I consider second to none, and one that enabled me to pursue almost any avenue of life beginning with the law.

After that my life was, in a sense, taken out of my own hands because of World War II and the fact that I had to go into the military. And, certainly, I don't regret my military career.

But coming out of the war, there might be a regret: spending ten years in the practice of the law. They were years that might have been more fulfilling, more fruitful if I had begun a career in broadcasting then. But there again, I did languish for a year after getting out of the service, and I tried to get into broadcasting but couldn't. So I had no recourse other than to turn to my profession. If circumstances had been different from what they evolved to be, I would have liked to have gotten out of the law ten years earlier and achieved success in broadcasting ten years sooner than I did. But, of course, 20–20 hindsight is the best kind.

In terms of the positions I have taken editorially on issues in sports, I don't have any regrets, except that I wish that, in certain instances, my reactions to them had been less intense. I suppose the most notable stand of my professional life was in support of Muhammad Ali when he was stripped of his title, and deprived of his license to fight. I certainly wouldn't alter that, though I must say it was not pleasant to endure the hate mail and the threats upon my life that followed my various broadcasts defending his position, and attacking the action taken against him.

Nor would I modify nor change my views on the U.S. Olympic Committee, the AAU-NCAA feud, on the evils of big-time college recruitment, on the major-league baseball franchise carpetbagging and all of the other issues on which I have taken a stand. I did what I thought was right, and I still think it was right.

There was considerable furor over my interview with Stan Wright, the Olympic sprint coach, who did not get his two runners to the starting blocks on time. I was deeply troubled by the outcry and went back to reread the transcript of that interview many times. Having done that, I wouldn't change a question. In fact, I wonder today what all the noise was about. This doesn't mean I have never been wrong, or anything like it. It certainly doesn't mean that I am above criticism. All it means is that I do what I believe in, and that I have to weather the consequences of what I say.

If I have one regret about my career, it would be that my

opportunity never came in the area of hard news, national and international. I feel that I would have had far greater challenges than I have ever faced in sports. But then, who is to say that I could have ever achieved the influence and success that I have achieved in sports? Maybe I'm better off.

As to having regrets over a failure to say a certain thing at a certain time in a certain show, that happens often, and it happens to all performers. Walter Cronkite will tell you that and so will Johnny Carson, just to take two ends of the television spectrum. But that's simply a detail that does not go to the heart of the question.

Q. What do you think of the trend of ex-athletes becoming motion-picture actors?

A. I think that the trend is more understandable than the trend toward sports announcing because by the nature of motion-picture making, the athlete can be protected and even made to look good.

The motion-picture medium is vastly different from the broadcast medium. In the main, sports broadcasts are live; it's happening now, and you tell it as it happens. There are no retakes and no editing.

In the making of a motion picture, there is the finest kind of direction, tight direction; there are retakes upon retakes, and then there are days upon days of film editing. You can do wonders with film, and inexperience is not guaranteed to show.

To a lesser degree, the same is true of television movies, and situation series. You can make almost anybody look better than he is.

I have discussed athletes as actors with two performers for whom I have the utmost respect, Karl Malden and Ernest Borgnine. Malden is convinced that the athlete brings to acting two basic ingredients: one is the ability to concentrate above the norm, derived from the years of training in concentration in sports. "Two," Karl observes, "They have a lot of confidence. They are not afraid of doing scenes with experienced actors. They probably get this from years of playing in front of vast live audiences, and getting used to crowd reactions when they succeed and when they fail. They are natural extroverts, just the way many performers in the arts are."

Ernest Borgnine doesn't agree. "It's not the same thing at all," he told me. "An athlete knows where he's supposed to go and what he's supposed to do on a given play and he learns it by rote. It's altogether different once that little light goes on and the camera starts clicking. And what happens if the real actor throws a line at him that he doesn't expect? Acting is a dramatic art, and while some people are born to it, they are very few in number. What helps the athlete is the film editor. Nothing else. He may be even less qualified to go into motion pictures than into your business."

I would agree with Borgnine, but again there are exceptions, and O. J. Simpson is one of them. Joe Namath wants, almost desperately, to become an actor. But he has had bad advice. He did a couple of movies and they were sad affairs. He is very much aware of that now, and ever since those experiences he has been determinedly taking acting lessons. With his natural personality and charm, maybe in the long run he will be able to make it.

But I keep hearing Ernie Borgnine: "Why not sign one up and let him play *Marty*?"

Q. How in the world did you ever get away with producing a television show about yourself—*Cosell At Large*?

A. I never did produce such a special. The executive producer of that show was Ed Sabol, president of NFL Films. The line producer was Steve Sabol of NFL Films. The two came to me out of a clear blue sky and asked me if I would cooperate on a special about me. I respect both men, and I think they have done very fine work about professional football. So I agreed, and I asked for no editorial prerogatives over the content of the show.

Thus, NFL Films did the show. I had no idea whatsoever what material they would use in it, or how it would turn out. They sold the show to Roone Arledge and ABC Sports, and I had nothing to do with that either

Ed Sabol paid me a $10,000 fee for my cooperation and I sent that $10,000 to Ara Parseghian, head football coach at Notre Dame, for multiple sclerosis research. Ara is deeply involved with this disease since it has struck down members of his family. He is doing marvelous work in raising funds for research so that one day, hopefully, the disease will be wiped out.

As to the show itself, I would be disqualified on grounds of bias from judging it.

Q. My kids look up to athletes as heroes. Don't you think they have a responsibility to all kids?

A. I think athletes have a responsibility to comport themselves as gentlemen in public; to be courteous, not to be profane publicly, not to appear in public in an intoxicated state and to keep themselves in the best possible physical condition so that they can put forth maximum effort on the playing field or in the arena.

I do not think the athlete should have to undergo verbal abuse from fans, young or old, when he is outside the arena. Nor do I think he has to submit to having his physical safety imperiled by hordes of youngsters, well-meaning or otherwise, who swarm all over him and endanger him in their quest for autographs or for answers to questions.

I think the athlete, like anyone else, has a right to his private life, unless by wrongdoing or unseemly behavior that private life becomes public.

I remember what Bob Gibson, the great St. Louis pitcher, said on this general theme: "I don't have any obligation to any youngster with regard to the way he grows up. His parents do."

I believe there is much to what Gibson said with respect to today's society. We all have a tendency to farm our children out, to wittingly or unwittingly seek to escape our own responsibilities as parents. We send a child to dance class, so that the child can learn to dance. That takes care of X number of minutes per week. Our children go to school so that they can become literate. Now the burdens are on the dance instructor and the schoolteacher. They go to see a game and the burden is somehow placed upon the athlete. But who will teach the children the basics of life, what morality is and what ethics are? Who will develop their characters and their faith? It seems to me the parents must, with some assistance from their church. But we are all so busy with the problems of living, we like to forsake our own obligations. Thus, with the overemphasized place that sports has in the society, and with a youngster's natural bent to become involved in sports, many parents subliminally attach to the athlete a kind of father image. It is not the job of an athletic hero to assume a parental role for youngsters, and I fear that this is what many parents are asking them to do. Not totally, of course, but in terms of filling a vacuum which the parents have created.

There is another element involved here—the assumption that the athletic hero is equipped to be something he is not. Three of the greatest sports figures of my lifetime have been Willie Mays, Hank Aaron and Mickey Mantle. All three came to the major leagues without education, without schooling. All three are to this day ungrammatical. They found themselves, because of their abilities to hit, run and throw, projected overnight into national prominence; they became superstars. But there was no way in the world that they had been intellectually prepared for this. They didn't even know what the big cities were like. Mantle was a hick kid from Commerce, Oklahoma. Yet, instantly, he owned the biggest city in the world, New York. He shared that ownership with Willie Mays, a black kid from the South. People expected them to speak at dinners. Mantle and Mays didn't even know what a tuxedo was, let alone how to talk.

I was with them both from the beginning. I was their lawyer at the beginning. I saw Leo Durocher, who understood the problem, do his best to protect Mays from public situations he couldn't possibly cope with. He was placed in the custody of Monte Irvin, with whom he roomed, and he was very carefully kept away from people so that he could concentrate on doing what came naturally, playing baseball.

The Yankees paired Mantle with Jerry Coleman, one of

the outstanding young men in American sports. They recognized the problem too.

Aaron came up with less fanfare, but with the same difficulty.

How could these three young men possibly deal with the demands of the public? They not only had the task of playing up to expectations, but of fulfilling a publicly imposed image that they couldn't possibly meet because of absence of adequate backgrounds. The remarkable thing about the three young men has been the way they have grown socially through the years. Each can handle himself now in any company. The sophisticated restaurants have become their milieu; the skyscrapers have long since ceased to awe them. Aaron and Mays have come to understand what Jackie Robinson was all about. Once they were willing to be second-class citizens in order to be baseball stars and achieve financial security. But they outgrew that several years ago.

Now all three understand their importance and know how to deal with it. But it took years. Yet, in the very beginning, the public demanded far more from these men than they could possibly give. There were times when they paid the price of bad publicity, and it was not their fault. It was the fault of parents, parents like the ones who ask: "Don't these athletes have a responsibility to my kids?"

I wonder how often such parents ask themselves: "What are my responsibilities to my kids, and am I meeting them?" The broader question is: "Who will tell the children?"

And the answer, I believe, is: The parents should, but too often they are guilty of inattention, and encourage the development of false heroes for their youngsters. Then they impose responsibilities on those heroes as a cop-out for their own failures.

Q. You are always knocking college football and basketball. Why?

A. I think this question, often asked of me, arises out of a misunderstanding. I do not knock college football and basketball as such. I think there is a perfectly proper place

for the conduct of both sports, along with a broad in-
tramural athletic program, in our colleges and universities.
But I am appalled by the national fetish over winning,
over being number one, when the practical result is the recruitment of young athletes in a manner that can only be
corrupting to all concerned—the boy, himself, his parents,
the coaches (who are victims of the system, because they
must win to survive in their livelihoods) and, finally, the
college or university presidents, because they, by allowing
illicit recruitment practices to take place, debase the
character and very purposes of their institutions. Further,
I have nothing but contempt for those alumni, the "old
grads," who never outgrow the juvenile need to have their
school be number one—those who contribute mightily to
the continuation of illegal recruiting procedures by cough-
ing up "under the table" emoluments to induce youngsters
to go to their alma maters.

I know something about this from long experience. I
once did a piece with a youngster and his parents for the
ABC Evening News. The lad's name was Steve Worster. He
was a fine running back for Bridge City High School in
Texas. The scene was set in the boy's home. And would
you believe, a representative of the University of Houston, on
camera, was exhorting the lad and his parents in this way:
"Steve, you play better with a temperature of 64 degrees,
you've got it. If you want it at 70 degrees, you've got it.
Because we have the Astrodome." That was only the beginning, and the rest was equally disgusting. By the way, Steve
went to Texas. Youngsters are flown to campuses all over the
country, placed in situations for which they and their parents
are unprepared and they are corrupted at the very beginning
of their college lives. They become participants in a meretrici-
ous breaking of the NCAA regulations concerning recruitment, and learn early on that almost everybody is doing it.
What effect does this have upon a young man's character?
How can he respect those above him?

What about the coaches? Most whom I know are fine
men. They are men who have to wrestle with themselves
every night of their lives, question themselves, search their

own consciences and integrity. Ara Parseghian does it;
John McKay does it; Joe Paterno does it and so do most
of the others. They know they have to make recruitment
trips, talk to youngsters and their parents. They try to do
it cleanly, stay within the rules, tell a boy and his family
why they think their institution is the right one for the
boy. But they are aware that there are others who are not
doing it so cleanly, that there are competing offers that
cannot be met. They are also aware that the sense of values of
both the young man and his parents suffer. The latter become
demanding, develop a misplaced sense of importance, and all
too often young athletes arrive on campus impervious to
authority and with an almost patronizing attitude to the
coaches, conscious that if they don't like what they find, they
can go elsewhere and get more. How can you blame the kids?
Blame the system which erodes character at a tender age.

Once I sat in a New York restaurant with a college
basketball coach whom I deeply respect. He is a long-term
friend. At the time, his wife was terribly ill. He should
have been with her, but she understood. It was his job. He
had to make one last visit to the home of a kid who hap-
pended to be 6-feet 11-inches tall. My heart went out to
him. He was sick and disgusted with the whole routine.
He wanted to tell everyone in the system to go to hell. But
coaching basketball was all he knew. That and the fact that
he had to win to keep his job. He went to visit the kid and
his parents.

Not too long ago, *The New York Times* ran a week-long
series on the evils of recruitment in big-time college sports.
I wish their series had been more specific, more revelatory,
naming names. But however lacking it may have been in
terms of specifics, it more than made up for it in motivation. It was about time for a great newspaper to get back
to the basics of character, morality and ethics in sports.
Later, to its credit, *Sports Illustrated* ran an excellent, and
very pointed, group of articles that named the school, and
named names—Long Beach State and its football and basketball coaches.

In my opinion, this kind of journalism is not only necessary, but should be continuing. You don't write about a

problem for a couple of days or a week, that seems eternal, and then forget about it for years. You keep the pressure on, make the public aware and maybe you can force correction of an ugly system, or at least produce some amelioration.

I wonder how many people remember the college basketball scandals of the 1940s, 1950s and 1960s. I wonder if they think there will never be another. I wonder who they blame for those scandals. Just the kids, themselves? Hell no, blame the system. Those kids were corrupted in the very beginning by the inducements presented to them when they entered college.

I wonder how many people read David Wolf's fine book about Connie Hawkins of the Los Angeles Lakers entitled *Foul!*? I wonder how many know that Connie got a scholarship, and other things, to go to the University of Iowa, when he was at sixth-grade reading level. I wonder how he was expected to cope. You see, I know Connie, and I knew him when he was at Boys High School in Brooklyn, though he would never remember that.

I am sometimes amused at what can only be called the naïve sports syndrome of this country, by the publicly expressed notion of some that the average young athlete goes to a college today because he wants to play for a certain coach. There may be such kids here and there, but they are rare exceptions, almost an extinct breed. They can help their parents by taking the best offer. Why practice idealism? Yet you will hear people in Los Angeles tell you that the great UCLA basketball team, with its unending stream of victories, occurred because great young players from all over the country gravitated to the Westwood Campus in their desire to play for Coach John Wooden.

Did you ever hear of a youngster from Provo, Utah named Vrett Roman? He is 6-feet 11½-inches tall. He will be a freshman at UCLA this year. John Wooden made sure of that with his third visit to Provo. "It used to take me only one visit," he said, after the boy announced that he was going to UCLA.

At a time in the history of this country when we are all concerned about our moral fiber as a nation, when the credibility of our very government has been called into question, I wonder how many people stop to think about where that moral fiber is supposed to come from. It can only come from the character of each and every one of us, and those characters are formulated and developed in our youthful years.

As one who has spent countless hours on the campuses of this nation, who has had session after session with honest-to-goodness students, I can tell you that they don't appreciate the special treatment and the blandishments given to the athletes. They don't cotton to the fact that many young people today, good students, do not gain admission to the colleges of their choice, while athletes with lower scholastic qualifications are accepted.

This brings one to the root question: What is the purpose of a college or university? It is to educate and train, to prepare its student body for the great tasks of life, to make doctors and lawyers, engineers and artists, writers and poets, statesmen and historians and, in the process, to build character. The last thing in the world a college or university should be concerned with is being number one in football or basketball if the price one pays for that is the corruption of character and the undermining of true student morale on campus.

And believe me, that is the price.

I have a nephew named Greg who was graduated from Francis Lewis High School in Queens in June 1974. He is 6-feet 4-inches tall and a fine athlete, good enough at baseball to have received feelers from major-league teams, including Pittsburgh and Cincinnati. Good at basketball, too. Frank McGuire, head coach of basketball at South Carolina told me that Greg had fine potential. So he could have gone to a big-time sports college on a free ride. Greg is also an outstanding student. He has elected, instead, to go to Amherst. It won't be easy for my brother financially. But it will be worth it. Greg will doubtless play shortstop for the Amherst baseball team, and he will be playing it for fun. There will be the same distances between bases, the same ground balls, the same pop flies, the same game that is played when USC goes against whomever for the national title. And when Amherst meets its rivals, Williams and Wesleyan, you couldn't want for a more traditional competition. There won't be headlines, and there won't be national fame. There'll be a kid from Queens playing a game he loves, at one of the best colleges in this country, and he'll be graduated from Amherst four years hence. Hopefully he'll be prepared to realize his potential in his chosen field, free of exposure to the hypocrisy and moral corruption that attends many recruitment practices in big-time college sports.

He'll be playing college basketball and baseball the way I think they should be played. And I like both games.

Q. What do you think of beer promotions at ball parks to stimulate attendance?

A. Because of situations like that "ten-cent-a-beer night" in Cleveland this season, when the fans erupted onto the playing field and went after Texas right fielder Jeff Burroughs, I am against such promotions. The undue consumption of beer undoubtedly played a part in causing the upheaval that night, and similar promotions in the future could produce more of the same.

However, I do not believe for one moment that beer, and beer alone, was the sole cause of the violence. One of the more disturbing aspects of the sports scene in America today has been the development of a pattern of wanton and disorderly behavior by some fans that often jeopardizes the physical safety of an athlete, or even of other fans in attendance. When Pete Rose of the Cincinnati Reds was the target for debris thrown by the fans at Shea Stadium, beer was not involved. When Bob Watson of the Houston Astros lay cut and bleeding on the outfield grass in Cincinnati and was pelted by objects thrown by the spectators, a ten-cent beer promotion was not involved. When Hank Aaron was hit on the head by an orange while sitting in the dugout in Los Angeles, it wasn't because of a beer promotion. And when they went after Pete Rose in San Francisco, it wasn't because of a beer promotion.

In my opinion, the roots of fan disorder go much deeper than that. People are frustrated these days. The times are vexing, the inflation ever escalating, the problems of daily living overwhelming. Sports, for the masses, are a prime means of escape from those problems. It is at the playing arena that people can let their emotions loose, or at least so they think. And they degenerate, some of them, into profanity and ill-temper.

Another of the deep roots underlying such actions, it seems to me, is the disproportionate stress we place upon sports in this country, producing a mania for winning. Some fans get so aroused over the failures of the teams they root for, or the successes of an opposition team or opposition players, that they depart from all reason and drift into actions that can endanger those around them and the athletes.

It is a terrible thing to see mob disorder, a terrifying thing, and I have witnessed it often. People become half-crazed, and act without regard to consequences. This is why I so often speak of a mix and a balance in one's approach to sport; a proper evaluation of the role of sport in American society. One can't take fans as a total group and say, "Look here, there's more to life than your football team, or your baseball team, or your star players." You can't change people or educate them overnight. Their imbalanced view of sport derives from years of encouragement in the curious notion that they can use sports as an outlet for every hostility that springs from their daily social lives.

And this leads me to the third root cause of fan misbehavior. For all of the years that I have been in sports, the media—broadcast and print—have explicitly propagated the idea that if a fan pays his admission price to a contest, then there is an accompanying license to do just about whatever he pleases. Only in recent months have some sports columnists begun to take a deeper look into the continuing evidences of fans' disorder. It's about time. As I have pointed out elsewhere, whenever there is a confrontation between players and owners in any sport, and there is the threat of a strike or a lockout, most media people are quick to say that the two parties should forget their differences at any cost. They reason that the fan doesn't give a damn, because it's the fan who pays the way and who must be served. Any thinking person can see the imbecility of such reasoning. Owners and players have the same individual rights as citizens that fans have. And nobody has ever demanded that the fan give up a single right of his, whether it be the right to strike or anything else.

In summary, I disapprove of "ten-cents-a-beer nights," but I think the time has come when all of us in the media should embark upon a crusade to educate the fans to the realization that they have obligations and responsibilities as well as rights; that a key responsibility is to respect the rights of others and to behave in a decent, orderly and civilized manner when they attend an athletic contest. This does not mean, in any sense, that their enthusiasm should be inhibited, or their right to cheer or boo obviated. Let the bands play and the banners wave. And once and for all, let the sports operators meet their obligations by having sufficient security forces to control physical outbursts by fans.

Q. With all the leagues, all the teams and all the sports now, don't you think there is danger of oversaturation?

A. I certainly do. This was the real thrust of Russell Baker's column in *The New York Times* not long ago entitled *Turn the Sports Off*. On a broadcast, time does not permit reporting scores of all the contests that take place, and even most newspapers do not have the space to print all of the results. One is hard put to remember the names of the teams; the various nicknames are unfamiliar, and the national images of some sports are diminished by the proliferation of teams in areas where interest in the sport is often slight. I wonder who really cared about the Memphis Tams?

Every time and every place you turn on television, it seems there is a sports event on. One can no longer keep track of all of the tennis tournaments that are being shown and now, in addition, there is World Team Tennis. The same is true of golf. In football, Canadian football and the World Football League are on the air before the National Football League preseason games are even scheduled to begin. Baseball is on television one-half of the year. The number of motor races being televised is growing. Hockey and basketball are television staples. And don't forget college football and college basketball. Even lacrosse can now be seen. Plus all of the myriad events seen on *ABC's Wide World of Sports* and the *CBS Sports Spectacular*.

One would have to anticipate that, at some point, there will be a general decline in interest in some, if not all of these sports at least in terms of television watching. And yet nearly all of them rely upon the money they receive from television for economic prosperity or even survival.

On the other hand, one would have to admit that the organization of new leagues, the expansion of existing leagues, the development of new major-league sports markets and the presence of new and willing investors is evidence of a continuing sports boom in this country. So it is hard to say that the saturation point has yet been reached. I can't conceive of baseball, for instance, not returning to Washington and Seattle. Markets like Jacksonville and Hawaii and Memphis should prove out in football. And Tampa and Seattle figure to have successful new franchises in the National Football League.

Where and when will it all end, this unceasing inflation of sports in America? Certainly, it will not end because of a shortage of athletes or a decline in quality of play. Competition is the thing that spectators react to. If games are competitive, the average fan cannot detect the pure level of excellence being registered by the individual performance. And with the nation's bursting population, more and more young athletes will be developed so that filling team rosters will not be a problem.

It will end when enough people become sufficiently disenchanted with sports and with the sports proliferation to "turn the sports off," as Russell Baker has done. And I think more and more people will do exactly that. After all, who wants to see the Whippets play the Spurs, whoever they may be. And how do you keep rooting when the Senators become the Rangers, the Pilots become the Royals, or was it the Brewers, and on and on and on?

Q. If you could interview any one person in the world, who would it be?

A. The person who made the biggest contribution to Richard Nixon to help the president pay the taxes he did not pay. Maybe, in that way, I could get a better understanding of the root causes of the political apathy that grips this nation.

Q. What's your favorite sport to watch?
A. Football, college or pro.

Q. What's your favorite event to broadcast?
A. A heavyweight championship fight. In my experience, there is nothing to compare with it in terms of anticipation and excitement.

Q. Who are the three greatest athletes you have ever seen?

A. This question is unanswerable. Any reply would be subjective and would lead to argument. I can say that Jackie Robinson was the greatest I have ever seen because he excelled not only in baseball but also in football, basketball, track and field, and, having seen him play golf and tennis, I am sure he could have been outstanding in both. But apart from Jackie, there are any number of athletes who, I think, could have been exceptional in sports other than the ones they were stars in.

Looking back, I think Joe DiMaggio probably could have been outstanding in any sport. So could a healthy Mickey Mantle. I have seen films of a young Joe Namath, when his legs were firm, and he was a super baseball and basketball prospect. Willie Mays could have done anything. So could Jimmy Brown, who starred in lacrosse, played varsity basketball at Syracuse, and might have become the heavy-weight champion had he gone into boxing. Unquestionably, O. J. Simpson is a superb all-around athlete. So is Bob Seagren, and so were Rafer Johnson and Bob Mathias. Muhammad Ali could have done anything. There are others, and there were others, too numerous to list. And there will always be new ones.

This is one of the wonderful things about sports. Every generation produces its own great performers who can capture a total population with the magnitude and beauty of their exploits. Elliott Gould, the actor, told me once in an interview that he considers athletes the greatest actors in the world for this very reason. "They can command more attention, more immediately, than any actor on stage or screen or television when they perform within the arena, which is the greatest stage of all," he said.

Q. Where did you get the nerve to call your first book *Cosell*? That's conceit if I ever heard of it.

A. The title for my first book was selected by Bill Adler, executive editor of Playboy Press. The title I wanted for the book was ditched.

I first thought of writing a book during the Munich Olympics of 1972. I discussed the idea with Mel Durslag of *The Los Angeles Herald-Examiner.* He suggested the title, *I Never Played the Game.* I thought it was perfect on two counts: First, I have never played the game of politics in my company. Second, I had taken a lot of flack the first year of *Monday Night Football* because I had never played the game. So that was my title.

Bill Adler has been in the publishing business for many years. He knows a lot more about it than I do. Accordingly, he conducted his own research, and advised me that a book with the title *Cosell* would sell much better than a book entitled *I Never Played the Game.* I acceded to him.

That's how *Cosell* was born.

Q. Why have you advocated government control of sports? Don't we have enough government bureaucracies already, without fouling up sports?

A. I often wonder if those who ask these simple, naïve questions are among the superpatriots who were calling me when I was in Munich, demanding to know what was happening to our kids over there.

It is true that I testified before a Senate Commerce Committee in 1972, in favor of an "omnibus bill" that would have created a National Sports Commission, overseeing, in some respects, certain areas of professional and amateur sports.

It is also true that I testified before a Senate Commerce Committee in 1973 in favor of another "omnibus bill" that would have created a national commission to oversee, in some areas, the structure of amateur sports. And it is similarly true that I testified favorably before the House Special Committee on Education and Labor on a like bill that they were considering.

While I dislike covering old ground, I did it for these reasons: First, I have been there. I have been through two Olympics, and I have seen our young athletes frustrated again and again, victimized by injustices over which they have no control, and without recourse. I have watched the United States Olympic Committee fail to discharge its supposed functions time and time again. I know the members of the committee to be, in the main, part of the past, ceremonial in attitude, empty of substance. I have had athlete after athlete appeal to me to try to do something about it. Nobody can figure out, yet, how one so unqualified as Bill Bowerman could wind up being our head track-and-field coach at Munich, or why there were no members of the committee at the Russian-American basketball fiasco, or why Bob Seagren was deprived of his pole without a staunch fight being made by the committee on his behalf or why, why, why on many other issues.

Nobody can understand, yet, why certain young men of Jewish persuasion could not represent the United States in the basketball competition in the Maccabiah Games, except that the NCAA would not certify the event because the AAU already had. Why couldn't America's best indoor high jumper leap against the Russians in a dual meet at Richmond? Why couldn't our basketball players play against the Russians in America, until government pressures forced a change, at least in that case? Why? Because of the insane, unending feud between the NCAA and the AAU, a dispute that has lasted longer than the Vietnam War and resisted the peace making efforts of the late General Douglas MacArthur, and so skilled a labor mediator as Theodore Kheel.

Why do people only get excited about the mess in amateur sports every four years, and then cry out against a federal bill that seeks to bring justice to the athletes? What do these people do to produce change and improvement? Who is going to produce that change, if not the federal government? The United States Olympic Committee shows scant willingness to change. All they say is: If there is government control, the International Olympic Committee will kick us out of the Olympics. To that, I say nonsense. In the first place, the United States Olympic Committee gets its authorization to exist from the federal charter Public Law 805. In the second place, who can rationally argue, despite the subterfuge they employ, that the Russian sports structure is not governmentally controlled? In the third place, and quite bluntly, what would the Olympics be without the United States? In the fourth place, how is anyone ever going to end the NCAA-AAU feud voluntarily?

Before anyone writes a letter about government control of amateur sports, I would suggest that he should know about the proposed legislation. Very few do. Senator John Tunney of California, who has been extremely active in this area, has worked long and hard in studying the evils of our amateur athletic structure. He held a special press conference in New York in 1973. He came up from Washington with some members of his staff, his avowed purpose being to try to educate some of the sportswriters with regard to what was actually in the proposed legislation, and what it would do. Not one single sports columnist attended the press conference. The only New York newspaper that had a correspondent present at the hearings in 1972 and 1973 was *The New York Times,* Leonard Koppett in

1972 and William Wallace in 1973. Wallace was the only sportswriter of any note present at Tunney's press conference. Tunney was dismayed. I was disgusted.

The senator made the vital point that no single competition would be changed or controlled by passage of the proposed legislation. He patiently explained it. It would end the NCAA-AAU feud, improve the Olympic Committee. It was to no avail. Within the next couple of days I read columns by men who hadn't been at the press conference, and who probably had no idea of what was in the bill, decrying the thought of "government regulation." Once I asked Paul Zimmerman of the *New York Post,* who follows amateur sports, if he were going testify before the Congress. "What for?" he asked. "They're just a bunch of cheap politicians interested in publicity." What a blanket denunciation! And how does such an attitude produce, or tend to produce, the elimination of wrongs and injustices?

At the moment of this writing, legislation is again scheduled to come up on the Senate floor. I wish most of my broadcasting and writing colleagues would, just once, go to Washington and learn what the proposed bills are all about. If they did, maybe then the American public would get the information they need in order to form a judgment adequately.

But the answer is not in a superficial negative, "We don't want government control."

Q. What do you think will be happening in sports 20 years from now?

A. 1. The New York Giants will open their great new stadium in Easton, Pennsylvania. It will be a magnificent domed structure, seating 125,000 people, financed, jointly, by the taxpayers of New Jersey and Pennsylvania at a cost of $1.5 billion. Wellington Mara, the Giants' owner, will explain that the Jersey Sports Complex, completed only 17 years earlier, could no longer conveniently service Giant fans. Now they would be taken care of properly, he will say, and the value of the Giants to the public will finally be recognized. The stadium authority, headed by Sonny

Werblin, will provide a 99-year lease, tax free. Mr. Mara, in a sentimental gesture, will announce that the team will still be called the New York Giants. New York writers assigned to cover the Giants will hail the move. Sonny Werblin will take them all for helicopter trips from Times Square to the Lafayette College campus right next to the new stadium in just 45 minutes. The writers will write that it is easier to get to Easton than to drive to the Jersey Sports Complex from Scarsdale, New York.

2. Before 60,000 screaming fans, most of them women, Billie Jean King, 51 years of age, will beat 66-year-old Pancho Gonzales in three straight, bristling sets of tennis. Gloria Steinem and Betty Friedan, immediately after the match, will announce that once and for all the male chauvinists have been destroyed.

3, Baseball Commissioner Peter O'Malley, son of the late Walter O'Malley, will appoint a committee to study the question of whether the spitball should be legalized.

4. Authorities at the Indianapolis Motor Speedway will announce new safety measures for the brickyard designed to keep deaths to a minimum in the face of average speeds in excess of 275 miles per hour. Racing enthusiasts will hail the move as still another evidence of the sport's concern for human life.

5. There will be four football leagues, three baseball leagues, five basketball leagues, four hockey leagues; World Team Tennis will have 40 teams and World Championship Tennis will have eight divisions playing in a total of 400 tournaments. All told, more than 200 American cities will be involved, as will 14 foreign countries. And the American newspapers will not be able to print the scores and standings because of absence of space.

6. The North American Soccer League will announce that it is convinced that the American people will adopt soccer as a major sport. They will point to recent attendances which had moved as high as 6000 per game.

7. *ABC's Wide World of Sports*, now seen 7 days a week, will add 12 demolition derbies, increasing its total number to 72. All will originate in East Islip, New York.

8. Muhammad Ali will arrive in Houston to help the promotion of the upcoming heavyweight championship fight. Now 52, it will be Ali who continues to provide the color in boxing. In a long discourse, Ali will tell how he has taught the challenger Ali's famous "anchor" punch, the one that was taught to him by Stepin Fetchit for the fight against Liston in 1965. Nobody saw it then, Ali will say, and nobody will see it tomorrow night.

9. The Super Bowl game will be played between Des Moines and El Paso. Commissioner Pete Rozelle will express satisfaction that, finally, Middle America will be represented in the "big game." It will be played in Mexico City, with an anticipated sell-out crowd of 150,000 people. "This game, as no other in the history of sports," Rozelle will note, "will prove that football, and only football, reaches the hard core of the rural communities and is, at the same time, sophisticated, international and contemporary."

10. Former President Nixon will call Ara Parseghian, still at Notre Dame, to congratulate him on the victory over USC. ghian, still at Notre Dame, to congratulate him on the victory over USC.

11. *The New York Times* will discover the evils of big-time college sports recruitment, and do a series that will be called "revelatory."

12. Tom Seaver will be at his home in California, explaining what happened to his pitching rhythm 20 years earlier.

13. Former Governor Howard Samuels of New York will call for legalized betting on all sports. "Make the illegal legal, and you'll drive the gangsters out."

14. Streaking will stage a comeback at sports events.

15. Major league baseball will be looking for a qualified black to manage.

16. Professional football will be looking for a qualified black to play quarterback.

17. Average salaries of all athletes will be $100,000 a year.

18. Representatives of the AAU, the NCAA and the United States Olympic Committee will testify before the Senate

Commerce Committee in opposition to a bill designed to relieve the athletes of the injustices wreaked upon them by these ancient bodies. "We can settle our own problems. We don't want government control." But in the 1992 Olympics, eight American youngsters had their gold medals taken away because of mistakes by members of the United States Olympic Committee, and 16 American basketball players could not play against the Peoples' Republic of China because the NCAA would not certify the event.

19. The New York Jets will call a press conference to announce that Joe Namath, minus both legs and with only one arm, his left, will play one more year.

20. The National Football League will deny that it has a drug problem.

21. George Allen will have a number-one draft choice.

22. The National League will announce that it needs more time to study the "designated hitter rule" before it can adopt it.

23. No basketball team will have more than one white player. He will be able to handle the ball at least three times in any game.

Q. The time frame in which you have been successful has been in 1960s and 1970s. Given your personality, your particular approach to broadcast journalism and your emotional makeup, do you think that you would have been successful had you been working during an earlier era?

A. I'd like to think that I have the brains and the talent to have succeeded in any era, but I must admit that the 1960s and early 1970s were exactly right for me. The contemporary years have been years of disenchantment, especially for those who grew into young adulthood during this period. From the beginning these young people have been smothered by turmoil; slowly twisting in the wind, so to speak. Three assassinations within five years. A new word, "ecology"—worry about the very air one breathes. The unending racial anguish, busing, and will the blacks ever really get equal educational and housing opportunities? The horror of Vietnam and military conscription for so many young males. The disturbance of our young people, and tragedies like Kent State. Narcotics addiction at every social stratum, everywhere one turns, poor, middle income and rich. I remember nights when my younger daughter Hilary came home shaken by the discovery that some friends were smoking "joints," some were on "speed," one was actually a "pusher." Disillusionment everywhere.

And then, the breakdown in government. The vice-president of the United States, a confessed felon. A number of the former president's closest and personally appointed aides either confessed felons, duly sentenced, or under indictment. The president of the United States himself facing impeachment proceedings, and finally resigning. The loss of belief in government, and almost everything else.

Under such extraordinarily trying circumstances, a whole new generation has come of age. And under such circumstances, they could hardly be expected to subscribe to the long-cherished and long-propagandized fiction that in all the world only sports was clean and pure. It has been a time to puncture myths. And that's what I believe these young people have seen: the myths of the past punctured everywhere around them, in politics, in economics, in sociology, and yes, even in sports. They want things to believe in, and people to believe in.

And so, I think that the time in which I have prospered has been uniquely right for me. Whether or not I am disputatious, I do have opinions and I do take stands, some of which are not always popular with everybody. The bulk of the television viewers and radio listeners respect that. They want people around today who, at the very least, tell it like they think it is. This is what I have done.

I also happen to believe that the same approach would, in the long run, succeed in any era.

Q. You so often talk about what's wrong in sports. Do you ever find any joy in it?

A. Outside of my family, sports have been the joy of my life. I could not have been involved with sports for the past 18 years of my life if this had not been so. The joy, of course, has been in the people I have known, the places I have been and the events I have witnessed.

I was a friend of Jackie Robinson and it affected my entire life. I saw Jackie in his first game at Ebbets Field. And I saw him on the last day of the season in 1951 at Philadelphia, with darkness descending, and the Dodgers needing a victory to tie the Giants who had already won. I saw Eddie Waitkus hit a line drive over second, and I saw Jackie fling himself headlong on the ground and make the game-saving catch—I'll never know how. Then I saw him a few innings later—it was downright dark—hit a home run against Robin Roberts to gain the Dodgers a tie for the pennant. Jackie's whole life was mirrored in that game. He was unconquerable. Jackie Robinson was, for me, the joy of sports.

I saw Bob Beaman jump further than any man will jump in this century.

I saw Mark Spitz win seven gold medals.

I saw Bobby Thomson hit a home run on October 3, 1951 against Ralph Branca. The Giants won the pennant. I saw Ralph Branca become a man.

I heard Branch Rickey talk about his days at Ohio Wesleyan, about his youth and about his view of death.

Vince Lombardi respected me. I'm very proud of that.

I saw the Baltimore-New York sudden-death game, with John Unitas at his very best.

I saw Joe Namath and the Jets beat the Colts, 16–7.

I saw Joe DiMaggio, Stan Musial, Sandy Koufax, Don Drysdale and Ted Williams. I was there when Willie Mays and Mickey Mantle broke in.

I saw Jimmy Brown run, and now I am seeing O. J. Simpson.

I saw Sid Luckman and the Monsters of the Midway.

I saw Davis and Blanchard; I have seen Notre Dame and U.S.C. I have watched the Crimson Tide, and I saw Notre Dame and Michigan State play that 10–10 tie.

I have been to two Olympiads, in Mexico City and in Munich.

I have watched Henry Aaron all his baseball life.

I have seen racing drivers die; I have also seen them live.

I saw Pete Reiser crash into outfield walls and succumb.

I have seen Enos Slaughter crash into outfield walls and not succumb.

I have seen Lee Evans run and Bill Toomey win the decathlon when it seemed all but impossible.

I saw Citation and Count Fleet and Secretariat win the Derby.

I was there when Bill Mazeroski hit the 1960 home run that beat the Yankees in the World Series.

I saw Gallant Man lose to Iron Liege in the Derby, when Willie Shoemaker misjudged the finish line.

I saw Louis beat Schmeling. I saw Frazier beat Ali.

I saw Sugar Ray Robinson at his best.

I saw Arnold Palmer make golf a major sport. Then I saw Jack Nicklaus adopt it as his own.

I saw Bill Russell and I'll never forget it. Bob Cousy, too. Pancho Gonzales has been part of my life.

I was there when Patterson knocked out Johannson.

I have seen A. J. Foyt drive—and Jackie Stewart and Jim Clark and Stirling Moss and Juan Fangio.

I saw Mickey Ownen drop a third strike in a world series.

I saw Britain defeat West Germany to win the World Cup, and England turn delirious.

I have been to Monaco, a fairyland principality that is a monument to opulence. I can still see the dashing, romantic face of the late Peter Revson.

I have been to Stockholm, and seen the people stop Floyd Patterson in the streets, just to touch him in a fond, gentle way.

I have been to Germany, Switzerland, Italy, Austria, Spain and Yugoslavia. I have swum in the Adriatic, eaten fish in Trieste, walked the Via Venito in Rome.

I have been to Paris in the springtime.

I have been to Mexico and to Canada, to Caracas, to Rio, to Panama and to the Caribbean Islands.

I have been behind the wall in Berlin.

I have ridden a bike through the streets of Amsterdam; visited Hamlet's castle in Denmark; eaten at La Belle Terrace in Tivoli Gardens.

Ireland is as green as they say.

I have been to Los Angeles, San Francisco, Oakland, San Diego, Dallas, Houston, Atlanta, Miami, Denver, Kansas City, St. Louis, Chicago, Pittsburgh, Cleveland, Cincinnati, Philadelphia, Boston, Toronto, Montreal and Seattle. Las Vegas has been part of my beat. New Orleans has its own flavor. I have been to all of these cities and more. Baltimore *does* have great osyters. Washington *is* beautiful, regardless of what the politicians do there.

Always I come back to the city I love, my city, New York.

But I'm glad I've been to the others. It has made for a rich, full life.

It has been the joy of sports.

PART III

BROOKLYN REVISITED

CHAPTER 12

THE HOME OF IRA FELDBLUM

"Howard, you're making my cousin, Ira, famous."

It was Monday night, October 29, 1973. The place was Rich Stadium, Buffalo, New York, and more than 80,000 people were watching the Buffalo Bills rout the Kansas City Chiefs. They were doing more than that. They were enjoying a civic celebration. For the first time ever, *Monday Night Football* had come to their often maligned city, and they had waited for it for a long, long time. They had more banners than we had ever seen in any one ball park. They had horns and hats and hoopla that made the place seem like 30 circuses in one. And on the football field, they had O. J. Simpson, who had also been waiting for this night for a long, long time.

O. J. took advantage of the occasion. He carried the ball on almost every play. He carried it so often he set a new record for carries in one game in the National Football League. He wanted 40 million people to see him the way they used to see him at the University of Southern California—only better. And that's the way the people saw him. Buffalo was big league in every respect, and "The Juice" made sure that America knew it.

As he spun off one sensational run after another, there came a point at which "Dandy" Don and I had the following colloquy:

"Ha'hrd, how would you like to have had O. J. on your Eastern Parkway team?"

257

"Well, 'Dandy,' we didn't need him. We had the greatest speedster of all time, Ira Feldblum."

"Ira who?"

"Ira Feldblum."

Don't ask me why I mentioned Ira Feldblum. "Dandy" and I have had so many talks about Brooklyn—where I grew up—and I have kidded him so much about my youghful athletic exploites, it just seemed the natural thing to do. Ira Feldblum was one of the kids in our gang during those early years, and while I hear from him occasionally—he's an insurance man now—I haven't really seen him socially for more than 25 years.

Ira was a tall kid, and a pretty good street athlete. Because he was taller than the rest of us, we would send him out deep as a receiver, and he could outjump the defenders—what the on-air jocks of today would call "isolating him one-on-one in a mismatch."

For the same reason, although he was not a good shooter, we made him the center on our basketball team.

In stickball, he could hit the long ball, but only if you bounced the pitch to him on the outside. He had a bad batting stance, locking his arms and wrists in close to his body, and the inside pitch destroyed him.

Ira and I used to spend our summers together, along with a lot of the other guys, at Manhattan Beach in Brooklyn. He wasn't a bad swimmer either.

He went to Erasmus Hall High School in the years when they had Sid Luckman. I went to Alexander Hamilton High School in the years when they had "Dolly" King, who later became the center of a phenomenal Long Island University basketball team. But in football, Luckman prevailed, and Ira was a pain in the ass with his boasting about "the Buff and the Blue" (Erasmus's colors). I can still hear him on the streets of Brooklyn leading the old Erasmus cheer:

Vivo, Vivo, Vivo Ves,
E R A S M U S."

I grew to hate the damn thing.

Then, too, Ira went to law school, just as I did. Only he went to St. John's, and I went to N.Y.U. He spent the whole three years of law school complaining to me that St. John's was tougher because their final exams were not essay questions, but true/false or yes/no questions. We took the bar examination at the same time, and one half of the New York State Bar examination utilized the true or false format. Ira flunked. I didn't. The true or false issue was put to rest forevermore.

But he was a good friend, and a hell of a guy. I guess that's why I mentioned him during the Buffalo telecast. This is the Age of Nostalgia, after all.

Two or three days after the Buffalo game, I got a letter. It was from Ira Feldblum, and it carried with it a picture taken of the two of us on Eastern Parkway when we were in our teens. I knew I had been a skinny kid, but not *that* skinny. I kind of liked the picture, though. I had a marvelous head of hair when I was 16. The letter recalled old times together, and Ira told me of the many phone calls he had received after I had spoken of him.

Then it was Monday night, November 12, 1973. The place was Arrowhead Stadium, Kansas City, Missouri. The Chiefs were killing the Chicago Bears. It was a terribly dull game. There came a moment when Meredith and I had this exchange:

"Watch the ABC Evening News with Harry Reasoner and Howard K. Smith. Ha'hrd, did you know that Howard K. Smith was a Rhodes Scholar?"

"Not only that, 'Dandy,' he was a good athlete—a hurdler at Tulane."

"Is that where your good friend Ira Feldblum went?"

That did it. It was Don's Turn.

On the following Monday night, November 19, we were in the Regency Hyatt House in Atlanta, Georgia, hosting a pregame cocktail party for the *Monday Night Football* sponsors. Atlanta was to upset Minnesota later that evening in what I think was the best game we have ever had on our Monday night series.

Sue and Don Meredith arrived at the party brandishing a letter Don had received. It was from Ira Feldblum. It carried with it a picture of Ira and me taken at Manhattan Beach back in the 1930s. In a bathing suit, I was a toothpick. So was Ira. And between us in the picture was Ramona, the vocalist at the time for Paul Whiteman's orchestra, which was performing daily at the beach. Actually, I remembered when the picture had been snapped. It was a glorious moment, an instant of high glamour for two kids to be photographed with a "star." I was so excited I stayed around the bandstand all day, never going over to the pool or the basketball courts, or to any of my normal haunts.

Ira's letter to Don was epic in its modesty. He explained that I had perhaps overstated his speed, but that in all other respects, yes, he had been an extraordinary performer. Sue and Don were really taken with the letter, and I was taken with the picture. So Don gave me the picture, and he and Sue wrote Ira a letter.

The next morning, I had to go to Rich's Department Store on Peachtree Street to sign books for purchasers of my earlier book, *Cosell*. You always worry about those book-signing affairs. You worry about whether anybody will show up. You don't want to be embarrassed. But Rich's was a happy experience. Crowds of people on line. I went merrily about the business of autographing, delighted as I was by the turnout, when a man came up with four books that he had purchased and wanted signed. When someone buys four books at $8.95 per copy, plus tax, he deserves special treatment, so I greeted him with joyous magnanimity.

He smiled back and said, "Don't you remember me?"

I said no.

Then he told me. "I'm Ira Feldblum's cousin, Victor. You remember, Brooklyn?"

"Of course," I boomed out. "Any cousin of Ira Feldblum's is a friend of mine."

I signed the four books, shook his hand warmly, turned to Emmy and said, "You know, Ira was one helluva guy."

We made a 4:00 P.M. plane out of Atlanta to New York that afternoon, and as we were entering our apartment at 7:15

P.M. the phone was ringing. I rushed in to take the call.

"Howard?" the voice said at the other end.

"Yes?"

"Howard, it's Milton."

"Yes?"

"Howard, it's me, Milton Berle."

Recognition dawned. "Oy hes, Miltie, what's up?"

"Howard, you're making my cousin Ira famous. Stop talking about him on the air."

Suddenly, I recalled the first time I ever met "Mr. Television." It was in the late 1940s, when I was practicing law, and I represented a committee working for an independent state of Palestine. The late Senator Homer Capehart of Indiana and the late Congressman Joseph Clark Baldwin of New York headed up the committee. They were organizing a dinner to raise funds for the committee. And who could do the job of master of ceremonies better than the hottest property in show business, Milton Berle?

He was appearing at the time at a long-defunct nightclub in New York called the Carnival. But how in the world could we get to him? The answer was simple. Ira Feldblum was Milton Berle's cousin. Ira would introduce me. Ira did, and that's how I first met "Uncle Miltie." Berle, by the way, never did emcee that dinner. But now, on the phone all these years later, we got a big chuckle out of the reminiscence, and Milton could not believe it when I told him of Ira's cousin Victor being in Rich's Department Store that very morning.

"He always did have a lot of relatives," Milton laughed. "You know, the Feldblums were the hoity-toity ones. German Jews, too good for the rest of us."

The next weekend, Emmy and I were at our home in Pound Ridge for a day or so before moving on out to the next football game. We went to our favorite restaurant in the area for dinner on Saturday night, Nino's of Bedford Village.

When we got there, as usual, there was a line waiting for tables. A man smiled at me and said, "Hello." I nodded and greeted him. He looked vaguely familiar but I couldn't place him.

"Don't you remember me?" he asked. "I'm Jerry Gans, 263

Eastern Parkway, Ira Feldblum's cousin."

It was too much. I shook his hand, told him "Sure, I remember," walked off to my table with Emmy and said, "That's it. I've got to go back to Brooklyn, if only to see where Ira Feldblum once lived."

CHAPTER 13

NOSTALGIA STREET

"Oh, how I loved that team."

On a cloudy, uninspiring day in June 1974, my wife and I climbed into a car for the drive from Manhattan to Brooklyn. It had been 25 years since Emmy and I and our daughter, Jill, then four years old, left my parents' apartment at 175 Eastern Parkway and moved into Peter Cooper Village, a Metropolitan Life Insurance Company development in Manhattan. Our visits back to Brooklyn after that were only occasional, mostly to see my parents. Usually, they came to Manhattan to visit us. That was always one of the odd things about Brooklyn. Although it was part of New York City, it was a separate, different world with its own identity, its own pride, its own tradition. Most people who lived in Brooklyn were accustomed to riding the subway to Manhattan every day, in order to go to work. For Brooklynites, this was no trip at all. But people who lived in Manhattan would talk of the "other borough" as if it were a foreign land, and the prospect of ever going there carried with it all the hardships of a safari.

As we were driving downtown to Canal Street, there to take the Manhattan Bridge to Brooklyn, my mind inevitably wandered over the past 25 years. God, the things that had happened in the world during that time. It wasn't even the same world. During that quarter century, the Salk Vaccine was discovered and the atom bomb became part of our culture; children grew up with the realization that we could all be destroyed at any time. Korea and Vietnam erupted. Sexual mores changed; premarital sexual intercourse began to stop shocking parents into irrational actions directed against the child; homosexuality became an openly discussed topic, and even accepted by many as a fact of life; movies became infected by a spate of openly pornographic pictures. Jet transportation would make the whole world as one. Man invaded outer space, and men walked on the moon. The British Empire disintegrated. A new nation called Israel grew and fought three wars for survival. A Supreme Court decision was rendered, *Brown* v. *Board of Education of Topeka,* that sought to strike down, forever, inequality of educational opportunity for blacks, but instead provoked a long and bitter episode in the racial anguish of this country, an episode that is far from over. America negotiated détentes with the People's Republic of China and the Soviet Union. Assassination and violence became commonplace in the 1960s. The possible impeachment of a president was beginning to occupy the minds of most Americans.

All this and more had happened in the 25 years since we had left Brooklyn. Now, driving to my old domicile, I looked back on all of it. My dad died in 1957, so he missed most of it. But I wonder if he could have accepted the world the way it is now. He liked things the way they were. But they couldn't be that way in Brooklyn now. As the world had undergone enormous waves of change, so had the great old borough, I was sure of it in my own mind and from all I had read by writers, like Pete Hamill, who still live there.

We turned left on Canal Street and headed for the bridge. Once Canal Street, which separates Chinatown from the Lower East Side, was a very important and active thoroughfare. Now it looked run-down and seedy. An old landmark was gone, Lum Fong's Chinese Restaurant. Bargain signs were posted in discount and variety stores. The buildings looked generally dilapidated.

The Manhattan Bridge hadn't changed, just the Manhattan skyline. To our left were all the high-rise projects that had been constructed in the years since I had left Brooklyn—low-income housing that looked like low-income housing. And the bridge itself seemed to rock, as it always had, with the weight and the noise of the flood of trucks that endlessly crossed it.

When you leave the Manhattan Bridge, you go on to the Flatbush Avenue Extension, a wide street that was always notable for two things: its volume of traffic and the Brooklyn Paramount Theatre. Brooklyn Tech High School was once there, too, but that was long gone. It had been an antiquated facility and a new Brooklyn Tech was built in a different section many years ago.

The only thing that hasn't changed on that avenue is the volume of traffic. The Brooklyn Paramount Theatre isn't there any more. Long Island University is. A hell of a place for a university, I thought—a converted theatre now an office building, no campus, no visible evidence of university life, just bricks. How different it had been when I was a kid, jumping onto the subway at the Eastern Parkway-Brooklyn Museum IRT Station, riding down to Nevins Street, and then walking over to the Paramount. The subway ride was a nickel, admission to the theatre before 2:00 P.M. was a quarter.

What shows we used to see. It was a great age for movies and a marvelous age for vaudeville and stage shows. The first time I ever saw Eddie Cantor was at the Brooklyn Paramount. He came out in that bouncy little way of his, clapping his hands together, popping those banjo eyes, and singing *Whoopee*, the title song of his hit musical on Broadway in the late 1920s. Eddie Cantor, like most of the other great comedians of those years, meant a very great deal to people. He and the others were a buffer against the Great Depression. People were selling apples on corners, the bonus army was marching on Washington. But you could forget about those things with people like Eddie and Lou Holtz and Joe Cook and Phil Baker. When Cantor would sing, *I'd Love to Spend this Hour with You,* it was a joy and a comfort, a respite from the worries at home, like whether dad would be fired or not. That was always on our minds, and there were periods when he *was* out of work. That was when my mother's burden was heavy, indeed, having to hold the house together, keep us all encouraged and not let my father down. Somehow she would do it, and I will never know how she managed to give me the 30 cents to cover subway fare and the admission price so that I could go to the Paramount.

The first musical comedy I ever saw was at the Paramount. There was a time when musical comedies would be shortened for the stage show which accompanied the movie at the great motion-picture houses. The show I saw was *50 Million Frenchmen* and the hit song, *You Do Something to Me,* became a classic.

The last time I went to the Brooklyn Paramount was in 1944 with Emmy. It was shortly before we were married, and we went to see a war movie. What else? It was that time. I don't remember the name of the picture, but I do remember that Emmy lost $40 from her purse. The other memories are better: the Radio Rogues, the Nicholas Brothers, all of the wonderful vaudeville acts of the era.

But now, where DeKalb Avenue and the Flatbush Avenue Extension meet, there is Long Island University.

There is one remaining treasure of the past, however. Diagonally across the street there is a saloon, and the sign above it says, "Dodgers Bar." I hope they never take it down.

A little further down on DeKalb Avenue, the old RKO Albee is still there. In its day, it was just like the Paramount, the Brooklyn Fox, the Brooklyn Strand and the Loew's Metropolitan. Those five were the "Broadway" of Brooklyn in a movie sense, and I loved them all. At these theatres I first saw Milton Berle, Jack Benny, Jack Oakie and many of the big bands of the time.

It's funny how, suddenly, you remember things apparently long forgotten, and places, too. Flatbush Avenue Extension, between DeKalb Avenue and Fulton Street, used to have a Minsky Burlesque House and a movie house called Werba's Brooklyn Theatre. That was where the picture *Wings,* starring Richard Arlen, had a very long run. I'll never forget that movie, any more than I'll ever forget *Hell's Angels.* They were the two spectacular pictures about American pilots in World War I. Movies were a big factor in the lives and growth of young people then, as television is now.

Werba's and Minsky's are part of a distant past. So is a place called the Fulton-Royal, which was an upstairs restaurant and nightclub where Harold Stern and his orchestra held forth. You may never have heard of Harold Stern, but in the 1930s he was an important entertainer in Brooklyn. Every summer he and his orchestra would play at Manhattan Beach, about which I'll have more to say later. Stern's music was geared to his audience and to the times. I can almost hear Ravel's *Bolero* now, followed by *My Silent Love.*

Flatbush Avenue Extension intersects Fulton Street, the old, famous shopping street of Brooklyn. The renowned Fulton Street has vanished. Abraham Straus, the big department store of the borough is still there. So is May's. But if you look to the left as you cross Fulton Street, the Brooklyn Strand is missing. The Strand was where I saw Clark Gable for the first time. He was in a movie called *Night Nurse,* starring Barbara Stanwyck, and he played a small role as a kind of leering chauffeur. I never guessed, then, that he would become the biggest star in Hollywood. But in later years, I would think back to that picture often. You see, Ira Feldblum was about as homely as I am, which takes some doing, and yet he labored under the illusion that he looked like Clark Gable. He would tell us about it every day on Eastern Parkway, and when Gable was making those pictures with Joan Crawford, I am convinced that Ira fantasized that he was kissing Miss Crawford instead of "The King's" doing so.

After the Fulton Street intersection, the Flatbush Avenue Extension becomes just plain Flatbush Avenue. This is where I got my first taste of the decay of Brooklyn. Flatbush Avenue, from Fulton Street to Grand Army Plaza, had always been one of the most active and attractive business streets of the area. It was the link between the rich Grand Army Plaza and early Eastern Parkway sections, and downtown Brooklyn. Good shops lined the avenue on either side. As one would approach Fulton Street, coming down from those sections, there would be the Brooklyn Fox Theatre. Like the Paramount and the Strand, it no longer exists. Neither do the stores of yore. In their place are crummy, broken-down, bargain-type establishments, bars of a honky-tonk nature, and most of the places are shuttered and protected by metal screens or bars that bespeak the threat of burglary and vandalism. Everywhere one turns there is graffiti. I don't know to what the psychiatrists attribute the graffiti passion—whether it is supposed to be the protest of some young people against the society, an expression of frustration or even, in some strange, curious way an outlet for inhibited art—but I do know that the graffiti on Flatbush Avenue in Brooklyn is the most unsightly I have ever seen anywhere in this country. I was appalled by it. That whole run, from Fulton Street to Grand Army Plaza, with two exceptions, had the feel of a cavity-stricken tooth (in a state of advanced decay), and now the abscess was there, naked, for all to see.

This couldn't be the street I used to walk along, where there had been fine haberdashery shops, dress shops, sporting-goods stores and hardware stores. But it was. The two exceptions to the downtrodden look were the Williamsburg Savings Bank building and Michel's Restaurant. The bank building is still impressive, with a fine tenancy. Indeed, an old neighbor and dentist friend, Dr. Fred Shiplacoff, still has his office there. Across the street, the Long Island Railroad Terminal, where Walter O'Malley once wanted a new stadium for the Brooklyn Dodgers, looked like a disaster area. But Michel's Restaurant, all the way up at Sterling Place, just a couple of short blocks from Grand Army Plaza, was obviously still the same: A classy establishment with a fine menu in the window and the look of care that usually promises good food. I used to take Emmy there when we were dating. We got out of the car, looked into the place and I thought, "If we ever come back this way again, we'll eat here."

Two movie houses near Michel's are still open, the Carlton and the Plaza. The Carlton was showing *The Exorcist.* It used to be a nice spot. Now, like the avenue, it appears run-down. The Plaza was exhibiting X-rated movies, which should give you an idea.

Standing at the corner of Flatbush Avenue and Sterling Place, I took a long, lingering look down the avenue. Park Place, Prospect Place, St. Mark's Avenue, Bergen Street. They were all my home away from home when I went to Public School 9, just one block away at Vanderbilt Avenue and Sterling Place. My mind roamed back to the kids in my class, names

I hadn't thought of in 40 years. Matty Kolb, Willie Sandberg, Eddie Grey. These were some of the gang that used to meet at lunch hour every day right at the very spot where I was standing. We would choose up sides and play ring-o-levio, the old game where one group would be the pursuers and the other the pursued. When you captured one of the pursued, you would put him in "jail," which was an area guarded by one of the pursuers. The jailee could be freed if one of the pursued could sneak into the jail, scream "ring-o-levio" and dart off with the former prisoner. In the course of three-quarters-of-an-hour during lunch period, we must have covered miles of ground on all those streets I have already named, plus others.

I wonder what's become of all of those kids? I know what happened to one of them, a boy named Gene Slutzky. He became Gene Kelly—not the dancer, but a sportscaster who, for a time, was the voice of the Philadelphia Phillies.

We went up one block to P.S. 9. I was shocked by two things, the smallness of the place and the horrible graffiti. I looked in the schoolyard where I used to play basketball and handball. It seemed so tiny, and yet I remembered it as being big. This, I suppose, is the difference between a youngster's and an adult's physical perspective. Recently, when Emmy and I had a party for our 30th wedding anniversary, our grandsons, Justin and Jared were there, meeting about 50 people for the first time. Jared was overwhelmed with fright. The poor little two-year-old, looking up at all those tall people and strange faces and loud voices, suddenly found himself in a land of giants. Back in the schoolyard, I was a giant in a lilliputian world. I stared at the building, and couldn't believe that it was so unimpressive. When I was a kid the classrooms had seemed large and even foreboding. Year in and year out, P.S. 9 had held the PSAL track and field championship of New York City. I, myself, had finished second in the city championship meet in the standing broad-jump event. (Emmy still has the silver medal on her charm bracelet). How, I mused, could this little building have spawned so many fine athletes? And then I reflected back to the hours after school, day after day, when we would go over to the big circle at Grand Army Plaza, which was circumscribed by a cinderpath on which we practiced, and practiced and practiced. If we made the team and won a medal in the city championship meet, we would get gray sweaters with a yellow circle over the heart and the number 9 enclosed within it. The sweaters would be presented to us at assembly with the student body singing our sing, *March, march on down the line, shouting for number 9.* . . . It was taken from the old Yale song, of course, and I'll never forget the pride that swelled within me when I got mine.

When I went to P.S. 9, it was in a great neighborhood. Lovely, beautifully tended brownstones ran up Sterling Place toward Underhill Avenue. Now, the street had deteriorated. The corrosion of time, sociological change and inattention made it seem like dry rot had set in. And everywhere you glanced was that damned graffiti. Blue, green, yellow, red, orange and black—profane and ugly.

During my years at P.S. 9, we lived on Lincoln Place, between Underhill and Washington Avenues. It was a narrow street, as I remembered it, and it was even narrower than I had remembered it when I went back to look at it. Number 329 was where we lived. It seemed a nice, happy place then. It didn't now. But the memories are still bright.

We used to go down to the cellar, open the window slightly, fronting on Lincoln Place, take out our pea shooters, and plague passers-by with the sting of our carefully aimed missiles. Then we would scurry away with exultant chuckles at the discomfort of our targets. We would build snow huts every winter in back of Dixon Harwin's house next door. His family had money (his father was a doctor) and they had a private home right next to our apartment building. As if to prove their wealth, they even had a pool table in a downstairs playroom. Dixon went on to the University of Pennsylvania, and all the guys on the block envied him. He was one of the older guys on the block, my brother Hilton's age.

Hilton is four years older than I. Lincoln Place was a wonderful world of sports, dominated by Hilton's age group. There were guys like Jack Storm and Al Thorner, pure stylists when it came to punchball. Al was a master at looking at first while he punched the ball over third. Jack was one of a kind. He could do everything, a white Willie Mays of the street.

I was lucky if I could even get into a game because I was so much younger. That's why I remember a day when I was the last one picked just to fill out a team. They put me in short left field, close up to the third baseman, and Jack Storm hit a screaming liner right at me. In self-defense, I put up my hands and the ball stuck in them. I was an instant hero. The next inning I made two errors and got kicked out of the game.

I loved everything about those days at P.S. 9 and on Lincoln Place, and the flashbacks kept pouring into the forefront of my mind; I imagined the open lot across the street where we used to play baseball, until Turner Towers was built. The lot stretched from Lincoln Place to Eastern Parkway, but Turner Towers killed it off. It is, to this day, the tallest residential building on Eastern Parkway. I remember how we used to roast potatoes over a fire on that lot, "micks" we called them. I can still see my grandfather, my mother's dad, walking up the street to give me a Hebrew lesson. He was a rabbi, but there was nothing Old World about him. He would take me out of whatever game I was playing at the time, despite my resistance, go through the lesson with me and then insist upon our playing rummy. He used to murder me. He played to win, even against a 12-year-old boy.

I got my introduction to music in those years—if you could call it music. Every Sunday morning, my dad would get out his fiddle and play. He loved light opera; Victor Herbert and Rudolf Friml were his pets. It got so that I would hum *My Hero* from *The Chocolate Soldier* for an entire week. He alternated between that and *The Donkey Serenade* for an hour or more, screeching away, until my mother would finally say, "Izzie, that's enough. You're driving us crazy." Then he would smile sheepishly, put the violin in its case, and take Hilton and me rowing on the Prospect Park lake. After that we would have a milkshake. Those were the days. Some Sundays we would have to visit my paternal grandparents, and other Sundays my maternal grandparents. My brother and I rebelled at all these visits because we wanted to be out playing, but we were quashed. The one redeeming feature was when we went to Brownsville to see my dad's folks. There was a candy store nearby that made the best milkshakes I have ever tasted, creamy and rich.

Hilton went to Alexander Hamilton High School at Albany Avenue and Bergen Street. Before it adopted that name it had been famous as Boys Commercial. I don't know if Hilton really wanted to go to Hamilton, but I don't believe he had a choice. My mother did not believe in coeducation. If Hilton had a choice, it was between Hamilton and Boys High. Mother was fixed in her conviction that a boy could not possibly pay attention to school work if there were girls around.

This was surprising because she was a very liberal woman for her time. She was born Nellie Rosenthal in Worcester, Massachusetts, and was raised in Passaic, New Jersey. As a young woman, she was strikingly attractive, and even today, going on 80, she retains a positively beautiful complexion. She has had many setbacks physically, the most recent being a fall with subsequent hip surgery, but she's a fighter and she's walking again.

When I say she was liberal in her attitudes, I mean that she didn't hold us close to the womb. She used to let me go to Manhattan on my own when I was only 12 years old, armed with my subway fare and the price of admission, so that I could see the new movies when they hit Broadway. I used to tell the other kids, with a great deal of patronizing that, yes, I had seen Norma Shearer, Lionel Barrymore and Clark Gable in *A Free Soul* at the Astor Theatre. I would also boast of having gone into New York by myself to catch Phillip Holmes in Theodore Dreiser's *An American Tragedy*.

My dad was not a good-looking man, but he had great dignity in his bearing and in his face. He looked a lot like Henry Morganthau, Franklin Roosevelt's secretary of the treasury, with the same rimless, pinched-nose glasses, the same smile. Dad had one habit that drove us all mad. Every Sunday morning, before he would start to play the fiddle, he would take every shirt he had out of his bureau drawer, carefully examine them, refold them and put them away. Don't ask me why.

The real arguments in the house would occur over other things though, things like his preoccupation with his family; the fact that as controller for a credit clothing chain of stores, he was almost always on the road; the further fact that his job was neither high paying nor secure. As I have mentioned earlier, there were times when Dad was out of work, and the family didn't have a dime. When I would hear and see my parents quarrel I would cringe. I made a vow, then and there, that when I married, my children would never witness an argument between my wife and me. That has turned out to be the case almost, not quite, but almost.

I fell in love for the first time in my life on Lincoln Place. Her name was Dorothy Schroeder. She was a beautiful, Scandinavian, blonde, about 11 years old, and lived on the same floor we did in the apartment building next door. It happened in a thoroughly orthodox way. One night I was in our kitchen and she was in hers. The shades were not drawn. I looked through our window at her, and she looked back at me. I smiled, and so did she. And then, heaven knows why, we started matching kitchen utensils through the windows. I would hold up a pot, so would she. Then a knife. Then a fork. It went on for 15 minutes, until there was nothing left in the way of objects. I finally mustered up all my courage, blew her a kiss, and she blew one back at me. After that, every night for the next two weeks I would go to the kitchen, look over to see if Dorothy was there, and hope for a reprise. It never happened. My love went unrequited, and I never had the nerve to talk to her when I would see her in the street.

But even so, apart from the joy of living, I had another love affair, the Brooklyn Dodgers. Unless you grew up in Brooklyn in those years, it is impossible to describe what the Dodgers meant to everyone, kids, teen-agers, adults—everyone. They were the heart and soul of the borough, the spirit of the territory, the tie that bound every ethnic group together. It didn't matter that for most of those years the team was forlorn in its performances. All that mattered was that they belonged to Brooklyn; that they gave Brooklyn an identity separate and apart from Manhattan. They made Brooklyn big league.

Each of us had his own hero, and mine was Johnny Frederick, the center fielder with a fluid, left-handed swing. But I had others, too. The first baseman, Adelphia "Del" Bissonette, another power hitter, attacked the ball with a peculiar violence that sprang from a crouching batting stance that made him a difficult target to pitch to. Babe Herman, who couldn't run bases, but could get hit in the head with a fly ball was, nonetheless, one of the greatest hitters I have ever seen. And then the Dodgers got Frank "Lefty" O'Doul in a trade with Philadelphia. "Lefty" could have written books on hitting; he was that much of a stylist at the plate. On Sundays, you could see Clarence "Dazzy" Vance pitch.

I never waited for Sundays, though. On days when there was no track practice, I would run to Ebbets Field, and if I couldn't get the turnstile man to let me in, or turn his back while I sneaked in, I would scoot around to Bedford Avenue, lie on the ground and look under the center-field fence. That way I could at least see Johnny Frederick's back.

Oh, how I loved that team. On days when they won, I was jubilant. On days when they lost, I was morose; miserable to everyone around, and I would get into fights with my brother. This was not unique. All the people in Brooklyn felt the same way. The Dodgers were a civic enterprise. The ground of Ebbets Field was as hallowed as Gettysburg.

Thus, when we moved to 852 Classon Avenue at the corner of Eastern Parkway, I was not dismayed at leaving Lincoln Place. I was two-and-one-half blocks closer to Ebbets Field. And, although I did not know it then, right around the corner, on Lincoln Place between Classon and Franklin Avenues, lived Ira Feldblum. He had been on my street, only a block-and-a-half down from where I lived all the time I was in elementary school.

However, 852 Classon Avenue was a problem. I felt it, instinctively. It was a four-story graystone, and as Emmy and I looked at it, we could both understand why. On the corner of Eastern Parkway, it was surrounded by the fine, modern, doorman-attended, elevator-equipped, six-story buildings of Eastern Parkway. Eastern Parkway was for the rich people. We were not that. Eastern Parkway had the rich Jews, the successful merchants of the garment center, the kings of the textile industry, the fabric merchants. I used to think about how much the heads of the families would bring home each week. Maybe as much as $400. "Who would be my friends?" I began to wonder. "With whom could I play? Would I be accepted as one who lived on Classon Avenue in a four-story walk-up?"

I described all this to Emmy as we got out of the car and began to look around. There was still another gnawing trouble in those years. I had graduated from P.S. 9 and I wanted to go to Erasmus Hall High School. But my mother was steadfast. Hilton had been graduated from Hamilton High School. He had liked it, and there was no way she would permit me to go to a school that had girls. Since Hilton had been happy with Hamilton, I should go to Hamilton. I went to Hamilton. Nearly all the kids on Eastern Parkway went to Erasmus. That school even had a campus. Hamilton was four stories of cement. Not being in Erasmus would make me an even greater interloper in the swish atmosphere of Eastern Parkway.

"Lord, what fools these mortals be!" Ira Feldblum was one of those who came to the rescue. He lived on Lincoln Place, but played on Eastern Parkway. How can one repay him for that? Irv Berkowitz lived on Franklin Avenue, a block away. He played on Eastern Parkway while his parents ran a fruit store on Franklin Avenue. If he belonged, so did I. Buddy Youmans and Herb Grant lived on Washington Avenue. If they could make it, so could I. I became a part of Eastern Parkway. I was "in" with the crowd. The hell with Erasmus. "The Scarlet and the Gray" was my bag. Hamilton became my torch, Eastern Parkway my arena.

CHAPTER 14

EASTERN PARKWAY ALL-STARS

"You can't take my boy. What about all the others?"

Eastern Parkway is a very broad, three-lane boulevard, with islands separating the main, or middle, lane from the two side ones. The middle lane is the big one and it handles the bulk of the traffic. The side lanes are relatively narrow and are used for parking and for commercial traffic. The islands have trees spaced about ten yards apart and, of course, benches. Those benches were the social center for the women of Eastern Parkway. When the weather was warm and bright and clear, they would gather on the benches and gossip. Everybody knew everybody else's business, and no one was immune to the vicious scuttlebutt of the wagging tongues. Young mothers, populating the islands with their baby carriages, were no different. It used to get so intense that all the women were afraid to miss a day. They knew that if they were absent, they would be the victims of the daily venom.

The Parkway begins at Grand Army Plaza and continues all the way down to the beginning of Brownsville. As Emmy and I began to walk along it, even she was on familiar ground. During World War II, after our older daughter Jill was born, we moved into 175 Eastern Parkway with my folks. We stayed there five long years, years of apartment shortages and economic struggle. On our walk, we went from Classon Avenue to Washington Avenue, then past 175 Eastern Parkway, past 135, which was Turner Towers (as kids we would talk about that building in hushed tones, because the richest people in Brooklyn lived there) and on to Underhill Avenue and, finally, to Grand Army Plaza.

On the surface, the street hadn't changed that much. The apartment buildings are not as well maintained as they used to be, but certainly they are most respectable looking. The same is true of the ones on Plaza Street. And from Grand Army Plaza to Washington Avenue, on the other side of the Parkway, there is still beauty. The Brooklyn Public Library is a model edifice. The Brooklyn Botanical Gardens is glorious in its greenery. The Brooklyn Museum is, as it always was, a magnificent structure. Across the street from the museum, little Guider Park, where Emmy used to take Jill, remains an attractive pocket of grass in a sea of asphalt. I thought back 40 years, and remembered the Parkway at its best—Memorial Days, when they would hold the great veteran's parades and the street would be lined with thousands upon thousands of people, and the windows would be open with people waving gaily at the men who had fought in World War I. Then some of the Spanish War veterans would go by, and people would "ooh" and "ah," and burst into prolonged applause. They still have the parade every year, but I wonder what it looks like now. I suspect the Vietnam War has changed the feel of the whole thing, even as it has changed so much of the mood of the country.

It is when you leave Eastern Parkway and walk down Washington or Underhill Avenues that you come upon the new scene in this part of Brooklyn. You enter a whole new world—a black world. In the 1930s and the 1940s, the blacks were carefully contained. They could not move beyond Fulton Street. But, as new sociological forces swept the United States in the 1950s and the 1960s, Brooklyn was not to be excluded. The blacks and the islanders from Puerto Rico, Jamaica and Haiti would "transgress." They would climb the wall of Fulton Street, and they have. According to my mother, who only moved out of Brooklyn two years ago, even Eastern Parkway has been forced to open its doors to our citizens of dark skin. The fact that decent housing for black people is long overdue doesn't alter the hideous reality that white people still scurry like a horde of lemmings out of the neighborhood when the blacks approach it. And despite denials by landlords, they permit the buildings to run down as their black tenancies increase. In the meantime, they continue to raise the rents. In net effect, what has happened to this part of Brooklyn is a tragic commentary on the wretched racial problem that continues to haunt our nation.

In retrospect, I have to ponder what the matter was with all of us during those years of growing up; how we could have been so blissfully unaware of the discrimination and the consequent plight of the disadvantaged. What worried me then was anti-Semitism, not racism. Hitler was alive and well in Munich, and there was a band leader named Fritz Kuhn in New York.

But Eastern Parkway, my part of it, was a world of its own. Emmy and I looked at the buildings again as we walked back to our car. Each had its own roots in my personal history. 201 Eastern Parkway—Adelphi Hall. Margie Reich lived there, a terribly good-looking girl who captured one beau after another. She was probably the most popular girl on the block. Phyllis Bregstein lived there. She married, you guessed it, Ira Feldblum. Elaine Scheffries lived there. She reintroduced herself to me recently at a Friars' Roast of Don Rickles. She still looks good and has apparently married well. She came up to me at the dais and asked, "Don't you remember me?" I didn't, until she told me who she was. Then I recalled how concerned her parents were when I took her to the New York Paramount on a Saturday night date.

255 Eastern Parkway was another building of special import. Evelyn Bag, Betty Behrens and Muriel Mandell lived there. All three were attractive, and, for me, especially Evelyn Bag. She looked like Maureen O'Sullivan, the film star, and I had a secret crush on her for years. But I never made it with any of them. I was shy, late in learning how to dance, and all of my outlets lay in street athletics, scholastics and speech. Besides, they all went to Erasmus. I was a at Hamilton, angry with my mother for the enforced confinement. I was absolutely convinced that if I had gone to Erasmus my social poise would have been assured.

We played stickball on the outside lane of Eastern Parkway adjacent to Guider Park, on the block between Washington and Classon Avenues. Traffic was at a minimum. A belt of two sewers or more would wind up, if not caught, on Washington Avenue and bounce on up to the area fronting the Brooklyn Museum. When we had finished, ususally about 5:30 in the afternoon, we would run the long block from Classon to Franklin Avenues and rush to the newsstand at Ludell's stationery store to see how the Dodgers were doing while they were on the road. Brooklyn had its own newspapers then, the top one being *The Brooklyn Daily Eagle*. The others were *The Brooklyn Daily Times* and *The Standard-Union*. The Eagle was a vital part of my young years. One of the finest baseball writers of my lifetime covered the Dodgers for *The Eagle*. His name is Tommy Holmes, and when *The Eagle* died, Tommy went to work for *The New York Herald-Tribune* which was to perish later. But Tommy was my authority on baseball. I lived and died by him. Brooklyn has no newspaper of its own now, which has to be a significant reason for its decline in identity. But it is *The Eagle* that is mainly missed. And just to show you how important Tommy Holmes was, Brooklyn Tech High School had a terrific ballplayer named Kelly. He changed his name to Tommy Holmes, and went on to lead the National League in hitting with the Boston Braves. Briefly, too, he became a big-league manager.

When we would get to Ludell's newsstand, if the late afternoon editions of the papers hadn't arrived, we would wait for them. The newspaper deliverymen would drive up, and when they got out of the trucks, we knew immediately how the Dodgers were doing. If they were smiling, we were ahead, if they were glum, we were losing. Sometimes, though, you couldn't be sure. That was when the visiting team's turn at bat had not yet been recorded. The paper might show the Dodgers leading 2–1 over St. Louis after four-and-one-half innings. But what had the Cardinals done in the bottom of the fifth? Were they rallying? Did they only have men on base? Or had the Dodgers just made out in the fifth when the papers had had to go to press? You have no idea of the torment involved as we wrestled with these uncertainties, uncertainties not resolved until Stan Lomax came on with the scores on radio at 6:45 P.M.

We played football on the same outside lane of Eastern

Parkway where we played stickball. But we played across the street, between Classon and Franklin Avenues, right in front of Bishop McDonnell Memorial High School. We played there because it was a much longer block, and we used the trees on the adjacent island as yard markers. Thus, with the trees spaced about ten yards apart, we had a perfect 100-yard gridiron for touch football. I liked football then, and the Brooklyn Football Dodgers were beginning to occupy my attention. But in those days, baseball was the whole bag, even in the off-season.

And stickball was the game for the streets of *all* of New York. I remember one summer, before the years when I went to Manhattan Beach, and when most of the Eastern Parkway gang was away at camp, when Hilton and I played stickball with the fellows on Lincoln Place between Classon and Franklin. It wasn't like Eastern Parkway. The residents would call the cops and they would come and chase us. But we would be back playing the next day, and one time we broke a window and fled. Hilton and I thought we were safe at home on Classon Avenue when there was a knock at the door. It was the cops, and they started to take Hilton to the local precinct. My mother chased after them down the street screaming, "You can't take my boy. What about all the others?" The question was logical. Magnanimously, the cops released him.

Union Temple was built in 1925. It is a tall building at the very beginning of Eastern Parkway just off Grand Army Plaza. I always dreamed of someday belonging to it. But that never happened. My folks just couldn't afford it. I wanted to be part of it because the temple had a gymnasium, a basketball court and a swimming pool. The only way I could get there was as the guest of a member. Here, I was lucky. Joe Peters, who lived on 255 Eastern Parkway, was a member and he would take me to the temple often. So, the temple and basketball became part of my life on Eastern Parkway. On Sunday nights there would be basketball games, and I would go as often as I could. Union Temple had a fine team. Those were the days of the old club teams, and they attracted a lot of attention. Pro basketball, as we know it today, had not even been born. And even the college game, as we know it now, was just beginning to invade Madison Square Garden. The club game was the thing. The Crescent Athletic Club was tough, so was the 92nd Street YMHA. Eighth Avenue Temple of Brooklyn had some very good players. These were the groups that Union Temple would play, and I was absorbed with them.

The temple building looks as good now as it ever did. When Emmy and I looked at it, our thoughts drifted back to 1946, when I was separated from the service and joined the Corporal Sydney Rosenberg Legion Post, which had its headquarters at the temple. I succeeded a good friend, Arthur Levitt, now controller of the State of New York, as the commander of the post, which was influential in Brooklyn politics. Some of the important judges in Brooklyn were members and so were some of the leading politicians. That was when I was thinking about a career in law and politics, and I don't think Arthur Levitt has ever really forgiven me for deserting both.

It was time for Emmy and me to leave Eastern Parkway. We got back into the car and drove down to Franklin Avenue; on our way to the old site of Ebbets Field. The Franklin Avenue IRT station is at the corner of Franklin Avenue and Eastern Parkway, and the stairwell was a reminder of how frequently I used to stand there, waiting for visiting ballplayers to come walking up. "Red" Barber often came that way, too.

As we swung into Franklin Avenue I was shocked. It had become a horror scene. The first thing I noticed was that Radin's Delicatessen was gone. What a great place that had been. It was the "Stage Delicatessen" of Brooklyn, the eatery for ballplayers. Hot dogs (crips, all-beef ones), were always ready on the grill. The hot pastrami was unfailingly lean. You never had to ask, the tongue would be cut from the center. And the service would be by huge Lenny Radin, who had the build of Carl Eller of the Vikings. Lenny was a complainer, a whiner, even though he was a nice guy. The Dodgers were his life, too, but he would bitterly bemoan the fact that he could only serve them, never see them. Franklin Avenue without Radin's had to be like a man without a country.

The Franklin Avenue trolley was also gone, but that was to be expected. Brooklyn once had more trolley lines than any other city in the country: Flatbush Avenue, St. John's Place, Bergen Street, Kingston Avenue, Church Avenue, Gravesend Avenue and on and on; Nostrand Avenue, Rogers Avenue. There were almost as many trolleys as streets. In fact, some of the sports historians, in reciting how they came to be known as the Dodgers, will tell you that the nickname of the ball club derived from the longer expression "Trolley Dodgers." People had to dodge trolley cars all the time, and presumably, the Dodgers were once called the "Trolley Dodgers" for just that reason. Then the name was shortened to the Dodgers. They are all gone now, those trolley lines, and the buses have taken over, which is a good thing for motor traffic. As for nostalgia, that's something else. I remember the Franklin Avenue Trolley. On days when the Dodgers were at home, the trolleys on Franklin Avenue were teeming tenements, each and every one of them. So many fans would swarm on to each car that they would have to hang out the windows, ride on the backs of the cars and even on the sides; the conductors would do nothing about it, nor did they try.

But more than Radin's and the trolley lines were gone. The whole atmosphere of well-being, the prosperous small shops, the beauty parlors were absent, too. In their stead was a ramshackle, almost derelict environment: graffiti on the walls of the buildings, a low-cost rental apartment under construction, some sleazy-looking bars and even garbage in front of where the construction was taking place. There was no change all the way down past Union Street, President Street, Carroll Street, Crown Street and up to Montgomery Street where we turned left. The left-field stands of Ebbets Field used to border Montgomery Street. The left-field foul line was bounded by tiny little McKeever Place, named in honor of Steve McKeever, an old owner of the Dodgers. We turned into McKeever and went down past Sullivan Place, another small street that bounded the right-field stands, and continued on to Empire Boulevard, where we again turned left. I looked eagerly for something I could recognize. It was not to be found. One of the notable landmarks had been Freddy Fitsimmons's Bowling Alleys. You remember "Fat" Freddy, an excellent pitcher with the Giants for many years who wound up with the Dodgers and pitched well for them in the late stages of his career. While enjoying his rebirth with the Dodgers, he opened his bowling-lane operation on Empire Boulevard. Now it was an automobile dealership.

As we turned left on Bedford Avenue, I felt empty. Everything that I had loved in my youth seemed gone. Good Lord, I thought, even the Bond Bread plant with the big clock on top of it wasn't there anymore. Couldn't something have been left even if Ebbets Field had had to go?

During our drive, we had, of course, passed the apartment project where Ebberts Field had once been located. Now moving up Bedford Avenue we reached the point where the right field-wall had been, the most famous right-field fence in baseball history. This was the fence that defied Tommy Henrich in the 1947 World Series. This was the fence that Carl Furillo adopted as his own. This was the fence that Babe Herman, Lefty O'Doul, Johnny Frederick, Dolph Camilli, Dixie Walker, Pete Reiser and Duke Snider used to love. It was a short fence, only 297 feet from home plate along the foul line. Herman, O'Doul, Frederick, Bissonette and Harvey Hendrick used to hit over it so often, they had to put a screen up on top of it to make the home runs harder to come by. The screen never stopped Camilli, nor did it bother Duke Snyder.

But on this June day of 1974 as the remembrances tumbled forth, there was instead a sign, a great big series of white letters neatly laid out against the brick of the buildings wall. It said, "Ebbets Field." And next to it was a tremendous baseball laid into that wall which had these words between the stitches: "Jackie Robinson Apartments." My eyes became moist.

"Let's get the hell out of here," I said. "Let's move on to Hamilton High School." As we drove up Bedford Avenue, I mentally noted that Brooklyn Prep had vanished, too. A fine preparatory school in its day, it had been situated at Bedford Avenue and Crown Street. I didn't even notice what was there now.

We crossed Eastern Parkway, went down to Park Place and turned right. I felt hopelessly depressed. Somehow, some way, the Brooklyn Dodgers had been Brooklyn and Jackie Robinson. They had been America, and they could never be replaced.

Park Place added to my depression. Once a beautiful street,

it, like so many others, had become seedy. We followed it past Brooklyn Avenue, looked over at the Children's Museum and, unbelievably, there was graffiti on the building. We got to Albany Avenue and Bergen Street, and there was Alexander Hamilton High School. Only now it had a sign on the entrance that read: "Alexander Hamilton Vocational and Technical High School." Physically, from the outside, it looked much like it did when I went there. I got the same feeling that I had had earlier that morning when I was in the P.S. 9 schoolyard. It seemed tiny. I walked up the steps to the entrance, looked through the windows and saw the same halls and the same stairways that I had walked for four years of my life. I wondered about the gymnasium, which was really unusable for basketball because the court had big steel structural poles all around it and a couple on it. When we played on that court, we got to know exactly where those poles were so that we could use them effectively in seeking to get free of the men guarding us. If they rammed into the poles, that was fine. If we hit them, it was another thing. As I walked back down the entrance steps, I looked, compulsively, in both directions for the knishes stands at the two corners of Albany Avenue that were always there when school was out. I don't know why in the world I would have thought that they would be there now, all these years later, on a summer day when school was closed. Force of habit, I guess.

Before we started off, I reminisced about those four years, and about some of the teachers who had helped to shape my life. An English teacher named Joe Boland, who was also a member of the St. John's University faculty, was one of them. He was a tough Irishman, with a swaggering walk and teeth that always seemed to be gritted. I'll never forget him. It was Joe Boland who gave me confidence in my ability to speak. Whenever we had exercises in two-minute extemporaneous speeches on any subject he would begin by calling on me first. "Show them how to do it," he would say. He got me interested in Shakespeare, as I had never been before, when we studied *Macbeth*. He made John Milton come alive. He taught me the difference between liberty and license.

He was a rabid sports fan and deeply loyal to the Hamilton teams. He never missed a football game and even wrote a new marching song for the team. I remember the words, "Cheer the team, cheer the team, to the last white line. We are out to win today, our offense is immense, we've a stonewall defense, so fight, fight, fight for the victory. . . ." It was corny stuff, but very vital to the spirit of all of us at the time.

There was another English teacher, Miss Kaiser, who is indelibly recorded in my memory. It was she who got me interested in the Romantic poets, Keats, Byron and Shelley. Forty years later, I still read Keats and he remains my favorite poet.

A history teacher named Mrs. Shean was still another. She was dramatic in her presentation. She had traveled in England and on the Continent, and she made European history come alive. When we studied the Sinn Fein Rebellion in Ireland, by the time she was done, I felt a sense of having lived through Victor McLaglen's performance in John Ford's classic film, *The Informer*.

Aaron Shapiro was my teacher for algebra and plane geometry. He made it easy. The year I took the geometry Regents it was a very difficult examination. Marks were inordinately low, and the Board of Regents of New York State ordered that the marks be raised on a percentage basis. But Mr. Shapiro had prepared us well, and I scored a 97 on the test. It was raised to 98. Ira Feldblum didn't like that. He and another friend, Julie Mirsky, had taken the same Regents exam that I had. Both flunked. Maybe they should have gone to Hamilton instead of Erasmus. Maybe my mother had been right. But I never thought so, then or now.

Tony Bove was the football coach at Hamilton, as well as being my Spanish teacher. He was a square-set man with a powerful frame and a ruggedly handsome countenance. He wore tweeds all the time, and they were exactly right for his outdoorsy look. He also smoked a pipe and had it clenched between his teeth almost always, even in class. He was very kind to me, would often drive me to football and basketball games and encouraged me to work on the school paper, *The Ledger*. When I became sports editor of the paper, he sent me a congratulatory note which said, "You may be doing this the rest of your life." The way it turned out, he was nearly right. He passed away a number of years ago. I owed him a lot.

Bove had a great sense of humor, too. There was a kid in school named Archie Dubois, a giant of a guy, about 6-feet 3-inches tall and 230 pounds. Tony wanted him for the football team, but Archie's parents would not sign a letter of consent. Football was too dangerous for their frail lad. So Tony went back at them. "What about lacrosse?" he asked. That was fine with them. They knew nothing about lacrosse, which is more physical and dangerous than football. Thus it was that Archie played lacrosse, and helped lead Hamilton to the city championship. After that, they allowed Archie to play football, and he anchored our line. He never did get hurt, but we never won a football championship. Bove used to tell the story in class and chuckle, while he held his pipe in his hand.

Emmy and I got into the car and we started to drive to Williamsburg. My thoughts were still riveted upon Hamilton and upon a fellow in my class. His name was Bill King. We called him "Dolly." "Dolly" King was one of the best built athletes I have ever seen in all my years in sports. In high school, he was 6-feet 4-inches tall and weighed 220 pounds. His physique was perfectly proportioned. The waist was narrow, the shoulders broad, the thighs and legs in perfect proportion to the rest of he body. As big and as strong as he was, he was that mild of disposition—except in athletic competition. There, he was a tiger, a fierce competitor with uncanny anticipation and instinct. Certainly "Dolly" King was the finest high school athlete I have ever seen.

He was the star of our football team, our basketball team and our baseball team. He brought me thrills that match any I have ever had in watching the great professionals of my time. He was an All-Scholastic in all three sports.

Sitting in the car with Emmy, it was easy to visualize "Dolly" back in the 1930s. I had a mental image of him against Manual Training High School on Columbus Day—we always played Manual on Columbus Day. They had a better football team than we did, but that never bothered King. We were trailing by a touchdown, but "Dolly" had been studying the Manual quarterback. With his keen reading of the opposition, he sensed a flat pass, tore in, picked it off and went 80 yards for a touchdown. Once he got in the open, no single tackler could bring him down. "Dolly" set a record for touchdown interceptions that year.

As good as King was in football, I always thought that baseball was his game. He was a catcher, and what an arm he had. He would get the ball away without even straightening up from his crouch and it would go on a line, three feet above the ground, right to second base. They couldn't steal on "Dolly," not even in high school. He was as quick as a cat under a pop fly, a predecessor in this respect of the Roy Campanella yet to come. At the plate, all he did was break Lou Gehrig's long-standing New York City high school home-run record. In the whole history of Commercial Field, which was our home field, nobody had ever hit a ball over the left-field wall. It was 420 feet away. I was there when "Dolly" King did it.

One day I will never forget. We were playing James Madison at Madison for the division title; the winner to move on in the tournament for the city crown. Madison was the favorite to win because their pitcher was a southpaw named Harry Eisenstat, who had spent the season striking everybody out. It was no accident, because Harry later became a big-league pitcher. The rickety wooden stands at Madison's field were packed. I was in the top row behind third base. The Madison ball park was big, the left-field fence was particularly distant. No ball had ever been hit out of the Madison ball park. "Dolly" was a right-handed hitter. On his first turn at bat, he gave Hamilton the lead. He hit the ball over the left-field fence. On his third turn at bat, King clinched the game. He hit the ball over the left-field fence. When he did it the second time, the fans in my section of the stands went wild, pounded their feet and kept jumping up and down. The stands collapsed. We fell in a bunch, body on body. Incredibly, no one was seriously hurt. And the bruises were forgotten in praise of "Dolly."

King was black. I believe to this day, that if the opportunity had come to him, "Dolly" could have been the first black man ever to play in the big leagues.

His saga did not stop there. Until he got to high school, King had not played basketball. He went out for the team, and because of his size, he made the squad as a center. At first, King seemed awkward and clumsy. But not for long. Within two years he was the best center in the city. Hamilton was in a three-way playoff for the Brooklyn title with New Utrecht and Abraham Lincoln. Utrecht had a remarkable center in "Ash" Resnick, big, tough and mobile with a fine assortment of shots. "Dolly" not only stopped Resnick, but "Ash" fouled out. As I left St. Peter Claver's gym, where the game was played, Resnick was crying. It was something I'll always remember because it probably had never happened before, and doubtless has never happened since. Resnick is one of the original hard-boiled guys of the world. That's why you'll find him now working as an executive at Caesar's Palace in Las Vegas, Nevada. He knows all the guys in all the rackets, and he can handle them. Whenever I see "Ash" we talk about that game and about Bill "Dolly" King.

After King went on to Long Island University and led them to a national title, he faded out of sports. He became recreation director for a housing project in Harlem, and then, in the 1960s, he died prematurely. I ran into him occasionally when he was working in Harlem. He was as mild-mannered as ever, a perfect gentleman. When he died, I was deeply touched. It was as though a part of my life had gone with him.

The car was moving through Williamsburg now, and sure enough there were the Hassidic Jews, with their black hats and suits and their telltale *païs* curling down their cheeks. Williamsburg had always meant two things to me, the Hassidic Jews and Peter Lugers Restaurant. Peter Lugers is still there, close to the Williamsburg Bridge, spotlessly clean, a place visited by Manhattanites and people from all over the country. It continues to be one of the greatest steak houses you'll find anywhere. There was a time, when I was very, very young, four or five, when my dad's parents lived in Williamsburg, and we would go to visit them. I even dimly remember that sometimes we would cross over the bridge to Delancey Street on the Lower East Side to get kosher cold cuts at the Sussman-Volk Delicatessen. I remembered one other thing about Williamsburg: Eastern District High School was there, and it had the same kind of tiny gymnasium with the same poles all around the court and on the court as Hamilton. I thought of a game we played there, when Red Auerbach, the general manager and former coach of the Boston Celtics, played for District. He was as guileful then as he is now, and if you know Red Auerbach you know that's saying a lot. But all his shrewdness was to no avail in that contest. "Dolly" King killed them.

We drove back up Bedford Avenue to St. John's Place, two blocks short of Eastern Parkway, and turned right. I wanted to go to 500 St. John's Place where we had moved when we left Classon Avenue. 500 St. John's Place was a brand new building when my folks leased an apartment there in the 1930s. It was directly across the street from a firehouse and just down the block from St. Teresa's Church and School. My recollections of living there are two: The ceaseless screaming of the fire engines as they pulled in and out of the firehouse, and the Irish kids from St. Teresa's who, as was unfortunately normal in those days, had a running battle with the Jewish kids of the Eastern Parkway neighborhood. Of course, I still went up to Eastern Parkway to play.

I have one other terrible memory of 500 St. John's Place. It was while we lived there that my brother, Hilton, developed a cough. He had grown tall even more quickly than I, and he was also thin. He was 6-feet 3½-inches tall and must have weighed about 150 pounds. He worked during the day and went to college at night. And then came that cough. At first, none of us paid any attention to it. As it lingered, my parents had him visit the doctor in the building. It was diagnosed as a post nasal drip. The cough got worse. Finally Hilton went for X-rays. He had tuberculosis. In those days, the word filled one with fear and horror. Medical science did not have the drugs it has today. What about contagion? Would Hilton have to go to a sanitarium? Where in the world would the money come from to pay for his treatment? My parents had struggled for so long; it seemed too devastating a blow to bear. But a friend recommended a doctor famous for chest work. His name was Milton Louria, and he proved to be a genius and a saint. Hilton never left home. Dr. Louria collapsed his infected lung by a process known as pneumothorax. The lung was allowed gradually to expand back to normal only after the infection had been killed. Hilton's sanitarium became an upstairs porch at 1023 President Street between Franklin and Bedford Avenues, just two blocks from Ebbets Field, where we moved into a two-family house.

All of this filled my mind as I stood at 500 St. John's Place, which is utterly shabby now. The firehouse is still there and so is St. Teresa's. In fact, St. Teresa's is a bastion of cleanliness in what is now a neighborhood of corrosion.

Emmy and I started toward 1023 President Street. As vividly as though it had happened yesterday, I could see those empty boxes of cough drops—Smith Brothers and Luden's—that we had found in Hilton's pockets when we emptied out his suits. There would be no more cough drops. Somehow Dad got the money to pay Dr. Louria. Hilton now weighs 220 and my mother has never gotten the nursing award of the year which she earned.

How different 1023 looked from what I remembered. In my mind it had been a warm, tree-lined street; a street of two-family houses, each carefully maintained by its owner, the grass neatly mowed, the hedges precisely clipped. Many of the houses had flower gardens. Now the whole damn street was of a different genre. In the first place, the houses looked tiny, the porches had the appearance of small balconies, and the whole feeling was one of neglect. Yet my entire family sat on our porch in nice weather, and it seemed idyllic then. Everything is relative.

When we moved to President Street, Ira Feldblum moved to Eastern Parkway between Bedford and Rogers Avenues, virtually around the corner from us. We were never far apart.

Thus far in our odyssey, Emmy and I had seen nothing but Brooklyn in decline. As we wended our way toward Prospect Park West and the Park Slope section, we saw nothing to encourage us. Girls Commercial and Bishop McDonnell Memorial High Schools, both handsome buildings, were marred by graffiti. Only the Brooklyn Museum and the Brooklyn Public Library seem to have escaped it.

Prospect Park West, like Eastern Parkway, has its beginning at Grand Army Plaza. The Knights of Columbus building was at the corner, and it still is, only it is now "The Madonna Residence".

Prospect Park West up to about Third Street is still lovely. It is marked by fine private homes interspersed with attractive, beautifully maintained apartment buildings. The Brooklyn Ethical Culture School is there. Frankly, I was always in awe of Prospect Park West. Some of the top judges in Brooklyn lived there, and so did former Congressman Emmanuel Celler. Eighth Avenue, just below Prospect Park West, is another bright spot. After World War II, when Emmy and I were apartment hunting, how we wished we could afford to live there. In fact, all the way down to Sterling Place, below Flatbush Avenue, there is a general air of caring. Brownstones are being renovated, and one gets a sense of well-being.

Methodist Hospital of Brooklyn on Sixth Street, where our daughter, Jill, was born, has grown tremendously; now, with a new wing, it occupies the entire block. A vacant lot across the street has a big sign indicating that still another structure will be erected. Incidentally, I go back further than Jill with Methodist Hospital. I had my tonsils and adenoids removed there when I was six.

There were more places to see, more neighborhoods to examine, more memories to be drawn upon. Emmy and I moved on to Flatbush and Erasmus Hall High Schools, on Flatbush Avenue just beyond Church Avenue. Some of the old landmarks of that immediate area still remain, like the movie houses, the Kenmore, the Astor, the Albemarle and Loew's Kings. Some are gone, like the Garfield Cafeteria and Newman's Soda Shop where so many kids used to go for lunch. But the most important historical building was intact, the Dutch Reformed Church and the old cemetery by its side. We looked at it and remembered going there the first Easter Sunday after we were married.

They tell me that the student body of Erasmus isn't what it used to be. I suppose they mean there are many more blacks in the school, and as we stopped in front of it, there were eight or ten summer-school students, all of whom were black. Looking through the entrance arch into what was called "the campus," nothing had changed. It was clean, attractive and had a much nicer environment than Alexander Hamilton.

We cut over to Ocean Avenue and started toward Sheepshead Bay. Ocean Avenue was pretty, an apparently desirable area in which to live. New apartment buildings are going up, the old ones are still attractive; the lawns and trees are healthy and the atmosphere bespeaks solid middle-class prosperity. My mother, before she finally left Brooklyn (a traumatic experience for her), considered moving to Ocean Avenue. We talked her out of it. At her age, it was time to be close to us.

We meandered through Flatbush, gravitating over to East 28th Street between avenues I and J where my mother's parents lived, and then down a couple of blocks on that very street to the late Gil Hodges's church. It seemed like only yesterday that I had been there for Gil's funeral service along with "the boys of summer." All of this neighborhood has kept its style and character. As we got to King's Highway the impulse to visit James Madison High School was irresistible. I just had to return to where "Dolly" King had hit those two home runs against Harry Eisenstat.

Then we went back to Ocean Avenue and drove to its terminus, Sheepshead Bay. It was still there, one of the traditional landmarks of Brooklyn, Lundy's Sea Food Restaurant. Originally, Lundy's had been a wooden building, built out on a pier right over the bay itself. It was a superb seafood restaurant, the fresh fish being brought in daily from the fishing boats that were docked in the bay. And the atmosphere added to the pleasure. You could smell the Atlantic Ocean, which was just a few short blocks away. Eating dinner there after a full day at Manhattan Beach, was a treasure of life, a soothing, comforting experience to be savored delicately, a tribute to civilized behavior.

Lundy's reputation grew. Patrons came from everywhere. It was a time when Manhattan and Oriental beaches were the most populated summer places in the entire country. The wooden building would no longer do, so they built a new Lundy's, one block long, right across the street. This one is a gigantic stone-encased structure. It was still hard to get a table. The crowds were overflowing. The new place never had the atmosphere of that smaller, wooden building; you weren't looking right out on the bay, watching the fishing boats come in, but the food was worth the travail. The lobsters were sweet and tender; the catches of the day were a gourmet's delight; the steaks were rare and juicy, done just the way you wanted them, and they had a flair for French fried potatoes that made them seem like no other French fried potatoes in the whole world.

It would have been a crime for Lundy's ever to leave Sheepshead Bay. I had a warm feeling as I left. Emmy and I are going to go back there for dinner—and soon. We'll take our chances with the crowds.

The first time I ever went to Lundy's was when I was a young teen-ager. It was in the old, wooden restaurant. I was the guest of Mr. Max Feldblum, who was giving a birthday dinner for his son, Ira.

To go to Manhattan Beach, we used to take the BMT Brighton Express. From there it was a 20–25 minute walk to the beach, unless you took the bus, which I couldn't afford. The pedestrian route took us right past Lundy's and across a wooden foot bridge which spanned Sheepshead Bay. The bridge is still there. So are the old, nicely manicured lawns and homes on attractive, shaded streets that bear such names as Amherst, Coleridge and Exeter. Driving past these streets with Emmy, I remembered that the famous criminal lawyer, Sam Leibowitz, later a judge, lived on one of them. Manhattan Beach is a lovely residential area.

Originally, while some of the Eastern Parkway gang had season lockers—a season went from May 30 through September 15—I could never get one because of the cost. My folks had enough trouble making ends meet in those depression years. The breakthrough came because I had a rich uncle, or at least I thought he was rich for those times. Lou Soman was married to my mother's sister, Ethel. They lived in Brooklyn, too, and Lou had a paint store at the corner of Washington Avenue and Fulton Street that was quite successful. In the early years, the Somans lived above the store. But after he accumulated enough money they bought a beautiful home in Flatbush. (My cousin, Bernie, Lou's son and a brilliant student, went to Harvard.) Lou was a smart businessman. He took his profits out of the paint business and put them into real estate. Then he watched his assets grow.

In the early days of the automobile industry, Lou awed all of us with his manifestation of wealth. He bought a Willys-Knight, and on some Sundays he would take us for a drive all the way out to Sheepshead Bay. Once he gave me a real thrill. The Holland Tunnel had just been built, and he drove Hilton and me through it for the first time.

Of course, my uncle had a season locker at Manhattan Beach, and on some hot summer days he was kind enough to take me to the beach as his guest. Finally, there came a year when he did more than that. A season cost $25, but for kids under 16 there were smaller special lockers that could be purchased for the season for only $15. Uncle Lou treated me to a $15 season locker as a gift. Hilton, because he was four years older, was never with me at Manhattan Beach. He went his own way with his own friends, and was part of a softball team that hung out at Rockaway Beach.

Manhattan Beach was one of the joys of my youth. It had an incredible variety of activities and entertainment that could absorb you from 9:30 in the morning until 7:00 at night. The Atlantic Ocean was there to swim in if that was your wont. If not, there was the olympic-size pool. There were baseball fields, softball fields, tennis courts, hand-tennis courts, basketball courts, and there was a wide open mile-long stretch of sand at the end of the beach which we used to call, "the desert." It was an isolated area, off by itself, an ideal place to spread a blanket and, if you were romantically inclined (and successful), to neck with a girl. It was also a perfect place to play tackle football.

We had organized softball leagues, basketball leagues and football leagues. It was a summer paradise. One day, we were out on the desert ready to chose up sides for a game of tackle football. We were short a man, but there was a lifeguard, a rugged-looking guy, standing by. "Wanna get in the game?" someone asked him. "Why not" he replied.

In the very first series of plays, I carried the ball and the lifeguard hit me. When I came to, I was staring straight into his face above me. "What's your name?" I asked him. "Alex," he said. "Alex what?" I persisted. "Alex Wojciechowicz," he replied. As I staggered to my feet I asked him, "Why the hell didn't you tell us?" He laughed. Alex was the center on Fordham's Seven Blocks of Granite, later to star with the Detroit Lions and become a pro-football hall of famer. He had the grace to withdraw from the game.

Quite apart from all the athletic activities, Manhattan Beach had a bandstand. It was the center for the greatest entertainment in the world. Harold Stern and his orchestra were only the beginning. Rudy Vallee and his Connecticut Yankees came in, and Alice Faye was his vocalist. She was so beautiful that we just stood at the bandstand and gaped at her adoringly. The rumors were heavy then of a romance between Rudy and Alice, and when he would take his megophone and croon at us, I hated him.

Paul Whiteman and his orchestra became a staple at Manhattan Beach. What a group! Johnny Mercer was one of them, and I was transfixed when he sang, *Here Come the British with a Bang, Bang.* The big bands were in vogue and one after another they paraded through. Benny Goodman, "The King of Swing," had come east from Chicago, and we all stood there stamping our feet as they pounded out, *Stomping at the Savoy.* The songs of the time were a reflection of youthful romance: *I'm in the Mood for Love, Love in Bloom, Love Thy Neighbor, East of the Sun and West of the Moon, Is It True what They Say About Dixie?* and many, many more. The Lucky Strike *Hit Parade* was a big radio show, and the bands would play the songs listed on the hit parade.

Great entertainers would appear. Al Jolson was one. One day as Al was about to come on stage, the rains came down in torrents. In the area surrounding the stands where literally thousands of people were massed, nobody moved. We got soaked, but we wanted to hear Jolson. As he looked at the audience and the rain had begun to angle in under the bandstand roof pelting him, he said, "If you're willing to stand out there in that rain, I'm willing to stand up here all afternoon and sing." That's exactly what he did. He sang *Rockabye My Baby,* he sang *Sonny Boy,* he sang *With My Eyes Wide Open I'm Dreaming.* He sang, and sang and sang, and the rains never let up. It was one of the most wonderful afternoons imaginable.

All this for $15 a season if you were under 16, and for $25 a season when you reached 16. There's never been anything like it before or since.

But Brooklyn was growing and more beach was needed. Brighton Beach, down near Coney Island, had become passé. Manhattan Beach was becoming overcrowded. If you wanted to play handball, you couldn't get a court. If you wanted to play tennis, you couldn't get a court. If you wanted to lie on the beach where the ocean was, you couldn't find blanket room.

Joseph P. Day, the man who owned all the land out on the oceanfront of Brooklyn, opened a brand new beach just past Manhattan Beach. It had two magnificient, olympic-size swimming pools. The 1936 Olympic swimming trials were held there. Those two places, Manhattan and Oriental beaches, were the only places to be. That's where I was, summer in and summer out, with Ira Feldblum, Julie Mirsky and a swarm of others. No, my Uncle Lou was not paying anymore. My parents were.

Do you know what is there now, where Manhattan and Oriental beaches used to be? The Manhattan Beach Public Bath and Kingsborough Community College. We drove away from the memories to Coney Island.

Once one of the amusement capitals of the world, Coney Island is now a study in blight. Steeplechase and Luna Park, the two internationally famous amusement centers, don't even exist anymore. The only amusement place there is called Astroland. It's a scrubby looking operation, but it does have the ride that used to terrify us all, the "Cyclone." This was the one that you'd begin by going up, up and up (it seemed forever), and then abruptly down, almost in a vertical line. You would hold on to your safety rail for dear life, crazy things would happen in your stomach, your heart would pound with fear, and then, suddenly, you would be on your way back up again. That ride and the parachute jump were the courage testers. But now they tell me the Cyclone is coming down.

As I remember Steeplechase, we used to be able to buy combination tickets, ten rides for a quarter. Luna Park was a little more expensive. I never understood why. But we had glorious times at both in a mixture of excitement, elation, fear and challenge and hot dogs. Hot dogs are the one remaining attraction at Coney Island. The original Nathan's is still there. Emmy and I stopped for lunch, and the hot dogs were the same as ever—the best I've tasted in my life. The French fried potatoes were still special and the root beer was a dream. But the minute we finished eating we left Coney Island. It was a tawdry scene that could only blemish my nostalgia.

It was time to head for the Brooklyn Army Base where the most important happening of my life took place.

CHAPTER 15

THE ROAD TO MANHATTAN

"I took the shape of my life from Brooklyn."

On our way to the Brooklyn Army Base, we skirted the Bay Parkway section of Brooklyn. Abruptly, I recalled the old semipro baseball teams, of which the Bay Parkways had been one. The best known of all the teams was the Bushwicks, and occasionally, the Dodgers would bring up a player from the Bushwicks for a trial. They played their games at Dexter Park, the Bay Parkways, at Erasmus Field. The bearded House of David team played in this company, too. So did the Cedarhust Grays, who had Ken Strong, the Hall of Fame football player. In a way, all those teams related to the Brooklyn Dodgers, because, as I have mentioned earlier, baseball was then in its golden age. And Brooklyn was baseball. Thus, the semipros drew good crowds. Few, now, can recall that they ever existed.

We swung back past Fort Hamilton, where Emmy was quartered during World War II. She had enlisted as a WAC, had had basic training in Nagodoches, Texas, and then was assigned to Fort Hamilton for secretarial work at the Brooklyn Army Base where the headquarters of the New York Port of Embarkation was located. The Brooklyn Army Base was at First Avenue and 58th Street.

Fort Hamilton is beautiful. It overlooks the Atlantic Ocean, the Verrazzano Narrows Bridge, an engineering beauty, and the Narrows as you come into the world's greatest harbor. It was impossible to go past it and not feel a twinge. I had been there so many times during World War II. It was one of four

298

staging areas, within the command of the New York Port, the others having been Fort Slocum and Camps Kilmer and Shanks. Then, too, it was the return point for Emmy when we were dating. And that was nightly.

Fort Hamilton is at the tip of the Bay Ridge section of Brooklyn, which has the look of being the borough's finest section. There are lovely private homes, fine new apartment buildings. All of them seem to be on or around Shore Road, overlooking the Narrows and Staten Island. Bay Ridge has a sense of pride and prosperity.

The Brooklyn Army Base no longer exists. Neither does the New York Port of Embarkation. They were wartime creations. But the same buildings are there at First Avenue and 58th Street, the same fences and the same sense of the military because of the security guards posted at the entrances. We got out of the car and walked up to the guards. There was a sign over the security building adjacent to the gate. It said "Military Ocean Terminal." I was at the base when the security building was hastily constructed. At that time, we used it as an administration building and I had an office on the second floor when I came back from Officer Candidate School as a second lieutenant. I asked the guards when the name had been changed from Brooklyn Army Base to Military Ocean Terminal. They didn't know.

I looked over their shoulders to the old Administration Building which had been headquarters for the collective command known as the New York Port of Embarkation. Now there was a sign that read, "Administration Headquarters, Military Ocean Terminal." I asked the guards who worked there and what the function of the place was. They told me that down on the piers the International Longshoremen's Association held forth. "There are some navy people and a handful of army people in Building B," they told me. "And there are some navy people in Building A." Buildings A and B are two of the hugest warehouse buildings anywhere in the world. They extend, within the confines of the terminal, all the way down to 64th Street. During World War II, we used some of the floors of Building B for offices, and even part of one floor as quarters for the enlisted men. The rest was for storage. The same was true of Building A.

The piers down at the waterfront housed transports, which were used to ship troops, supplies and material overseas. The Brooklyn Army Terminal was one of five within the jurisdiction of the New York Port of Embarkation. The others were Staten Island Terminal, Bush Terminal, Piers 86 and 90 of North River Terminal in Manhattan, from which we dispatched the two Queens, Mary and Elizabeth, and Caven Point Terminal in New Jersey, from which we shipped ammunition. Those were compelling days, urgent days; there was a sense of unity in all of us at that port that I have never found since. I remember nights down on the piers, watching the troops file up the gangplanks for embarkation and wondering what would happen to them. It was eerie. It was also sad.

I left the guards and went into the security building. There were more security officers in there behind a counter, and there was also a workman outside the counter. I asked one of the guards if he could tell me when the name of the base had been changed. He couldn't, but the man outside the counter said that he thought it had been in 1962 or thereabouts. I then asked the guard to describe the function of the terminal to me. He said it was, "down to almost nothing, everything was being moved out to Bayonne, New Jersey. Just some commercial action down on the piers. Nearly all the army is gone," he told me. "And just a few navy people are still here." I asked them both if they knew what was happening at the Brooklyn Navy Yard. The Brooklyn Navy Yard had always been a critical factor in the economy of Brooklyn, but some years back the government had pulled out on the grounds that the facility was no longer useful. It was a terrible blow to the borough because thousands of men lost their jobs. Now, according to the workman, commercial activity was increasing at the Yard. So, some men were getting employment.

I went into the terminal heading straight toward the second floor of Building B where the personnel division of the port had been located during World War II, and where my office had been. There was nothing there now but the warehouse floor. I remembered all the cubicles that had been built to serve as offices. One was for Lieutenant Colonel

Kolyer, in charge of military personnel, officers and enlisted men. And then there were the others: Major Lewiston, Captain Swaybill, Captain Shirkes. My own office—I was manpower control officer—was down the floor a way, and set off from the Military Personnel Division.

It all came back to me, the whole action and flow of the New York Port of Embarkation; above all, the first time I met P.F.C. Mary Edith Abrams, Serial Number A-220, 656. The first contingent of WACs to be assigned to the New York Port had arrived on Memorial Day weekend 1943. They received their assignments from Major Lewiston who, by the way, lived on East 28th Street in Brooklyn, my grandmother's street. Major Lewiston made Mary Edith Abrams his secretary. (She rose quickly in the ranks to sergeant.)

I stood in Building B at the spot where Lewiston's office was, and thought back to the day when I walked in and saw Emmy for the first time. She was cute, 22 and flip. Her eyes were limpid blue and alive. You could tell she knew she was attractive, and you could tell that she was pretty damned sure of herself. I hung around Lewiston's office longer than was necessary trying to attract her attention, and trying to let her know that I was pretty damned good, too.

From that day on, I couldn't get her out of my mind. But the problem was military. There was a strict regulation to the effect that officers couldn't date enlisted women, and I didn't have the courage to try to break the rule. Finally there came a Sunday when I was on special duty. So was she. I was through at about 2:00 P.M. She was still working. I decided the time had come to take the step. I waited until 5:00 o'clock when, finally, she was finished and left the building. I went out swiftly after her and caught up with her as she was walking up 58th Street. I talked her into going out with me, and we took the Sea Beach Express up to Manhattan to have dinner and see a movie. I took her back to Fort Hamilton by cab that night, inducing a cab driver—I'll never know how—to make the long trip in spite of the wartime gasoline shortage. Then he took me home to Eastern Parkway.

I was hooked. We would go out together almost every night, she in her WAC uniform and me as an officer. We tried to do it surreptitiously because of the army regulations. But we weren't kidding anybody. All of the WACs in her company knew about it, and so did most of the enlisted men and officers. We became an "item," the scandal of the port. There are a thousand anecdotes I could write of our attempts at a furtively conducted romance. Emmy would get sick of the pretense and tell me that she was going to drop me. One day she went out of her way to go to lunch with a former date, a good-looking guy named Murray, at the very place where I usually ate with Ralph Shirkes and Walter Swaybill. As I walked past her and Murray, I laughed sneeringly, confident that I had destroyed her. Inwardly, she had me worried. The guy was too good looking for my taste.

There was another day when I was passing her just outside of Building B. She was with two WAC friends, and did not salute me as her friends did. I wheeled around and said, "Sergeant, don't you salute when you see an officer?" She didn't answer. It took three days of apologies for me to get her to see the humor of the situation.

We found a little bar on Parkside Avenue in Flatbush that we made our courting place. They had good food and drink, and a kindly old gentleman waiter who viewed our romance benignly.

Ultimately, I was asked by my superior officer, Colonel Gillespie, if it were true that I was dating Sergeant Abrams. I confessed. He grinned and said, "We'll get you a letter of authorization from General Groninger." The general, who commanded the New York Port, wrote the letter and ordered Emmy's company commander to write a similar letter for her. We were home free, as far as the army was concerned.

But not as far as our parents were concerned. We wanted to get married. I had to meet Emmy's parents. They lived in Maplewood, New Jersey, and Emmy's father worked in Kearny, New Jersey, where Congoleum-Nairn had its general offices. He was the executive vice-president of the company, and Emmy had described him to me as a hard line, big-business Republican. It made me uneasy. I was sure he would prove to be anti-Semitic. But I had to face up to it.

We took the Pennsylvania Railroad to Newark, and Norman Ross Abrams was waiting for us in his car at the station. I was a captain then, and he had been a member of the First Division in World War I. He was an old army man. He treated me courteously, almost with deference, calling me "Captain." I could not relax. He was a handsome man, but his face was stern, unbending. Our conversation was cool, detached. It was about the war, of course. Emmy didn't make it any easier when we got to the house and I met her mother, sister and brother. She kept holding on to my hand, tightly, in the living room, at the dinner table, everywhere. It was her way of saying, "Here he is dad, and this is it." When I shook his hand upon leaving, I looked him squarely in the eye. He looked back at me, unyieldingly. I had the urge to tell him then and there that I loved his daughter, and was going to marry her. But I chickened out.

It wasn't any easier for my parents. All my life they had impressed upon me the idea that I should never marry a shikse. The mere thought was abhorrent to them. The first time Emmy came to my home at 175 Eastern Parkway, my mother was as tense as could be. She knew that Emmy was gentile, and she knew that if I had invited her to the house I was serious. I waited for Emmy at the IRT station. She came bouncing up the stairs flushed and nervous. I was in no better shape. We walked down to the building, went into the lobby, and damned if we didn't run into the biggest gossip in the house. I smiled and introduced Emmy. She smiled and eyed Emmy with the look of a jeweler using his spy glass to appraise a diamond.

My mother was prepared for the visit. She was perfectly charming, and she had drinks ready—gin and pineapple juice. You know, all shikses drink. To be polite, Emmy took a couple of them, and I could see mother glancing over, knowingly, at dad. Her worst suspicions were confirmed. But she held together and, in spite of herself, responded to Emmy. I knew it would happen.

The next day mother bumped into the gossip. "I saw Howard bringing a girl up to your apartment yesterday. He looked serious, and she's good looking. But is she Jewish?"

"No," my mother gulped, and then added defensively. "But she's a lovely girl."

It was time to leave the Military Ocean Terminal. I could

have stayed there the rest of the day, thinking back to Emmy and me and the New York Port of Embarkation; of World War II, another of the wars to end all wars.

Instead, we got back into the car and reflected. Four days earlier, Emmy and I had celebrated our 30th wedding anniversary, and we had a big party in Pound Ridge. Thirty years with the same girl and, truthfully, never a moment of regret. Only gratitude and love. "Dandy" Don Meredith once put it simply and correctly: "Ha'rd's strength is Emmy, and those daughters she gave him." Amen.

We drove downtown to Brooklyn Heights, just below the Brooklyn Bridge. Brooklyn Heights had always been a class section, and it still is. It's got the feel of Beekman Street in Manhattan, a glow of sophistication, an urban polish. There are brownstones and apartment houses intermingled, and you could be walking on an East Side street in Manhattan. When Emmy and I were married, we moved into one of those brownstones for six months or so at 202 Columbia Heights. It was a studio apartment, with an exquisite view of the harbor. As we drove past it, it looked as trim as ever.

Then we went to Borough Hall, and much credit is due to municipal officials for the job they have done in rebuilding the area. There is a new Supreme Court building, a new federal building, a new state building and a new real-estate project called Cadman Towers. I was most impressed, and if they could do that with "the Hall," they can do it in the sections where I found decay. And they can lend a hand to what the Kennedy family is trying to do in Bedford-Stuyvesant.

We returned to Manhattan over the Brooklyn Bridge. Five-and-one-half hours had elapsed. I sat back to collect my thoughts; to ruminate about what I had seen.

Ebbets Field was gone. *The Brooklyn Eagle* was gone. My high school was, in effect, gone. Manhattan Beach is gone. To all intents and purposes, Coney Island is gone. The Brooklyn Army Base is gone. Graffiti has arrived. And in some areas, decay. Thomas Wolfe was right. You can't go home again.

But you don't have to because of the things you have taken with you. I took the shape of my life from Brooklyn. Ebbets Field is with me. So is *The Brooklyn Eagle* So are P.S. 9 and

Alexander Hamilton High School. So is Manhattan Beach and Coney Island. So is Brooklyn Heights. So is the Brooklyn Army Base. So are people, people whom I'll never forget: my teachers, "Dolly" King, the friends who grew up with me.

Above all, I took Emmy with me, and, by the time I left Brooklyn, our daughter Jill. All the graffiti in the world can't change that.

I leaned over and kissed Emmy. "You know what," I said, "I'm going to have lunch with Ira Feldblum."